consumer
education
bibliography

U.S. Office of Consumer Affairs

Prepared by The Office of Consumer Affairs
and The New York Public Library
September 1971

For sale by the Superintendent of Documents, U.S. Government Printing Office
Washington, D.C.   20402 — Price $1

FOREWORD

As President Nixon stated in his Consumer Message sent to Congress February 25, 1971, "Legislative remedies and improved enforcement procedures are powerful weapons in the fight for consumer justice. But as important as these are, they are only as effective as an aware and an informed public make them. Consumer Education is an integral part of consumer protection."

Consumer Education is a valuable tool and must be made available for all Americans—young or old, rich or poor.

I have encouraged Consumer Education and am aware of the increased number of consumer programs. More needs to be done, however, particularly for the poor, foreign language speaking, and the elderly. It is hoped that this bibliography will be helpful to consumer educators, school and public libraries, and community information centers in establishing such programs.

Children are often overlooked as consumers and it is important that they learn how to be wise consumers at an early age; therefore, a new section on books for the education and pleasure of our young people is included.

This Consumer Education Bibliography is the result of the efforts of many. I am particularly indebted to Mr. John Mackenzie Cory, Director, the New York Public Library, Mr. Robert C. Sheehan, Principal Librarian, History & Social Science Department, Mid-Manhattan Library and my Consumer Education staff, Mr. Samuel B. Blaskey, former Director and Mrs. Doris Sasser Stalker, Director, who coordinated the development of this bibliography.

A special thanks is due Miss Germaine Krettek and Miss Eileen Cooke, American Library Association, for their professional counsel.

Also, a debt of gratitude is owed the professional bibliographic staff who researched literally thousands of possible entries. They are:

Loda M. Hopkins   Formerly Director of the Library
         Simmons College, Boston

Lydia B. LaFleur   Supervising Young Adult Specialist
         The New York Public Library

Lillian Lopez   Administrator, South Bronx Project
         The New York Public Library

Alieen O'Brien Murphy	Children's Literature Specialist Office of Children's Service The New York Public Library
Shirley Quement	Supervising Librarian History and Social Science Dept. Mid-Manhattan Library The New York Public Library
Faye Simkin	Assistant Executive Director New York Metropolitan Reference and Research Library Agency
Irene Patjens Singer	Formerly Branch Librarian 96th Street Regional Branch The New York Public Library
William Sloan	Film Librarian The New York Library

The members of President Nixon's Consumer Advisory Council, particularly Dr. Stewart Lee, Geneva College, and Dr. Carmen Busquets, University of Puerto Rico, gave invaluable and expert advice to the preparation of this document.

I am, also, most grateful to the numerous teachers and librarians throughout the country who offered suggestions and comments on this publication. I hope that I will continue to receive suggestions and comments for future editions.

The Yonkers Public Library, Yonkers, New York, under the direction of Mr. Grinton I. Will, Director, and Miss Irene Rogers, Coordinator of Adult Services, are to be commended for their pioneer work in producing the first Consumer Education Bibliography.

VIRGINIA H. KNAUER
Special Assistant to the President
for Consumer Affairs

CONTENTS

INTRODUCTION

This bibliography is a listing of over 4,000 books, pamphlets, periodical articles, audiovisual aids, and teachers' materials relating to consumer interests and consumer education. It was undertaken at the invitation of Mrs. Virginia H. Knauer, Special Assistant to the President for Consumer Affairs.

The recent proliferation of materials in this area has made it impossible to produce an exhaustive bibliography. We have instead attempted to give an overview of the field. For practical reasons of space, we have omitted those items which appear in university extension bulletins and those items which are readily available only in local areas. No attempt has been made to index every article appearing in consumer oriented periodicals. Annotations have been kept as brief as possible.

Wherever possible the most recent edition of each item has been listed. The nature of the subject, however, requires constant revision of materials, so the user should be sure to obtain the latest edition for the most up-to-date information.

It has been an honor for The New York Public Library to be consulted on this revision and to be associated with what is hoped to be a useful contribution to a field of such paramount importance.

JOHN MACKENZIE CORY, *Director*
The New York Public Library

Consumer Classics

Affluent Society, by John Kenneth Galbraith, 1958. 368 p. $6.95. Houghton Mifflin, Boston. Also available in paperback: 95¢ (cat. no. MT348) New American Library, 1301 Avenue of the Americas, New York, N.Y. 10019.

"A book which is as disturbing as it is brilliant. It is a book with which it is easy to cavil or to disagree, but which it is impossible to dismiss. . . . The general reader will relish a book whose style is polished and witty, but the professional will feel its sharp barbs." R. L. Heilbroner. *New York Herald Tribune Book Review*, June 1, 1958: 3.

American Chamber of Horrors; the Truth about Food and Drugs, by Ruth de Forest Lamb, 1936. 418 p. O. P. Farrar-Rinehart, New York.

"Miss Lamb tells the story of the Chamber of Horrors, folio upon folio, until the heart cries out in anguish. She tells it carefully, accurately, and with scrupulous documentation." Stuart Chase. *Survey Graphic*, v. 25, Apr. 1936: 254.

Backward Art of Spending Money, by Wesley Mitchell, 1950. 421 p. $5.00. Augustus M. Kelley, New York.

First published in 1937.
"Every student of social science who pretends to any intelligent interest in economics, and particularly in its orientation in the larger problem field, must welcome this collection of essays." F. H. Knight. *American Journal of Sociology*, v. 43, Jan. 1938: 668.

Consumer Cooperation in America, by Bertram B. Fowler, 1936. 305 p. O. P. Vanguard, New York.

"Mr. Fowler's engagingly written narrative is authoritative and penetrating but not in the least dogmatic . . . it should be read by everyone who is interested in our national economic reorganization." Manya Gordon. *Saturday Review of Literature*, v. 14, June 20, 1936: 3.

Consumer Interest, by Persia Crawford Campbell, 1949. 660 p. O. P. Harper, New York.

"The entire book deserves thoughtful reading by students and educators, governmental policy makers, and, obviously, consumers in general." M. B. Matson. *Survey*, v. 85, Oct. 1949: 555.

Consumer Movement, by Helen Laura Sorenson, 1941. 245 p. O. P. Harper, New York.

" . . . a history of and guide to the consumer movement. It is both comprehensive and accurate. It threads its way unerringly among the many organizations, distinguishing between the real and sham and between the quick and the dead." M. S. Stewart. *Nation*, v. 153, Aug. 16, 1941: 145.

Consumer Representation in the New Deal, by Persia Crawford Campbell, 1969. 298 p. $10.00. AMS Pr., New York.

First published in 1940.
"Dr. Campbell has made an important contribution to the literature of consumer economics. Although writing close to the events she describes, the author has sifted wisely and evaluated objectively." L. J. Gordon. *Social Education*, v. 6, Jan. 1942: 50.

Consumers' Co-operative Movement, Sidney and Beatrice Webb, 1922. 504 p. O. P. Longmans, London.

"They have an epic story to tell; but the great virtue of their book is that, while entirely admirable as a description of a very complex system of federal institutions, it has a most suggestive analysis of future possibilities." H. J. Laski. *New Republic*, v. 31, June 14, 1922: 80.

Consumers' Co-operative Societies, by Charles Gide, 1921. O. P.

Originally published in French in 1904. First English edition being a translation of the third French edition published in 1917.

"The book is a keen, critical study of the movement in its physical aspects. The well balanced, almost detached point of view . . . comes near to making sociology as absorbing as fiction." Albert Sonnichsen. *Nation*, v. 116, Jan. 3, 1923: 20.

Decline and Rise of the Consumer: a Philosophy of Consumer Cooperation, by Horace Meyer Kallen, new ed., 1946. 484 p. $4.00. Hendricks House, New York.

First published in 1936 by Appleton-Century. This edition has an introduction by S. I. Hayakawa.

"Charles Gide has furnished the standard structural analysis of cooperative enterprise. The Webbs produced the classic economic treatise from British experience. In formulating a social philosophy of the movement Dr. Kallen has undoubtedly fathered a new line of co-operative studies." P. S. Broughton. *Books*, Sept. 20, 1936: 21.

Eat, Drink and Be Wary, by Frederick Schlink, 1935, 322 p. O. P. Covici Friede, New York.

" . . . in essentials there is so much truth in his book, truth that needed badly to be said loudly and spectacularly, that the public owes him a debt of gratitude for writing it." Herschel Brickell. *New York Times Book Review*, Dec. 8, 1935: 22.

Economic Effects of Advertising, by Neil Hopper Borden, 1942. 988 p. O. P. Irwin, Homewood, Ill.

"The study is by no means the final word on the subject, but it is at least a point of departure for all future studies, and no scholar can afford to venture opinions on the incidence of advertising costs until he has familiarized himself with the material." G. B. Hotchkiss. *Annals of the American Academy*, v. 221, May 1942: 218.

Economics and Ethics, by John Atkinson Hobson, 1929. 489 p. O. P. Heath, Boston.

"I know of no other book in which crucial ethical concepts and issues are canvassed with such critical regard to their economic relevancy and promise." T. V. Smith. *American Journal of Sociology*, v. 35, Mar. 1930: 849.

Economics of the Household, by Benjamin Richard Andrews, 1923. 623 p. O. P. Macmillan, New York.

"Whether or not the volume be opened with expectation, it will be closed with profit . . . Mr. Andrews accentuates the significance to the nation that lies in a recognition of the full economic meaning of the homes of its people." G. B. Biddle. *Annals of the American Academy*, v. 111, Jan. 1924: 379.

Education of the Consumer, by Henry Harap, 1924. 360 p. O. P. Macmillan, New York.

A study and evaluation of the consumption habits of the American people.

Guinea Pigs No More, by Joseph Brown Matthews, 1936. Additional material by Oscar S. Cox. 311 p. O. P. Covici, Friede, New York.

"It is refreshing to have a book of this type which offers constructive suggestions as well as destructive. While the act offered by Mr. Cox may or may not be the correct one it at least supports a negative argument with a constructive alternative." *Christian Science Monitor*, Mar. 2, 1936: 18.

The Jungle, by Upton Beall Sinclair, 1906. 413 p. O. P. Doubleday, Page, New York. Available in paperback: 60¢ (cat. no. CP-130) New American Library, 1301 Avenue of the Americas, New York, N.Y. 10019.

"It was in 1906 that Upton Sinclair published *The Jungle*, the novel that Jack London described as the *Uncle Tom's Cabin* of wage-slavery and that was almost as important in its practical effects. This story of stockyards affected legislation, but rather because the public was shocked by its revelations of the food-supply than because of the author's disclosure of social conditions.

The story was a nightmare and all quite true—it was never disproved in any part—and the book worked mightily for the physical welfare of the nation." Van Wyck Brooks and Otto Bettmann, *Our Literary Heritage*, 1956. Dutton, New York. p. 187.

100,000,000 Guinea Pigs, by Arthur Kallet and Frederick Schlink, 1933. 312 p. O. P. Vanguard, New York.

"Speaking as one guinea pig to another I must admit that there is a lot of honest, well made, grade AA Swiss cheese in the argument of this book: it is full of holes. The emphasis, however, should be placed on the complimentary adjectives, because the facts presented are of greatest value." James Rorty. *New Republic*, v. 74, Feb. 15, 1933: 23.

Silent Spring, by Rachel Carson, 1962. 368 p. $5.95. Houghton Mifflin, Boston.

The book which shocked the nation into action concerning the misuse of pesticides. A powerful protest against the abuse of synthetic chemicals and a plea for maintaining the balance of nature. Of special interest to teenagers.

Standards and Labels for Consumers' Goods, by Jessie V. Coles,

1949. 556 p. O. P. Ronald, New York.

"For those who wish information as well as analysis, this book is a rich storehouse of facts as to who did (or said) what and when." Hazel Kyrk. *Annals of the American Academy*, v. 268, Mar. 1950: 235.

A Theory of Consumption, by Hazel Kyrk, 1923. 298 p. O. P. (Hart, Schaffner and Marx prize essays, 35) Houghton Mifflin, Boston.

"It's an odd world anyway in its irrationality, and Miss Kyrk's book will only help rob the reader of any sneaking suspicion he may have harbored of rationality in his own choices or in social choices—in a world of war and politics, and of love and sunshine." Henry Raymond Mussey. *Nation*, v. 118, Feb. 6, 1924: 146.

The Theory of the Leisure Class, by Thorstein Bunde Veblen, 1934. 404 p. $2.95. Modern Library, New York. Also available in paperback: 95¢ (cat. no. MQ-813) New American Library, 1301 Avenue of the Americas, New York, N.Y. 10019. Also available in various other editions.

"It is indeed ironic that our understanding of work and play today should owe so much to this mocking and forbiddingly austere son of the Scandinavian-American Midwest, who had such little use for luxury and frivolity." Eric Larrabee, ed., *American Panorama*, 1957. New York University Press, New York. p. 336.

Tragedy of Waste, by Stuart Chase, 1925. 296 p. O. P. Macmillan, New York.

"Stuart Chase combines Sidney Webb's encyclopedic passion for the facts with H. L. Mencken's scornful fervor. The result is a book which neither Mencken nor Webb could have written—a book that is at once exciting and informing." Evans Clark. *New York Times Book Review*, Nov. 15, 1925: 5.

Two-Thirds of a Nation, by Nathan Straus, 1952. 291 p. O. P. Knopf, New York.

"The book should lend itself to effective propaganda for better housing in the United States. No one reading Mr. Straus can doubt the desperate need for such propaganda—and no one can remain indifferent to the issues involved." Peter Blake. *New York Times Book Review,* Jan. 13, 1952: 18.

Unsafe at Any Speed, by Ralph Nader, 1965. 365 p. $5.95. Grossman, New York. Also available in paperback: $1.00. Essandess Special Editions, 1 West 39th St., New York, N.Y. 10018.

"The author has done prodigious research in a field mired in anonymity,

and has come up with a book that, hopefully, will change Detroit's ways, voluntarily or otherwise . . . " Eliot Fremont-Smith. *New York Times Book Review,* Dec. 5, 1965: 77. Of interest to some teenagers.

Your Money's Worth, by Stuart Chase and Frederick Schlink, 1927. 285 p. O. P. Macmillan, New York.

"Messrs. Chase and Schlink have written a very enjoyable book, gathered an accumulation of winning evidence, and no doubt stirred up national thought so that even the courts —the last resort of musty thinking— may in time be influenced to protect consumers from false representations and to force sellers to sell by standards and truth rather than by trade names and slogans." M. L. Ernst. *Nation,* v. 125, Aug. 10, 1927: 134.

Consumer and the Economy

Do You Know Your Economic A B C's? 11 booklets. Various prices; various catalog numbers. U.S. Dept. of Commerce, Supt. of Documents, GPO, Washington, D.C. 20402.

Describes such basic aspects of the American economic system as balance of payments, patents, profits, and economic growth. Of particular interest to consumer specialists are booklet 7, *"Measurement"* (cat. no. C 1.2:M 46; 25¢ each) and booklet 10, *"The Marketing Story"* (cat. no. C 1.2:M 34/4; 30¢ each).

Adam Smith, Consumer Tastes, and Economic Growth, by N. Rosenberg. *Journal of Political Economy,* v. 72, May 1968: 361–374.

The author points out how the taste and preference structure of the consumer is related to Adam Smith's explanation of the process of economic growth.

America the Inefficient. *Time,* v. 95, Mar. 23, 1970: 72–78.

A satirical look at our mechanized and materialistic society. Consumer products and services are among the areas considered. Of interest to some teenagers.

American Cooperatives: Where They Came from, What They Do, and Where They Are Going, by Jerry Voorhis, 1961. 226 p. $4.95. Harper and Row, New York.

Considers the consumer cooperative in its broadest sense and discusses its potential benefits to the public and the American economic system.

The American Market of the Future, by Arno H. Johnson and others, 1966. 138 p. $4.95. New York University Press, New York.

Three lectures concerned with the composition and level of consumer demand and its relationship to the American economy in the next decade.

Annotated Subject Index, v. I–VI, 1964–69. *Journal of Marketing Research,* v. 6, Nov. 1969: 511–556.

Serves as an abstract to the research articles published in the journal, some of which are separately annotated in this bibliography. The articles are technical, and serve as models upon which scholarly consumer research can be based. Written primarily from the marketer's point of view.

Better Deal for Ghetto Shoppers, by Frederick D. Sturdivant. *Harvard Business Review,* v. 46, Mar./Apr. 1968: 130–136.

Disheartening study of the Watts riots where bitterness towards retailers was apparent. The author urges incentives to encourage responsible chain stores to locate in ghetto areas to help counteract high-cost and unscrupulous retailers.

Bibliography on Marketing to Low-Income Consumers, 1969. 49 p. 55¢ (U.S. Dept. of Commerce, cat. no. C41.12: M34–4) Supt. of Documents, GPO, Washington, D.C. 20402.

An annotated bibliography of two hundred and thirty-six publications.

Business and the Consumer—a Program for the Seventies, 1970. 14 p. $1.00. Chamber of Commerce of the United States, 1615 H St., N.W., Washington, D.C. 20006.

An examination of the emerging consumer movement: the causes behind it, its future direction, and the role business should pay in its future relationships with the American consumer.

Business—Consumer Relations Program, n.d Six pamphlet series. Chamber of Commerce of the United States, 1615 H St., N.W., Washington, D.C. 20006.

Program developed to aid and encourage local Chambers of Commerce. Individual titles are:

Let's Revitalize Business-Consumer Relations, 30 p. $1.50

Model Community Consumer Survey, 8p. Free

Consumer conference guides:

Appliances, 14 p. $1.00
Clothing, 17 p. $1.00
Foods, 16 p. $1.00
Credit, 16 p. $1.00

"Business Responds to Consumerism." *Business Week,* Sept. 6, 1969: 94+

The many ramifications of the relationship between business and the consumer are discussed in depth. Spurred by fear of customer revolts or more protection laws, industry is now offering simpler products, new warranties and services.

Business Week. Weekly. $12.00. McGraw-Hill, 330 W. 42 St., New York, N.Y. 10036.

Contains brief but informative articles about consumer expediture surveys. A weekly column on "Personal Business" is aimed at the upper middle-income businessman. Other articles are of occasional interest to consumers.

Comparison of Prices Paid for Selected Foods in Chainstores in High and Low Income Areas of Six Cities, 1968. 15 p. Free. Consumer and Marketing Service, U.S. Dept. of Agriculture, Washington, D.C. 20250.

"Data collected during a survey of prices charged for food items purchased in stores of two chains in each of the six cities showed no identifiable pattern of differences between sample stores of the same chain operating in high and low income areas."

Competition for Consumers: a Study of the Changing Channels of Distribution, by Christina Fulop. 1965. 323 p. $8.25. Translantic Arts, Inc., 565 Fifth Ave., New York, N.Y. 10017.

Developments in recent years in Great Britain. One section discusses problems of consumer protection, resale price maintenance, and trading stamps.

The Consumer, edited by Gerald Leinwand, 1970. 190 p. 75¢ (paper) Washington Square Press, 630 Fifth Ave., New York, N.Y. 10020.

One of a series of volumes designed as text materials for urban schools. A shocking and informative exposé of the marketing and selling practices that are commonplace in modern America.

Consumer Affairs: Progress in Sight, by Sidney Margolius. *American Federationist,* v. 76, Sept. 1969: 1–6.

Comprehensive article about what has gone on in the consumer area during the 1960's and what problems continue to exist.

Consumer Choice in the American Economy, by Carolyn Shaw Bell, 1967. 429 p. $9.50. Random House, New York.

Focuses on welfare economics, consumer information, labeling, pricing, packaging, standards and consumer credit. Extensive bibliography.

Consumer Interests Drift in Vacuum as Business Pursues "Marginal Float," by Stanley E. Cohen. *Advertising Age,* v. 40, Mar. 24, 1969: 112+.

Perceptive analysis of some of the interactions between the consumer, the government and business.

The Consumer Movement in Historical Perspective, by Robert O. Herrmann, 1970. 32 p. Single copies free; additional copies 25¢. College of Agriculture, Dept. of Agricultural Economics and Rural Sociology, Pennsylvania State University, Weaver Bldg., University Park, Pa. 16802.

A brief discussion of the three eras of consumer activity: early 1900's; 1930's; and the 1960's. Provides an historical perspective for the consumer education teacher.

The Consumer Movement in the United States, by Lucy Black Creighton, 1968. 319 p. Dissertation, unpublished. Harvard University, Cambridge, Mass. 02139.

Available on interlibrary loan. Traces the history of the consumer movement. Subtitled: "A study of efforts to promote the role of consumers in the economy."

The Consumer Price Index. Monthly. Free. U.S. Dept. of Labor, Bureau of Labor Statistics, Washington, D.C. 20210.

"A monthly report on consumer price movements including statistical tables and technical notes." Issue for Jan. 1971 reports figures for Nov. 1970.

The Consumer Revolution. *U. S. News & World Report,* v. 67, Aug. 25, 1969: 43–46.

"Mrs. Virginia Knauer . . . tells what is causing the consumer revolution, and explains her plans for improving products and services through 'tell-tags', and other ideas." A question and answer interview.

Consumerism Reaches the Crossroads, by Isadore Barmash. *The New York Times,* Oct. 5, 1970: 67, col. 4.

Summarizes the present state of the consumer movement.

Consumerism: the Opportunity of Marketing, by Peter Drucker, 1969. 12 p. Free. National Association of Manufacturers, 277 Park Ave., New York, N.Y. 10017.

A noted business philosopher tells why he feels the consumer movement marks a failure in the marketing concept when it should actually create an opportunity for marketing.

Consumers' Capitalism and the Immutable Laws of Economics, by Al Lox, edited by E. A. Opitz, 1969. 236 p. $5.95. Charles Hallberg and Co., 110 W. Grand Ave., Chicago, Ill. 60610.

A book on comparative economic systems, with implications for the consumer. The author rejects government interference in economic activity and defends his system of "consumers' capitalism."

The Consumer's Freedom to be Wrong, by E. B. Weiss. *Advertising Age,* v. 39, Mar. 4, 1968: 53+.

Excellent discussion of the pros and cons of consumerism by businessmen. The position of the consumer is outlined clearly by the author.

The Consuming Public, edited by Grant S. McClellan, 1968. 219 p. $3.50. H. W. Wilson Co., New York.

Thirty-four articles reprinted from newspapers and magazines that offer a spectrum of views on consumer interests. Contents are grouped under headings: the citizen as consumer, the role of government as a protector, business and consumer protection, consumer concerns and the consumer interest movement. A seven-page bibliography is appended.

Consumption Economics, a Multidisciplinary Approach, by Marguerite Burk, 1968. 359 p. $10.95. John Wiley, New York.

Quantitative and technical presentation of consumption economics, presenting the micro- and macro-economics of consumption.

Co-ops on Campus, by Barbara W. Newell. *Nation,* v. 209, Dec. 8, 1969: 635–636.

Subtitle: "The militant consumers." The developing consumer movement on campus, due in large part to older students with families confronted with rising costs.

The Corporate Deaf Ear, by E. B. Weiss. *Business Horizons,* v. 11, Dec. 1968: 5–6.

The author believes that there will be more government legislation in the future if large corporations do not develop effective channels of communication with the growing number of sophisticated consumers.

Crusader Widens Range of His Ire. *Business Week,* no. 2056, Jan. 25, 1969: 128+.

Interesting biographical sketch of Ralph Nader and his new targets: federal agencies and law firms. Of interest to some teenagers.

The Customer—Business Partnership, by Frank E. McLaughlin. *Food, Drug, Cosmetic Law Journal,* v. 25, Dec. 1970: 519–524.

Reviews the changing nature of the relationship between business and its customers. The author is Director for Industry Relations of the Office of Consumer Affairs.

Do the Poor Pay More? by Charles S. Goodman. *Journal of Marketing,* v. 32, Jan. 1968: 18–24.

What kind of stores do the poor patronize and why? How well do they perceive differences among stores? These are some of the questions answered from a survey conducted in a Philadelphia redevelopment area.

Economic Report of the President; together with the annual report of the Council of Economic Advisers, 1969. 332 p. $1.50 (cat. no. PR36.9:969) Supt. of Documents, GPO, Washington, D.C. 20402.

A compendium of past, present and future economic policy. On page twenty-six the President states "I hope that this Congress will go down in history as the consumer-conscious Congress."

7

Economics of Food Retailing, by Daniel I. Padberg, 1968. 292 p. $9.00. Cornell University Press, Ithaca, New York.

A text prepared for a correspondence course for supermarket managers and food industry executives. It provides consumer economists with a useful overview of the organization of food retailing, competitive behavior and the overall performance of the industry.

Fact Booklets. 1971. 15¢ (or 8 for $1.00). Council of Better Business Bureaus, Inc., 1101 17th St., N.W., Washington, D.C. 20036.

A series of pamphlets explaining or commenting on various subjects of interest to consumers. Sample titles annotated elsewhere in this bibliography.

Farm to Factory, by Gilbert C. Fite, 1965. 288 p. $6.00. University of Missouri Press, Columbia, Mo.

Detailed accounts of its activities and the kinds of challenges that face the modern large-scale cooperative. Includes labor-management relations, and expansion into newer areas.

Five Myths of Consumerism, by Dallas Smythe. *Nation,* v. 208 Jan. 20, 1969: 82–84.

"Consumption is the goal of life" and "the consumer is king" are two of the five myths of the "buy something" society in which we live. Of interest to some teenagers.

Fortune. Published 14 times a year. $14.00. $2.00 per copy. Fortune Magazine, Time and Life Building, Rockefeller Center, New York, N.Y. 10020.

Comments on consumer spending and trends appear occasionally in the "Business Roundup Column." Long articles on individual industries and companies are useful to investors.

Growing Consumer Upheaval Seen Aspect of Fast Changing Society, by Stanley E. Cohen. *Advertising Age,* v. 40, Dec. 8, 1969: 20.

An analysis of the changes taking place in the modern "consumerism" movement.

A Guide to Consumerism, by George S. Day and David A. Aahen, *Journal of Marketing,* v. 34, July 1970: 12–19.

Heavily documented discussion of how consumerism evolved and where the movement is headed.

Handbook of Modern Marketing, edited by Victor Buell and Carl Heyel, 1970. unpaged. $27.50. McGraw-Hill, New York.

A monumental compilation of marketing information. Of special interest to consumer specialists: Section 14, "Customer Services"; Section 17, "Ethical and legal aspects of marketing".

Harassment Laid to Consumerism, by Peter Millones. *The New York Times,* Feb. 18, 1970: 1, col. 5.

An account of a rebuke to consumer activists given by Woodrow Wirsig, president of the Better Business Bureau of Metropolitan New York, Inc.

How to Organize a Co-op, 1969. 53. p. Free. Office of Economic Opportunity, 1200 19th St., N.W., Washington, D.C. 20506.

"Moving ahead together" describes the purposes and organization of a cooperative. Very simply written. Prepared by: the Cooperative League of the U.S.A. and the Office of Economic Opportunity.

Income in 1969 of Families and Persons in the United States, 1970. 136 p. $1.25 (Consumer income current population reports, Series P–60, No. 75, cat. no. C3.186:P60/75). Supt. of Documents, GPO, Washington, D.C. 20402.

Eighteen pages of descriptive material followed by one hundred and eighteen pages of a variety of tables on personal income.

Journal of Marketing. Quarterly. $10.00. The American Marketing Association, 230 Michigan Ave., Chicago, Ill. 60601.

Official publication of the American Marketing Association. Emphasis is on the marketer's point of view. Almost every issue, however, contains articles of interest to consumer economists.

Kiplinger Washington Letter. Weekly. $24.00. Kiplinger Washington Editors, 1729 H St. N.W., Washington, D.C. 20006.

A report to business men, taxpayers, and consumers on trends and developments affecting finance, jobs, and economic conditions.

Let's Revitalize Business-Consumer Relations, 1969. 32 p. $1.50. Chamber of Commerce of the United States, 1615 H Street, N.W., Washington, D.C. 20006.

Explains for the twenty-seven hundred local chambers of commerce the mechanics of setting up a business-consumer dialogue at the local level. Quantity prices available.

Let's Take the Politics out of Consumerism, by Arthur C. Fatt. *Nation's Business*, v. 57, Jan. 1969: 82–86.

The author claims that government bureaucracy, mainly for political reasons, is championing the consumer cause without understanding the consumer's real needs or the purposes of the American economic system. Steps are outlined to remedy this situation.

The Making of Economic Society, by Robert Heilbroner, 2d ed., 1962. 241 p. $6.75. Prentice-Hall, Englewood Cliffs, N.J.

An exploration of "economics of the past, bringing the reader through economic evolution of the Roman slave system, medieval feudalism, and the industrial revolution to the present-day market system." Current economic problems and the role of planning for the future are included.

Market Restraints in the Retail Drug Industry, by F. Marion Fletcher, 1967. 444 p. $10.00. University of Pennsylvania Press, Philadelphia.

Examination of the ways governmental regulations and occupational licensing obstruct free market competition in the retail sale of drugs. Instead of focusing on the price-fixing and market-controlling activities of the large drug manufacturers, this study emphasizes the activities of small companies and pharmacists.

Marketing Information Guide. Monthly. $4.50 (cat. no. C41.11:) Supt. of Documents, GPO, Washington, D.C. 20402.

A publication of the U.S. Department of Commerce, Business and Defense Services Administration, Marketing Division. Contains an annotated bibliography of current government and non-government materials. Of interest to those concerned with the sale or purchase of industrial and consumer products, business or personal services.

The Marketing Story, 1968. 48 p. 30¢ (cat. no. C1.2:M34/4). Supt. of Documents, GPO, Washington, D.C. 20402.

The marketing functions of the American economy are explained in layman's language. A valuable list of bibliographical references is included, primarily on marketing but some consumer source materials are included.

Markets of the Seventies, by the editors of *Fortune*, 1968. 118 p. $3.95. Viking Press, New York.

This collection of articles from *Fortune* provides a look forward to the unwinding American economy of the 1970's.

Mass Consumption Society, by George Katona, 1964. 343 p. $8.50. McGraw-Hill, New York.

A plea for the revision of many accepted economic theories based on three emerging characteristics of modern society: affluence of the many, consumer power, dependence on consumer motivation.

The Merchant and the Poor, by Marion O. Boner, 1970. 5 p. $1.50 (Exchange Bibliography 129) Council of Planning Librarians, P. O. Box 229, Monticello, Ill. 61856.

Selective bibliography on consumer credit and consumer protection, as they apply to low-income groups.

Monopoly, by Joseph C. Goulden, 1968. 350 p. $5.95. Putnam's, New York. Also available in paperback: 95¢ Pocket Books. 1 W. 39th St., New York, N.Y. 10018.

A critical survey of the operations of the American Telephone and Telegraph Company.

Monthly Labor Review. Monthly. $9.00 (cat. no. L2.6) Supt. of Documents, GPO, Washington, D.C. 20402.

The medium through which the Department of Labor releases many articles of interest to consumer specialists, including information on consumer costs, budgets, and labor developments.

NFCU 1970 Consumer Annual, 1970. 34 p. Free. Navy Federal Credit Union, 8th and M Streets, S.E., Washington, D.C. 20360.

Contains fourteen articles of general consumer interest.

The New Age of Consumerist Columnists. *Sales Management,* v. 104, Feb. 15, 1970: 42+.

A brief but interesting discussion of the increasing number of journalists writing consumer columns.

The New Industrial State, by John Kenneth Galbraith, 1967. 427 p. O. P. Houghton Mifflin, Boston.

Well-known examination of the role of industry, the state, and the individual. A new economic order is described where great corporate complexes carry on a special kind of planning to insure their continued positions of dominance.

The Old Country Store, by Gerald Carson, 1965. 330 p. $1.85 (paper) E. P. Dutton, 201 Park Ave., South, New York, N.Y. 10003.

An entertaining and informative history of the general store in America.

Over the Counter and on the Shelf, by Laurence Ayres Johnson, 1961. 140 p. $10.00. Tuttle, Rutland. Vt.

"Country storekeeping in America, 1620–1920." An exercise in consumer nostalgia.

Politics of the Consumer, by L. Tivey. *Political Quarterly,* v. 39, Apr. 1968: 181–194.

A British view of the role of consumers' pressure groups and their future prospects.

Reaching the Consumer through the Creative Home Economist, by Betty McDermott. *Forecast for Home Economics,* v. 13, Nov. 1967: F33.

How the home economist can assist manufacturers, retailers, and advertisers to reach their customers, improve their sales, and provide better products.

Rise of the Russian Consumer, by Margaret Miller, 1965. 254 p. $6.25; $1.95 (paper) Transatlantic, New York.

Examines the ways in which consumer demands are reshaping the Soviet economy and changing the living standards of the Russian people.

Shoplifting, the Pinch that Hurts. *Business Week,* June 27, 1970: 72–73.

Surveys the fastest growing larceny in the nation—shoplifting, a billion dollar a year bill charged to the honest consumer.

The Significance of Consumerism, by Milan D. Smith, 1967. 21 p. Free. National Canners Association, 1133 20th St., N.W., Washington, D.C. 20036.

Abstract of an address presented at the Mid-western Canners Sales Conference. Presents the canners' side in the conflict over the growing aspect of "consumerism" in the marketplace.

Take in a New Partner—the Consumer, by William G. Kaye. *Nation's Business,* v. 58, Feb. 1970: 54–57.

The former executive director of the President's Committee on Consumer Interests comments on ways in which business could improve its relations with consumers.

Toward Balanced Growth: Quantity with Quality, July 4, 1970. 228 p. $1.50 (cat. no. PR 37.8:N 21g 1R 29/970) Supt. of Documents, GPO, Washington, D.C. 20402.

Surveys the objectives of the American way of life. Chapter 7, p. 135–149 entitled: "Consumerism."

U.S. Consumer. Biweekly. $7.50. Student rate: 25 copies or more for 8 months at $2.70 per subscription. Group rate: 2 to 49 subscriptions at $5.50 each, 50–99 at $4.50 each, 100 or more at $3.75 each. All subscriptions payable in advance. Consumer News, Inc., 813 National Press Building, Washington, D.C. 20004.

A newsletter specializing in news about brand-name products, safety hazards and other consumer information. Of interest to some teenagers.

The Waste Makers, by Vance Packard, 1960. 340 p. $6.50. David McKay, New York. Also available in paperback: 95¢. Pocket Books, 1 W. 39th St., New York, N.Y. 10018.

Attacks "planned obsolescence" in industry, a practice which causes the consumer to waste untold sums of money on repairs and replacements. Suggests ways of combating this unfortunate trend in American business. Of interest to some teenagers.

Consumer Behavior

Anticipations and Purchases, by F. Thomas Juster, 1964. 303 p. O. P. National Bureau of Economic Research, 261 Madison Ave., New York, N.Y. 10016.

Conclusion of an investigation of consumer purchasing behavior initiated in 1957. Data obtained from a sample of 20,000 families, member-subscribers to Consumers Union.

Aspirations and Affluence, by George Katona, Burkhard Stumpel, and Ernest Lahn, 1971. 239 p. $12.95. McGraw-Hill, New York.

"Comparative studies in the United States and Western Europe" which survey the interaction between man and his economic environment.

Blue-Collar World, by Arthur B. Shostak and William Gomberg, 1964. 622 p. $8.95. Prentice-Hall, Englewood Cliffs, N.J.

Studies of the American worker as parent and provider, community member, moral and religious being, participant in physical and mental health experiences, and user and abuser of leisure time, unemployment and retirement.

The Child Consumer: a New Market, by James U. McNeal. *Journal of Retailing,* v. 45, summer 1969: 15–22.

An analyses of the marketer's process of "growing customers for future use." The author warns that marketers must take care not to offend parents.

Competition and Human Behavior, by Chester R. Wasson and others, 1968. 173 p. $2.95 (paper) Appleton-Century-Croft, New York.

Summarizes the human element in consumer decisions and considers the consumer in relation to the major principles of the behavioral sciences.

A Computer Controlled Experiment in Consumer Behavior, by G. David Hughes and Philippe A. Naert. *Journal of Business,* v. 43, July 1970: 354–372.

Author concludes that there is considerable potential for the application of the techniques of a computer controlled experiment to consumer behavior.

Consumer Attitudes toward Auto Insurance, 1970. 132 p. Free. Allstate Insurance Co., Northbrook, Ill. 60062.

Reports on two national studies of consumer attitudes toward automobile accidents and automobile insurance. The studies were sponsored by four major insurance companies.

Consumer Behavior, by James F. Engel and others, 1968. 652 p. $13.50. Holt, Rinehart and Winston, New York.

Comprehensive analysis of consumer motivation and behavior. Three areas are stressed: critical analyses of relevant evidence; generalizations drawn from the evidence; and pinpointing of areas in which research is needed.

Consumer Behavior: an Integrated Framework, by C. Glenn Walters and Gordon W. Paul, 1970. 548 p. $15.35. Richard D. Irwin, Homewood, Ill.

Intended as a basic undergraduate text on consumer behavior, but of interest to the general reader.

Consumer Behavior and Marketing Management, by James H. Myers and William R. Reynolds, 1967. 336 p. $4.25 (paper) Houghton Mifflin, Boston.

A survey of consumer motivations and buying behavior as these are related to marketing. Will be of interest to the general reader as well as the student. Extensive bibliography: p. 315–330.

Consumer Behavior and the Behavioral Sciences, by Steuart Henderson Britt, 1966. 592 p. $11.95. John Wiley, New York.

Three hundred and forty-eight selections from two hundred and sixty-nine authors concerned with varying aspects of consumer behavior.

Consumer Behavior; Contemporary Research in Action, edited by Robert J. Holloway and others, 1971. 458 p. $5.95 (paper) Houghton Mifflin, Boston.

"This volume reflects the editors' belief that it is time for this vital area of marketing to move to the next stage of its development, that is, that a research emphasis be introduced into the study of consumer behavior." Preface.

Consumer Behavior: Learning Models of Purchasing, by George H. Haines, Jr., 1969. 216 p. $7.95. Free Press, New York.

Discussion and analysis of contemporary theories. Technical in approach and advanced in subject matter. Designed for management scientists, marketing specialists, and economists.

Consumer Behavior of Children and Teenagers, by Robert O. Herrmann, 1969. 160 p. $5.00. American Marketing Association, Central Services Offices, 230 North Michigan Ave., Chicago, Ill. 60601.

A selective bioliography of research done from 1955 to 1970. Entries are arranged into twenty-one categories.

Consumer Choice Behavior: an Experimental Approach, by Flemming Hansen. *Journal of Marketing Research*, v. 6, Nov. 1969: 436–443.

A scholarly analysis of the process of consumer choice and predicting consumer behavior. Includes a description of experiments and a twenty-five item bibliography.

Consumer Demand in the United States, by H. S. Houthakker and Lester D. Taylor, 1970. 321 p. $10.00. Harvard University Press, Cambridge, Mass.

Comprehensive study of the composition and magnitude of consumer expenditures in the United States, with applications to other countries. Includes analyses for 1929–64 for over 80 commodities, projections of the demand for each in 1970 and 1975, and a detailed investigation of total consumption and savings patterns.

Consumer Markets in Mid-1970. *Federal Reserve Bulletin*, v. 56, July 1970: 555–563.

Study of consumer spending and saving patterns through mid-1970.

Consumer Patterns and Marketing Patterns in Low-Income Neighborhoods, by Robert J. Halloway and Richard N. Cardoza, 1969. 62 p. $2.00. University of Minnesota, Graduate School of Business Administration, Division of Research, Minneapolis, Minn. 55455.

"An exploratory study," includes general data, retail strategy, and consumer aspirations.

Consumer Response to Income Increases, by George Katona and Eva Mueller, 1968. 244 p. $6.75; $2.95 (paper). Brookings Institution, Washington, D.C.

A report of a series of interviews designed to measure responses of consumers to increases in income during 1964–65. The purpose was to measure the responses to the tax cut of 1964 as well as to the increases in income before the tax cut.

Consumer Search, Role Enactment and Market Efficiency, by Louis P. Bucklin. *Journal of Business*, v. 42, Oct. 1969: 416–438.

A study and analysis of comparison shopping, particularly as it applies to foods.

Consumerism: a Perspective for Business, by David W. Cravens and Gerald E. Hills. *Business Horizons*, v. 13, Aug. 1970: 21–28.

Business firms should understand consumer behavior through appropriate research, suitable marketing strategy, involvement in consumer affairs, and greater awareness in the ranks of top management.

Consumerism: the Mood Turns Mean. *Sales Management,* v. 103, July 15, 1969: 27–41.

Summation of the problems facing the consumer, his growing activities and continued resistance to anti-consumer forces.

Current Population Reports. Irregular. $8.50 per yr. (price includes eight series) (cat. no. C 3.186:P[Series no]). Supt. of Documents, GPO, Washington, D.C. 20402.

Taken together this series contains a wealth of statistical information on consumer behavior and predictions of consumer trends. It is widely available in public and academic libraries. Series P–60 and P–65 are of particular interest to students of consumer affairs.

Current Problems in Consumer Behavior Research, by David T. Kollat and others. *Journal of Marketing Research,* v. 7, Aug. 1970: 327–332.

Supplements other critical evaluations of consumer research by discussing several issues and problems that impede the development of a consumer behavior research tradition. Includes eighty-seven references.

Determinant Buying Attitudes, by James H. Myers and Mark I. Alpert. *Journal of Marketing,* v. 32, Oct. 1968: 13–20.

The meaning and measurement of attitudes which determine buying behavior.

Dimensions of Consumer Behavior, edited by James U. McNeal, 2d ed., 1969. 446 p. $4.50 (paper) Appleton-Century-Crofts, New York.

A selection of readings emphasizing the psychological and sociological aspects of consumer behavior and research techniques.

A Dissonance Approach to Repeat Purchasing Behavior, by Robert Mittelstaedt. *Journal of Marketing Research,* v. 6, Nov. 1969: 444–446.

Discusses the nature of the dependent variable in dissonance studies. An experiment in consumer choice is described.

Don't Sell the Buyer Short, [interview with] John A. Howard. *Nation's Business,* v. 58, Aug. 1970: 34–35.

An evaluation of consumer information intake as observed in three product surveys. Professor Howard has a high opinion of consumer intelligence.

Economic Behavior of the Affluent, by Robin Barlow and others, 1966. 285 p. $6.95. Brookings Institution, Washington, D.C.

This study is based on the results of a survey conducted in 1964, concerning the working and investment behavior of individuals with yearly incomes of $10,000 or more.

Expenditure Patterns of the American Family, edited by Fabian Linden, 1965. 175 p. $25.00 ($5.00 educator's rate). National Industrial Conference Board, 845 Third Ave., New York, N.Y. 10022.

Based on special tabulations of data from the Bureau of Labor Statistics' Survey of Consumer Expenditures, 1960–61. The volume includes 145 pages of statistics and the remainder consists of explanatory information.

Forgotten Generation. *Forbes,* v. 103, Jan. 15, 1969: 22−24+.

The over 65 market.

Handbook of Consumer Motivation, by Ernest Dichter, 1964. 486 p. $12.95. McGraw-Hill, New York.

The likes and dislikes of human beings whether they concern concrete objects or the world of ideas are explained. Dichter's studies in motivational research helped stimulate Vance Packard to write *The Hidden Persuaders*.

The Hidden Persuaders, by Vance Packard, 1957, 275 p. $7.50. David McKay, New York. Also available in paperback: 95¢ (cat. no. 77162) Pocket Books, 1 W. 39th St., New York, N.Y. 10019.

An investigation of the subtle methods of motivational research. Dated, but still a basic work in the field.

Household Decision-Making, edited by Nelson N. Foote, 1961. 349 p. $8.50 (Consumer behavior, v. 4) New York University Press, New York.

Papers and discussions from a conference held at the University of Michigan in the fall of 1958 on various aspects of consumer behavior by sociologists, psychologists, economists, market researchers, and other social scientists.

How to Predict What People Will Buy, by Louis Cheskin, edited by Van Allen Bradley, 1957. 241 p. $6.95. Liveright, New York.

By a trained psychologist who has specialized in color as a device for increasing sales. The author tells of many products whose sales increased because of a change in package design and color.

Information and Consumer Behavior, by P. Nelson. *Journal of Political Economy,* v. 78, Mar. 1970: 311–329.

Limitations of consumer information about quality have profound effects upon the market structure of consumer goods. Consumer behavior is also relevant to the determination of monopoly power in consumer industries.

The Intelligent Buyer and the Telltale Seller, by Dexter Masters, 1966, 252 p. $5.95. Knopf, New York.

A discussion of the "hard sell" commercialism of today.

Money and the Young Wage Earner, 1967. 32 p. Free. National Association of Bank Women, Inc., 60 E. 42nd St., New York, N.Y. 10017.

Reports on a survey made to determine the attitudes of young people toward money and finance.

A Multidisciplinary Analysis of Children's Food Consumption Behavior, by Lois A. Lund and Marguerite C. Burk, 1969. 221 p. $2.00. Technical Bulletin No. 265, Bulletin Room, University of Minnesota, Agricultural Experiment Station, St. Paul, Minn. 55101.

Appraisal of children's food consumption characteristics.

On Knowing the Consumer, by Joseph W. Newman, 1966. 248 p. $9.50. John Wiley, New York.

The result of a Consumer Behavior Symposium held by the Stanford University Graduate School of Business. Covers buying decisions, consumer-product relationships, market segmentation, and influences on consumer choice. Emphasizes the marketing approach.

Perspectives in Consumer Behavior, by Harold H. Kassarjian and Thomas S. Robertson, 1968. 568 p. O. P. Scott, Foresman, Clearview, Ill.

An overview of some of the basic thinking on consumer behavior. Presents a comprehensive set of readings together with a text.

Psychological Approaches to the Study of Saving, by Folke Olander and Carl-Magnus Seipel, 1970. 114 p. $3.50; $2.50 (paper) Bureau of Economic and Business Research, 408 David Kinley Hall, University of Illinois, Urbana, Ill. 61801.

Presents researchers in psychology, economics and allied fields with a synthesis of previous scholarship on the psychological aspects of saving. Two hundred and ninety references are cited. Based on a monograph published in 1967 by the Economic Research Institute, Stockholm School of Economics.

The Psychology of Consumer Behavior, by Rom J. Markin, 1969. 258 p. $5.25 (text ed.). Prentice-Hall, Englewood Cliffs, N.J.

Emphasizes that consumer behavior has its roots in socio-psychological phenomena. The theme of the book centers around a concept of existential behavior.

The Psychology of Pricing, by Benson P. Shapiro. *Harvard Business Review,* v. 46, July/Aug. 1968: 14–16+.

A storehouse of valuable information for retailers, manufacturers and consumers who want to know more about pricing. Footnotes contain numerous additional sources.

Research in Consumer Behavior, by James F. Engel and others, 1970. 688 p. $10.95; $6.95 (paper) Holt, Rinehart and Winston, New York.

A selection of articles drawn from the literature of the various behavioral sciences. All are related to the study of consumer behavior.

Risk Taking and Information Handling in Consumer Behavior, edited by Donald F. Cox, 1967. 667 p. $10.00. Division of Research, Harvard Business School, Soldiers Field, Boston, Mass. 02163.

A selection of papers which focuses on the perception of risk by consumers and the way in which consumers acquire and process information in order to deal with these risks.

'70's Consumer May Spur Status of Consumption Everett Warns, by John R. Everett. *Advertising Age,* Jan. 19, 1970: 36+.

Emphasizes that consumers will expect more from corporate giants, and that they will, at the same time, grow less prone to revere luxury and less enchanted with accumulating "things".

Shoppers' Movements Outside Their Local Retail Area, by Robert O. Herrmann and Leland L. Beik. *Journal of Marketing,* v. 32, Oct. 1968: 45–51.

An investigation of people who shop out of town, why and what they buy. The results suggest that concern about local prices was not an important motivator, but that the desire to examine a large and varied selection of fashion merchandise was.

Shopping Center Versus Downtown, by Christen Tonnes Jonassen, 1955. 170 p. O. P. Bureau of Business Research, Ohio State University, 1775 South College Road, Columbus, Ohio 43210.

Motivation research on shopping habits and attitudes in three widely separated and diverse cities: Seattle, Washington; Houston, Texas; and Columbus, Ohio.

Some Insights into Reasonable Grocery Shopping Strategies, by James M. Carman. *Journal of Marketing,* v. 33, Oct. 1969: 69–72.

Statistical presentation of a study to show whether "shopping around" resulted in lower prices being paid.

The Spenders, by Steuart Henderson Britt, 1960. 293 p. $7.95. McGraw-Hill, New York.

"Where and why your money goes." A carefully written defense of the American system of marketing.

The Strategy of Desire, by Ernest Dichter, 1960. 314 p. O. P. Doubleday, Garden City, New York.

An intriguing reply to the questions raised by Vance Packard's *The Hidden Persuaders* about the value and justification of the science of motivation. Ernest Dichter has been called the "father of motivational research."

Survey of Changes in Family Finances, 1968. 321 p. $1.00. Publications Services, Division of Administrative Services, Federal Reserve Bank, Washington, D.C. 20551.

A discussion of savings-distribution as related to income and age; determinents of total savings; and composition of savings. Questionnaires and statistical tables are included.

Theory of Buyer Behavior, by John A. Howard and Jagdish N. Sheth, 1969. 458 p. $5.95. John Wiley, New York.

Provides a theoretical structure for the buyer behavior specialist and the basic scientist in their approaches to the problems of purchase behavior.

The $30 Billion Negro, by Gibson D. Parke, 1969. 311 p. $6.95. Macmillan, New York.

A journalistic analysis of the American Negro market. Part I: "Understanding the Negro Consumer"; Part II: "Planning for the Negro market"; Part III: "Developing the market."

Understanding Consumer Behavior, edited by Martin M. Grossack, 1966. 339 p. $6.50. Christopher Publishing House, 53 Billings Rd., North Quincy, Mass. 02171.

A selection of papers on the potentialities and limitations of consumer research as performed by social scientists. Topics include acceptance of new products, measuring of TV commercials, household decision making and new product innovation.

Why People Buy, by Louis Cheskin, 1959. 319 p. $6.95. Liveright, New York.

Sub-title: "Motivation research and its successful applications." Basic research into why people buy. Emphasis is on color and shape of product. Controlled tests were used to determine why people selected a certain product.

INTERNAL INFLUENCES

Brand Assortment and Consumer Brand Choice, by Eli Seggev. *Journal of Marketing,* v. 34, Oct. 1970: 18–24.

How do consumers select brands? The author reports on a study in which a new approach to brand choice behavior was tested and shows how it can improve understanding of consumers' decision processes.

Buyer Attitudes and Brand Choice Behavior, by George S. Day, 1970. 219 p. $7.95. Free Press, New York.

Develops a theory of the attitude-behavior relationship, and incorporates this theory into an interpretive model to appraise the influence of environment on the brand choice decision.

Consumer Image and Attitude, by John G. Myers, 1968. 167 p. $2.00 (paper) Institute of Business and Economic Research, University of California, Berkeley, Calif. 90024.

Succinct monograph on the concepts of consumer attitudes in marketing and behavioral science literature.

Consumer Self-concept, Symbolism and Market Behavior, by Edward L. Grubb and Harriet L. Grathwohl. *Journal of Marketing*, v. 31, Oct. 1967: 22–27.

Considers the relationship between the psychological characteristics of a consumer and his purchase behavior. The authors establish a theoretical foundation for a model of consumer behavior based upon an individual's self-concept and the symbolic value of the goods he buys.

Household Correlates of 'Brand Loyalty' for Grocery Products, by Ronald E. Frank and others. *Journal of Business*, v. 41, Apr. 1968: 237–245.

Primarily written for those in marketing, this article will also be of interest to anyone concerned with consumer brand loyalties. Footnotes include numerous other sources.

Interproduct Household Loyalty to Brands, by Yoram Wind and Ronald E. Frank. *Journal of Marketing Research*, v. 6, Nov. 1969: 434–435.

A study of brand loyalty patterns in brand loyalty prone households. A technical presentation.

Judging Quality by Price, Snob Appeal, and the New Consumer Theory, by Roger E. Alcaly and others, 1966. 18 p. $3.00. Clearinghouse for Federal, Scientific and Technical Information, Springfield, Va. 22151.

Highly technical and mathematically oriented study of the theory of demand. Designed for the specialist.

Purchasing Behavior and Personal Attributes, by William F. Massy and others, 1968. 174 p. O. P. University of Pennsylvania Press, Philadelphia.

The relation of household, socio-economic and personality characteristics to brand-name grocery purchases are here examined with psychological, econometric and statistical techniques. The author found that personality factors and socio-economic characteristics provide only a limited explanation of variations in purchasing behavior.

Secrets of Marketing Success, by Louis Cheskin, 1967. 278 p. $5.75 Trident Press, send orders to Simon and Schuster, New York.

One of the most successful "motivational researchers" presents his views on the science and art of persuasive selling.

Social Class and Income as Indicators of Consumer Credit Behavior, by John W. Slocum, Jr. and H. Lee Mathews. *Journal of Marketing*, v. 34, Apr., 1970: 69–74.

Based on questionnaires mailed to a random sampling of commercial credit card holders in a large eastern metropolitan area.

Social Class and Life Cycle as Predictors of Shopping Behavior, by Stuart U. Rich and Subhash C. Jain. *Journal of Marketing Research*, v. 5, Feb. 1968: 41–49.

Concerned with applications of concepts of social class and life cycle to consumer behavior for the purpose of segmenting the market. Contains a twenty-nine item bibliography.

The Status Seekers, by Vance Packard, 1959. 376 p. $7.95 David McKay, New York. Also available in paperback: 95¢. Pocket Books, 1 W. 39th St., New York, N.Y. 10019.

"An exploration of class behavior in America and the hidden barriers that affect you, your community, your future."

A Study of the Influence of Image Congruence on Consumer Choice, by Al E. Birdwell. *Journal of Business,* v. 41, Jan. 1968: 76–88.

A statistical survey of why people buy the cars they do. Twenty-two concepts were measured, including sophistication, reliability, safety, excitement.

EXTERNAL INFLUENCES

Advertising

Advertising Age. Weekly. $6.00. Advertising Age, 740 North Rush St., Chicago, Ill. 60611.

A trade journal serving the American advertising industry. Carries frequent articles on consumer interests.

Advertising and Competition, by Jules Backman, 1967. 239 p. $5.95. New York University Press, New York.

Results of a study commissioned by the Association of National Advertisers. Author concludes that advertising promotes competition and that advertising does not increase the cost of goods and services advertised.

Advertising and Your Life, by Richard P. Frisbie, 1969. 41 p. 50¢. Claretian Publications, 221 W. Madison St., Chicago, Ill. 60606

Discusses the defects of advertising as a medium of information in modern American society.

Advertising in America, by Raymond A. Bauer and Stephen A. Greyser, 1968. 474 p. $9.00; $5.00 (paper) Harvard Business School, Soldiers Field, Boston, Mass. 02163.

A study of Americans' attitudes toward advertising based on a nationwide survey of consumers.

Advertising: Its Cultural and Political Effects, by Giancarlo Buzzi, 1968. 147 p. $5.50. University of Minnesota Press, Minneapolis.

The author probes deeply into the political, social and cultural questions raised by advertising, and presents ideas which are unorthodox, challenging and sometimes paradoxical. Published in Italy in 1963 under the title *La Tigre Domestica.*

Bait Advertising, n.d. 6 p. Free. Council of Better Business Bureaus, 1101 17th St., N.W., Washington, D.C. 20036.

Comments on the practice of advertising a product or service solely to attract consumers who can then be "switched" to a more expensive item. Available in quantity, $4.00 per 100; $30.00 per 1,000.

Consumer Response to Various Levels of Advertising for Fluid Milk, 1967. 12 p. 75¢ (cat. no. A 1.82:805) Supt. of Documents, GPO, Washington, D.C. 20402.

A Critique of Consumerism, by E. B. Weiss, 1967. 28 p. $1.00. Doyle Dane Bernbach, Inc., 20 W. 43rd St., New York, N.Y. 10036. (Single copies free to business executives or educational organizations.)

Critique stressing the importance of the effect of consumerism on advertising. The author is vice-president of a large advertising company.

Due to Circumstances beyond Our Control, by Fred W. Friendly, 1967. 325 p. $8.95. Random House, New York.

"Because television can make so much money doing its worst it cannot afford to do its best." This paradox summarizes the dilemma of commercial television today.

Ethics for Today, by Harold Hooper Titus and Morris Keeton, 4th ed., 1966. 573 p. $8.50 (text ed.) American Book Co., New York.

A leading textbook on ethics. Chapter 19 deals with "Ethics and the Mass Media."

The Federal Trade Commission and the Regulation of Advertising in the Consumer Interest, by Dorothy Cohen. *Journal of Marketing,* v. 33, Jan. 1969: 40–44.

Points out that knowledge of the behavior patterns of low-income groups would assist the FTC in performing its advertising regulatory function more effectively.

15 Ways Ads Try to Get You to Buy, *Scholastic Scope,* v. 13, Jan. 18, 1971: 4–11.

"Famous people say," "snob appeal," "youth appeal," "concern for public good" are some of the approaches used by advertisers to sell their products. This article demonstrates through the use of illustrations fifteen such approaches. Should make teenagers more aware of methods advertisers use to get them to buy their products.

Free Press and Fancy Packages, by A. Z. Mowbray. *Nation,* v. 205, December 11, 1967: 621–623.

Discusses the attempts to suppress information on the truth-in-packaging bill in magazines, newspapers, TV and radio, and the degree of success obtained.

Freedom of Choice—an Action in the Public Interest, 1968. 32 p. Free. Magazine Publishers Association, 575 Lexington Ave., New York, N.Y. 10022.

Compilation of advertisements sponsored by the Magazine Publishers Association.

From Those Wonderful Folks Who Gave You Pearl Harbor, by Jerry Della Femina, 1970. 253 p. $6.50 (text ed. $5.95) Simon and Schuster, New York.

An hilarious and urbane commentary on advertising agencies and their practices.

The Golden Fleece: Selling the Good Life to Americans, by Joseph J. Seldin, 1963. 305 p. O. P. Macmillan, New York.

An advertising man analyzes advertising men, the Madison Avenue symbol, advertising in a class society, built-in obsolescence, quack remedies, TV give-aways, motivational research and the exaggerated ungrammatical language of Madison Avenue.

Guides Against Bait Advertising, Adopted November 24, 1959, 1969. 3 p. 10¢ (Federal Trade Commission Reports, cat. no. FT1.8/2:B16) Supt. of Documents, GPO, Washington, D.C. 20402.

Highlights problems of price advertising which have proved troublesome to businessmen, who in good faith, desire to avoid deceiving the consumer public.

Guides against Deceptive Advertising of Guarantees, Adopted April 26, 1960, 1969. 5 p. 10¢ (Federal Trade Commission Reports, cat. no. FT1.8/2:G93/960). Supt. of Documents, GPO, Washington, D.C. 20402.

Enumerates the major principles applicable to advertising of guarantees and indicates that the greatest difficulty with this type of advertising has been the failure to state adequately what a guarantee is.

Honesty and Competition, by George J. Alexander, 1967. 315 p. $10.00. Syracuse University Press, Syracuse, New York.

"False advertising law and policy under Federal Trade Commission administration." This heavily documented study analyses legal aspects of descriptions of product assets, price information, testimonials, and sales information. Seventy-two pages of appendices include FTC guides and regulations against deception.

Madison Avenue, U.S.A., by Martin Mayer, 1959. 332 p. 75¢ (paper) Pocket Books, 1 W. 39th St., New York, N.Y. 10018.

A popular study of the advertising industry and the people who run it.

The Mechanical Bride, by Marshall McLuhan, 1951. 154 p. $12.50. Vanguard Press, New York. Also available in paperback: $2.95. Beacon Press, 25 Beacon St., Boston, Mass. 02108.

A penetrating analysis of the content of many advertisements.

The Morality (?) of Advertising, by Theodore Levitt. *Harvard Business Review,* v. 48, July-Aug. 1970: 84–92.

"In curbing the excesses of advertising both business and government must distinguish between embellishment and mendacity." An interesting in-depth article with valuable suggestions for businessmen and consumers to consider.

The One-Eyed Slicker; TV's Long Lasting Superstrength Half-Truths, by Daniel Henninger. *New Republic,* v. 162, May 2, 1970: 17–19.

A commentary on television "soft-core" semi-frauds. Several popular commercials are examined. Of interest to some teenagers.

The Permissible Lie, by Samm Sinclair Baker, 1968. 236 p. O. P. World Publishing Co., New York.

An esposé of American advertising which condemns the industry for plac-

ing profits before public service. The author states that "a lie that helps build profits is considered as a permissible lie."

The Role of Advertising, edited by Charles Harold Sandage and Vernon R. Fryburger, 1960. 499 p. $11.35 (text ed. $8.50) Richard D. Irwin, Homewood, Ill.

A book of readings from forty-five writers representing a wide range of skills and occupations. Each presents some aspect of the role of advertising in the economy.

Seven Glorious Days, Seven Fun-Filled Nights, by Charles Sopkin, 1968. 286 p. $5.95. Simon and Schuster, New York. Also available in paperback: 75¢. Ace Books, 1120 Avenue of the Americas, New York, N.Y. 10036.

The diary of "one man's struggle to survive a week watching commercial television in America."

Stormy Weather in Media City, by Jacqueline Eagle. *Media-Scope,* v. 14, Feb. 1970: 29–32+.

Advertising quality and ethics as they affect the consumer.

Text of Model State Deceptive Practices Act. *Advertising Age,* v. 39, Nov. 25, 1968: 26–28.

Final form of model statute on deceptive practices in advertising drawn up by the American Advertising Federation to be transmitted by members to their respective legislators.

Those Were the Good Old Days, by Edgar R. Jones, 1959. 448 p. $15.00. Simon and Schuster, New York.

"A happy look at American advertising, 1880–1930."

Victorian Advertisements, by Leonard DeVries, 1968. 136 p. $8.95. Lippincott, Philadelphia, Pa.

A pictorial survey of early consumer advertising. Of interest to some teen-agers.

The Vulnerable Americans, by Curt Gentry, 1966. 333 p. $4.95. Doubleday, Garden City, New York.

Describes questionable advertising procedures, confidence games, shady interest and credit terms, tricks of the drug trade, merchandising schemes, extortion, credit card swindles, telephone insurance frauds, and many others dubious practices.

Washington View: Tough Customers Ahead for Admen, by Stanley E. Cohen. *Advertising Age,* Jan. 19, 1970: 35, 40+.

Contends that a vast consumerism surge to save the environment will make consumers wary of advertising claims. The author makes predictions of consumerist aims for the coming decade.

With All Its Faults, by Fairfax M. Cone, 1969. 335 p. $6.95. Little, Brown, Boston.

"Advertising's most respected scold brings to life the controversies, the triumphs and defeats of forty years in the world of advertising."

Marketing techniques

Brand Strategy in United States Food Marketing, by William Applebaum and Ray A. Goldberg, 1969. 86 p. $2.00 (paper). Division of Research, Harvard Business School, Soldiers Field, Boston, Mass. 02163.

Two lengthy essays. Applebaum analyzes the competition between manufacturers' brands and distributors' brands. Goldberg examines the brand strategies of six major food chains in promoting sales of both private label and manufacturers' brands of white bread, frozen orange juice concentrate and margarine.

The Case against Trading Stamps, by Fred E. Waddell. *Journal of Consumer Affairs,* v. 2, summer 1968: 21–39.

Traces the cost of trading stamps to both consumer and retailers. The author predicts a declining use of trading stamps.

Developing Responsible Promotion, [an address] by E. L. Bond, Jr. *Vital Speeches,* v. 37, Dec. 1, 1970: 124–128.

Comment on corporate consumer information policies.

The Direct Selling Industry, by Harry M. Buttenham and others. *UCLA Law Review,* v. 16, Sept. 1969: 883–1031.

Empirical study of consumer protection and door-to-door selling. Locale is chiefly California.

Economic Report on the Use of Games of Chance in Food and Gasoline Retailing, 1968. 122 p. Free. Federal Trade Commission, Washington, D.C. 20580.

An FTC staff report prepared for the House Subcommittee on Activities of Regulatory Agencies. Presents many of the apparent malpractices present in games of chance.

The Economics of Trading Stamps, by Harold W. Fox, 1968. 176 p. $6.00. Public Affairs Press, Washington, D.C.

Examines the structure, conduct and performance of the trading stamp industry and analyzes the economic functions, costs, and benefits of its service. Many charts, graphs, and statistical information.

The Future of Trading Stamps and Games, by Fred C. Allvine. *Journal of Marketing,* v. 33, Jan. 1969: 45–52.

Discusses the question of whether the use of trading stamps and games has stabilized or is in the early stages of a major decline.

The Great Discount Delusion, by Walter H. Nelson, 1965. 237 p. O. P. David McKay, New York.

A survey of discount merchandising from an opponent of discount retailing. Included are interviews with economists, retailers and marketing consultants, and transcripts of congressional hearings.

Groceries, Gas and Games, by J. Cross. Nation, v. 208, Mar. 24, 1969: 370–372.

"Economic report on the use of games of chance in food and gasoline retailing."

Grocery Bills, by David Sanford. New Republic, v. 163, Oct. 17, 1970: 12–14.

Discussion of tactics of supermarkets which have converted to "discounting." Conclusion of one study is that discounting has not altered the cost of groceries.

How Housewives See the Discount Stores Today. Discount Merchandiser, v. 10, Mar. 1970: 77+

Findings of a recent marketing research study on the image of the discount house.

Loaded Odds. Time, v. 93, Apr. 18, 1969: 86–87.

"FTC investigation of promotional lures by food chains and oil companies."

On the Use and Economic Significance of Trading Stamps, 1969. 44 p. 30¢ (cat. no. FT 1.2: T67). Supt. of Documents, GPO, Washington, D.C. 20402.

Price Movements Following the Discontinuance of Trading

Stamps, by F. E. Brown. Journal of Retailing, v. 43, fall 1967: 1–16.

The conclusion reached in this study is that prices were not affected as a whole in those areas where trading stamps were phased out.

Private Brands—the Inside Story. Changing Times, v. 19, Nov. 1965: 25–29.

"Is a store's own brand as good as a nationally advertised one?" Discussion and chart listing private-label appliances and the manufacturers who make them.

Sperry & Hutchinson's Very Successful Stagnation, by Stanley H. Brown. Fortune, v. 70, Nov. 1964: 157–159+.

In depth analysis of a trading stamp company. Reveals a great deal concerning trading stamp companies and their operations, particularly the operations of S&H green stamps.

Trading Stamps and Their Impact on Food Prices, 1958. 42 p. 30¢ (cat. no. A 1.82:295) Supt. of Documents, GPO, Washington, D.C. 20402.

A study of the impact of trading stamps on the price of food. The data has aged, but the report still contains much valuable material.

Who Wins Marketing Promotion Games? by Thomas O'Hanlon. Fortune, v. 79, Feb. 1969: 104–108+.

"Nobody, really, but the promoters themselves, if you take the testimony of food-chain managers, gasoline dealers and disillusioned players".

What Consumers Think about Packaging Waste. Modern Packaging, v. 44, no. 3, March 1971.

Survey of consumers' attitudes concerning different types of packaging, disposal and recycling problems.

Consumer Protection

Buyer's Guide to the Law: Contracts and Consumer Frauds, by Howard T. Reben and Michael G. West, 1971. 45 p. $1.00. Pine Tree Legal Services, 158 Danforth Street, Portland, Me. 04101

Booklet contains basic information on contract law, interpretations of warranties, and consumer frauds.

Can "Cooling-off Laws" Really Protect the Consumer? by Orville C. Walker, Jr. and Neil M. Ford. *Journal of Marketing,* v. 34, Apr. 1970: 53–58.

Laws providing the consumer with a period of one to four days in which to rescind a contract to purchase goods or services.

Clearinghouse Review. Monthly. Free. National Clearinghouse for Legal Services, Northwestern University School of Law, 710 Lake Shore Drive, Chicago, Ill. 60611.

Each issue carries a section on consumer legal action.

Compromise on Who Can Sue in Consumer Actions. *Congressional Quarterly Weekly Report,* v. 28, Mar. 13, 1970: 747–750.

"The Nixon administration appears ready to back down in a legislative battle over consumer damage suits— a move likely to make the nation's businessmen unhappy."

Congress and Consumer Protection Proposals. *Congressional Digest,* v. 47, Mar. 1968: 67–96.

Provides broad coverage of the scope of federal activity and considers such controversial topics as truth-in-lending, fire safety act, and pipeline safety act.

Congress Probes Door-to-Door Selling. *Sales Management,* v. 99, Nov. 20, 1967: 38–40.

Discussion of proposed legislation to curb door-to-door selling.

Consumer and the Law in Canada, edited by William A. W. Neilson, 1970. 538 p. $10.00. Osgoode Hall Law School, Downsview, Ontario.

Thirty-three contributions make this a valuable source of commentary and opinion on the interaction of law and the advancement of the consumer interest. The editor states: "it is neither a scholarly treatise nor an exhaustive compendium of the subject field."

Consumer Law Bibliography, by Richard A. Elbrecht, 1971. 134 p. $4.00. National Consumer Law Center, Publication # A044. 550. Boston College Law School, Brighton, Mass. 02135.

Bibliography developed under a research grant from the Office of Economic Opportunity, Washington, D.C. 20506.

Consumer Legislative Monthly Report. Monthly. $4.00. Office of Consumer Affairs, Supt. of Documents, GPO, Washington, D.C. 20402.

A subject classified listing of legislation introduced in the Congress on consumer oriented subjects. Provides bill numbers, sponsors, a numerical index to bills, and lists of legislation of consumer interests passed by either house and by both houses. An indispensable resource for large public and academic libraries.

Consumer Protection, by Elizabeth Hanford. *Pittsburgh Business Review,* v. 39, Dec. 1969: 2–6.

An address given on Oct. 16, 1969 by the Deputy Director of the Office of Consumer Affairs.

Consumer Protection at Last Through Local Control of Retail Installment Sales Contracts, by Donald P. Rothschild. *George Washington Law Review,* v. 37, July 1969 : 1067–1116.

Considers the feasibility of local control over consumer affairs, primarily through municipal regulations and ordinances. The District of Columbia is used as an example.

Consumer Protection: Hearings before the Consumer Subcommittee of the Committee on Commerce, 1970. 533 p. Free. Consumer Subcommittee, U.S. Senate Commerce Committee, Washington, D.C. 20510.

The hearings on three bills concerned with consumer protection by amending the Federal Trade Act, including the "class action" bill.

Consumer Protection in Michigan. *Michigan Law Review,* v. 68, Apr. 1970 : 926–985.

Current methods in force in Michigan and some proposals for reform.

Consumer Protection in the States, 1970. 39 p. $3.00. Council of State Governments, Iron Works Pike, Lexington, Kentucky 40505.

Outlines the following consumer problems while defining the state role in them and reviewing what some States have done: public employee labor relations, consumer protection, narcotics control and drug abuse, law enforcement and crime control, and environmental quality.

Consumer Protection Program, by Louise Verr Hines and Edna DeCoursey Johnson, 1968. 12 p. Apply for price. Family Services Program, Baltimore Urban League, 2406 Pennsylvania Ave., Baltimore, Md. 21217.

"The story of how Baltimore is trying to meet a need."

Consumer Protection Responsibility. *Congressional Quarterly Weekly Report,* v. 27, Nov. 21, 1969 : 2349–2359.

Thirty-nine agencies and departments of the federal government that deal with consumer activities are listed here.

Consumer Protection: the Individual Can Act, by Howard Frazier [an address]. *Vital Speeches,* v. 36, Feb. 15, 1970 : 265–270.

Address by the president of the Consumer Federation of America at the Saturday Evening Forum, University of Arizona.

Consumerism: a New and Growing Force in the Marketplace, 1968. 34 p. Free. Burson-Marsteller Public Relations, 866 Third Ave., New York, N.Y. 10022.

Summary of consumer protection activities with emphasis on the 1960s. Includes a chapter on the attitudes of the business community toward this growing movement.

Consumer's Handbook, 1968. 26 p. Free. Consumer Division, Food and Drug Directorate, Dept. of National Health and Welfare, Tunney's Pasture, Ottawa 3, Canada.

A brief description of Canada's food and drug laws is presented, followed by a series of questions and answers from the consumer's viewpoint.

Consumers in Court, by Ronald G. Shafer. *Wall Street Journal,* v. 175, Apr. 30, 1970 : 1+.

Potential legislative action by consumers is discussed—bills to permit consumers to unite to sue companies, buyers with similar complaints could bring class actions.

The "Cooling-off" Period in Door-to-Door Sales, by Bryan D. Sher. *UCLA Law Review,* v. 15, Apr. 1968 : 717–786.

Defines the period during which the consumer may withdraw from purchase commitments made at home.

An Exploratory Analysis of Consumer Rights Cases of Low-Income Residents, Washington, D.C., by Ann Charlotte Erickson, 1967. n.p. Unpublished Master's thesis. College of Home Economics, Cornell University, Ithaca, N.Y. 14850.

A study of one hundred and ninety consumer rights cases handled by the four Neighborhood Legal Service Projects in Washington, D.C.

Fair Packaging, 1968. 4 p. 5¢ (cat. no. FS13.1281a:P12). Supt. of Documents, GPO, Washington, D.C. 20402.

A report extracted from the *Food and Drug Administration Papers,* October, 1967, outlining a synopsis of food packaging and labeling regulations.

Fair Packaging and Labeling, 1967. 126 p. $3.00. Commerce Clearing House, 4025 W. Peterson Ave., Chicago, Ill. 60646.

Describes the law, regulations, and proposed changes in the Fair Packaging and Labeling Act.

Fair Packaging and Labeling—When?, by Leland J. Gordon, 1968. 33 p. $2.00. Consumers Union of U.S., 256 Washington St., Mount Vernon, N.Y. 10550.

Discussion of the Fair Packaging and Labeling Act and the responsibilities

assumed by the Federal Trade Commission and the Food and Drug Administration.

Fair Packaging and Labeling Act . . . Approved Nov. 3, 1966. 5¢ (cat. no. 89–2: Public Law 755) Supt. of Documents, GPO, Washington, D.C. 20402.

"An act to regulate interstate and foreign commerce by preventing the use of unfair or deceptive methods of packaging or labeling of certain consumer commodities distributed in such commerce, and for other purposes."

Federal Food, Drug, and Cosmetic Act, with Amendments, June 30, 1906—Oct. 24, 1968, 1970. 125 p. 60¢ (cat. no. Y1.2: F31/10). Supt. of Documents, GPO, Washington, D.C. 20402.

Food, Drug, Cosmetic Law Journal. Monthly. $20.00. Commerce Clearing House, 4025 W. Peterson Ave., Chicago, Ill. 60646.

Published in association with the Food and Drug Law Institute, this journal records the progress of the law in the fields of food, drugs and cosmetics and includes constructive discussion. In conjunction with *FDA Papers,* this publication will keep one well informed about the administration and enforcement of food, drug and cosmetic laws.

The Great American Gyp; a Manifesto for Consumer Justice, by Ralph Nader. *New York Review of Books,* v. 11, Nov. 21, 1968: 27–34.

Seven out of ten people interviewed believe present federal legislation is inadequate to protect their health and safety. The majority think more laws are needed to give shoppers full value for their money. Nader questions whether the government is willing and able to do the necessary job.

Guide to Packaging Law, 1967. 75 p. $6.25. *Modern Packaging,*

330 W. 42d St. New York, N.Y. 10036.

Summarizes the basic laws affecting the packaging industry. Includes federal and state sources of legal information and packaging practices. Includes the texts of five federal packaging laws.

How to Sue in Small Claims Court in New York City, 1970. 27 p. Free. Department of Consumer Affairs, 80 Lafayette St., New York, N.Y. 10013.

"If you have been hurt or cheated by a person or a store you can sue in small claims court. You do not need a lawyer. The procedure is simple. This book tells you how to do it."

Labor Looks at the 90th Congress, 1968. 124 p. Free. AFL-CIO, 815—16th St., N.W., Washington, D.C. 20006.

An AFL-CIO legislative report, 11 pages of which are devoted to consumer protection legislation considered by the 90th Congress.

Law and the Consumer, by Robert Berger and Joseph Teplin, 1969. 101 p. $1.20 (paper). Houghton Mifflin, Boston.

Survey of the ways in which law relates to advertising, contracts, credits and other consumer problems.

The Law and the Low-income Consumer, edited by Carol Hecht Katz, 1968. 417 p. $1.00 (paper) New York University School of Law, 41 Washington Square South, New York, N.Y. 10003.

Discusses the legal rights and problems of the low-income consumer. Includes a twelve-page bibliography.

The Law Professor behind ASH, SOUP, PUMP and CRASH, by Joseph A. Page. *New York Times Magazine.* Aug. 23, 1970: 32–33+.

In-depth study of John Banzhaf, a lawyer and law professor, and his activities in championing consumer causes. He succeeded in placing anti-smoking commercials on television. Reply by R. H. Quinn published Sept. 23, 1970: 33.

Let's Rewrite the Probate Laws. *Changing Times,* v. 23, Jan. 1969: 39–42.

Arguments presented for a uniform probate code, so estates may be transferred with minimum delay and interference.

1971 Suggested State Legislation, 1970. 240 p. $5.00. Council of State Governments, Iron Works Pike, Lexington, Ky. 40505.

Statutes expressly concerned with consumer protection in the book are entitled "Consumer Information Act," "Automotive Repair Dealer Registration" and "Games of Chance." An index lists suggested laws from past editions which may still be appropriate for many states. Published Annually.

Notes on Government Action Taken to Enforce Consumer Protection Laws. *Consumer Reports,* v. 34, Jan. 1969: 34–35.

Specific cases of regulatory actions taken by federal agencies, such as the Federal Trade Commission, Food and Drug Administration and U.S. Postal Service; also state and local action to protect consumers.

The Package, Legislation, and the Shopper, by D. M. Gardner. *Business Horizons,* v. 11, Oct. 1968: 53–58.

A sociological approach to truth-in-packaging legislation. Emphasizes the need to investigate and understand the "shopper-package relationship" before interpreting existing laws or creating new legislation.

Product Liability. by David L. Rados. *Harvard Business Review,* v. 47, July/Aug. 1969: 144–152.

Discusses the changing law of product liability and indicates some of the ways in which management can respond. This law has been designed to protect consumers from inferior products.

Progress Made in the Fair Packaging Program, 1968. 9 p. Free. Office of Weights and Measures, National Bureau of Standards, Room A739, U.S. Department of Commerce, Washington, D.C. 20234.

Discusses the voluntary moves made by business to reduce the proliferation of package sizes.

The Proposed Federal Door-to-Door Sales Act, by William G. Meserve. *George Washington Law Review*, v. 37, July 1969: 1171–1217.

"An examination of its effectiveness as a consumer remedy and the constitutional validity of its enforcement provisions."

Rules, Regulations, Statement of General Policy or Interpretation and Exemptions under the Fair Packaging and Labeling Act, November 1, 1969. 21 p. Free. Federal Trade Commission, Washington, D.C. 20580.

A precise, detailed, and technical statement of FTC regulations.

Rush to Protect Consumers, *U.S. News & World Report*, v. 68, Feb. 2, 1970: 44–47.

The buying public now finds businessmen and politicians eager to listen to complaints about products and service. New laws, new agencies, both public and private, are taking shape.

Symposium on Consumer Protection. *Michigan Law Review*, v. 64, May, 1966: 272 p. The Michigan Law Review Association, University of Michigan Law School, Hutchins Hall, Ann Arbor, Mich. 48104.

Covers seven areas of consumer protection.

These Lawyers Work for Consumers. *Changing Times*, v. 24, July 1970: 17–19.

The story of the National Consumer Law Center with headquarters in Boston College Law School, Newton, Mass., and how it works with the Office of Economic Oppportunity to aid the poor.

Two Legal Reforms to Protect Shoppers' Rights. *Changing Times*, v. 24, Apr. 1970: 23–24.

Discusses two areas: "the holder in due course" legal concept, and consumer class action suits.

Unordered Merchandise, Shipper's Obligations and Consumer's Rights, 1969. 4 p. 10¢ (cat. no. FT1.3/2:2) Supt. of Documents, GPO, Washington, D.C. 20402.

Advises the consumer receiving unordered merchandise that he has no obligation either to return the merchandise or to pay for it under the Federal Trade Act.

Up against the Law, by Jean Strouse, 1970. 269 p. 95¢. Signet (cat. no. Q4315) New American Library, 1301 Avenue of the Americas, New York, N.Y. 10019.

The legal rights of people under 21 regarding school, parents, marriage, drugs, sex, driving, employment, contracts, and the draft are clarified through pertinent questions and answers. The appendix lists lawyers and legal organizations that will deal with the legal rights of young people. Of special interest to teenagers.

Fraud, Deception and Other Consumer Concerns

FRAUD AND DECEPTION

Aiding the Poor. *Wall Street Journal*. v. 171, Jan. 4, 1968: 18.

Numerous cases of unethical and fraudulent business practices involving the poor are cited. Possible social and legal actions aimed at remedying these conditions are discussed.

The Assault on Children, by Ron Goulart, 1969. 288 p. $6.50. Sherbourne Press, Los Angeles, Calif.

An "exposé" type of book presenting "the multi-million dollar 'kid market'" and the insidious techniques of the promoters and manufacturers who reap profits from it."

Bargain Hucksters, by Ralph Lee Smith, 1962. 236 p. O. P. Thomas Y. Crowell, New York.

Survey of the ways the public is gulled by fraudulent salesmanship. Automobiles, funerals, encyclopedias, household appliances and charities are the principal areas of investigation.

The Big Sell, by Pierre Berton, 1963. 239 p. $5.95. Alfred A. Knopf, New York.

"An introduction to the black arts of door-to-door salesmanship and other techniques."

The Billion Dollar Swindle, by Amram Ducovny, 1969. 252 p. $5.95. Fleet, New York.

"Frauds against the elderly", how to avoid them by knowing what to look for and who to contact when you have been cheated. Foreword by Senator Harrison A. Williams, Jr.

Buyer Beware!, by Fred Trump, 1965. 207 p. $3.50. Abingdon Press, New York.

Entertaining and informative guide to hoaxes and hucksters. "Get rich quick schemes", deceptive advertising, confidence men and other fraudulent practices are examined in real estate, investments, home improvements, insurance, etc. Notable feature is a guide to where to turn if you feel you are being exploited.

The Compleat Swindler, by Ralph Hancock and Henry Chafetz, 1968. 294 p. $6.95. Macmillan, New York.

"Lively survey of the art of conmanship from the short change gyp to the big time securities swindle." Case histories are drawn from official files. The book is dedicated to "the gullible American—may his numbers never dwindle."

Consumer Guide for Older People, 1968. 2.5 in. x 4 in. leaflet. 5¢ (cat. no. FS 17.308:C76) Supt. of Documents, GPO, Washington, D.C. 20402.

To be carried in wallet or purse, this handy reminder warns against merchandising frauds and swindles affecting the health and pocketbook of older people. To be used by all desiring protection when buying by mail, buying at the door, signing your name, and buying on credit.

Consumer Information Series, 1969. 6 p. leaflets. Free with stamped, self-addressed envelope. Council of Better Business Bureaus, 1101 17th St., N.W., Washington, D.C. 20036.

Leaflets prepared to alert consumers of potential frauds. Titles include: *Homework Schemes, Unordered Merchandise, Mail Order Profit Mirages, Truth in Lending, Fulfillment Complaints, Bait Advertising,* and *Considering a Franchise.*

Consumer Swindles and How to Avoid Them, by John L. Springer, 1970. 246 p. $5.95. Regnery, Chicago.

How to avoid being cheated in eight common consumer situations.

Curbing Fraud, by W. Stewart Pinkerton, Jr. *Wall Street Journal,* v. 175, Jan. 9, 1970: 1, col. 6.

A detailed description of the workings of the Department of Consumer Affairs of New York City. The department is headed by Bess Myerson Grant.

The Dark Side of the Marketplace, by Senator Warren G. Magnuson and Jean Carper, 1968. 240 p. $5.95. Prentice-Hall, N.J.

An angry investigation of the many areas in which consumers are exploited: cosmetics, home improvements, packaging, credit plans, small loans, drugs, and mail frauds. Tips are offered to aid the consumer.

Facts You Should Know about "Earn Money at Home" Schemes, 1956, 1967. 16 p. 15¢. Council of Better Business Bureaus, 1101 17th St., N.W., Washington, D.C. 20036.

A valuable discussion of the various kinds of false and misleading advertisements which are directed to people wanting to supplement their incomes. The victims are usually women.

Fads, Myths, Quacks—and Your Health, by Jacqueline Seaver, 1968. 28 p. 25¢ (Public Affairs Pamphlet no. 415) Public Affairs Committee, 381 Park Ave. South, New York, N.Y. 10016.

An elementary discussion of what to look for in many areas of health care.

Fight Back! 1969. 4 p. 10¢ (Federal Trade Commission Reports, cat. no. FT1.2:F44). Supt. of Documents, GPO, Washington, D.C. 20402.

"The ungentle art of self defense as recommended by the Federal Trade Commission." Alerts the consumer to be aware of the con artist in buying merchandise.

Five Common Frauds, and How to Avoid Them, by Don Wharton, *Reader's Digest,* v. 91, Dec. 1967: 69–72.

Frauds covered are: phoney bank-examiner swindle, home-improvement gyps, dishonest telephone solicitations, questionable charities, and pre-financed funeral plans.

Ghetto Merchants: a Study in Deceptions, by Philip G. Schrag. *New Republic,* v. 159, Sept. 7, 1968: 17–19.

Results of a study about low-income groups and merchants. Food is still more expensive and is still inferior to food sold in higher-income areas.

Health Education vs. Medical Quackery, 1966. 6 p. 10¢ (cat. no. FS13.122:13). Supt. of Documents, GPO, Washington, D.C. 20402.

This Food and Drug Administration Student Reference Sheet discusses medical quackery and presents examples of some of the most common types of medical frauds and swindles to be concerned about.

Health Quackery, 1966. [12 p.] 15¢. American Medical Association, 535 N. Dearborn St., Chicago, Ill. 60610.

A review of the various forms of medical frauds perpetrated on an unsuspecting public.

The Innocent Consumer vs. the Exploiters, by Sidney Margolius, 1968. 227 p. $4.95 ($.95 paper). Trident Press, Order from Simon & Schuster, New York.

Revealing report on the money traps, deceptive advertising, credit plans and packaging that the unsuspecting buyer encounters in the marketplace. Included are lists of Better Business Bureaus and local, state and national consumer organizations.

Mail Fraud Laws . . . Protecting Consumers, Investors, Businessmen, Medical Patients, Students, 1969. 20 p. Free. Chief Postal Inspector, U.S. Postal Service, Washington, D.C. 20260.

Describes the many types of mail fraud against which the law attempts to protect the consumer.

The Medical Messiahs, by James Harvey Young, 1967. 460 p. $9.00. Princeton University Press, Princeton, N.J.

"A social history of health quackery in twentieth century America." Quackery and home remedies are examined against the broader background of sociology, science, marketing and government.

The Medical Offenders, by Howard and Martha Lewis, 1970. 377 p. $7.95. Simon and Schuster, New York.

A readable account of the "corruption and malpractice" confronting the consumer when buying services from some unscrupulous members of the medical professions.

The Other Side of the Poverty Problem, by David Caplovitz. *Challenge,* v. 14, Sept.—Oct. 1965 : 12–15.

Points out methods used by many merchants in their dealings with the poor. Author's conclusion is that there is a clear need for legal safeguards to supplement poverty programs.

The Pill Conspiracy, by George Johnson, 1967. 175 p. 75¢ (paper) New American Library, 1301 Avenue of the Americas, New York, N.Y. 10019.

Exposé on hazardous drugs and pill profiteering.

A Primer on the Law of Deceptive Practices, by Earl W. Kintner, 1971. 593 p. $10.95 Macmillan, New York.

A leading expert in anti-trust and trade regulation law offers the layman an up-to-date introduction to consumer-oriented marketing legislation and regulation.

Stop the TV Repair Swindlers! by A. Hamilton. *Reader's Digest,* v. 94, Feb. 1969 : 100–103.

"Without forceful regulation, dishonest repairmen can clip the public mercilessly. Here's how one state (Illinois) cleaned out the frauds."

The Thumb on the Scale, by A. Mowbray, 1967. 178 p. $4.95. Lippincott, Philadelphia, Pa.

Illuminating portrait of supermarket packaging abuses and the efforts entailed in trying to pass an effective "truth-in-packaging" bill. Appendices include reprints of Senator Hart's strongly-worded bill and the watered-down version that became law.

Wolves, Widows and Orphans, by Dan Tyler Moore, 1967. 261 p. O. P. World Publishing Co., New York.

Entertaining book on swindlers and their victims, exposing the con man's many get-rich-quick schemes.

CONSUMER CONCERNS

Consumer Attitudes and Frustrations in Shopping, by Charles J. Colazzo, 1965. 148 p. $10.00. Retail Research Institute, 100 W. 31st St., New York, N.Y. 10001.

A marketing study of consumer frustration.

The Consumer Fights Back, by Lucia Mouat. *Christian Science Monitor,* Jan. 26, 29; Feb. 2, 5,

9, 12, 16, 19, 24, 26; Mar. 2, 5, 1970. Reprints available: University of Michigan, Reprint Dept., University Microfilm, 300 N. Zeeb Rd., Ann Arbor, Mich. 1–25 copies, $1.00 each; 26–100 copies 90¢; 101–and over copies 75¢.

A broad, sweeping journalistic study of the American consumer climate. The author considers such diverse topics as consumerism, automobile repairs, supermarket bargains, product safety, warranties, consumer protection, sales gimmicks, and consumer organizations.

Consumer Problems of the Poor, 1968. 68 p. Free. Committee on Government Operations, House of Representatives, Room 2157, Rayburn Bldg., Washington, D.C. 20580.

"Supermarket operations in low income areas and the federal response." Thirty-eighth report by the Committee on Government Operations.

Consumerism: a New Protest, by Virginia H. Knauer as told to James C. G. Conniff. *Bell Telephone Magazine,* v. 48, Nov/Dec. 1969: 26–31.

"A revolution among consumers over poor-quality products and shoddy service is forcing the market-sensitive businessman to revise his approach to customer needs."

Consumerism—an Interpretation, by Richard H. Buskirk and James T. Rothe, *Journal of Marketing,* v. 34, Oct. 1970: 61–65.

The forces underlying the present upsurge in consumer activity are analyzed, and some of the dangers of the remedies proposed by some consumer advocates are considered.

Consumerism: the Search for Consumer Interest, by David Aacker and George S. Day, 1971.

442 p. $10.95 ($4.95 paper). Free Press, New York.

Collection of articles and reports on varying aspects of consumer protection.

Consumerism—What is It? *Consumer Bulletin,* v. 53, Aug. 1970: 21–23.

An editorial comment on the present stage of consumer activism.

The Extra Cost of Being Poor, by T. Meyers. *Journal of Home Economics,* v. 62, June 1970: 378–384.

Research has proven that it actually costs more to be poor, from an economic, educational, psychological and physical standpoint.

Eyeball to Eyeball with Customers. *Nation's Business,* v. 56, Nov. 1968: 42–45.

Report of the efforts of businessmen in cities all over the country to initiate dialogues on what's bothering the consumer.

Food Marketing in Low Income Areas, by Bruce W. Marion and others, 1969. 79 p. Free. Cooperative Extension Service, Ohio State University, Columbus, Ohio 43200.

This publication received the American Council on Consumer Interests award for outstanding research on the consumer problems of families.

Food Prices: Before and After Distribution of Welfare Checks ... Low-Income Areas, Seven Cities, 1969. 1970. 22 p. 30¢ (cat. no. A1.82:907) Supt. of Documents, GPO, Washington, D.C. 20402.

Survey to determine if low-income area food stores increase prices after distribution of welfare checks.

Green Power: Consumer Action for the Poor, 1969. 65 p. Free. Office of Economic Opportunity, 1200 19th St., N.W., Washington, D.C. 20506.

Designed for use in planning and establishing Consumer Action Programs and their various components, including credit unions, consumer organizations, buying clubs and other cooperative enterprises.

Hot War on the Consumer, edited by David Sanford, 1969. 280 p. $5.95. Pitman, New York.

Collection of articles, most of which have appeared in the *New Republic* since 1965. Focuses a sharp light on the dark corners of American commerce and offers practical remedies for consumers.

Let the Buyer Beware, 1969. 19 p. 25¢. United Automobile Workers Education Department, 8000 E. Jefferson Ave., Detroit, Mich. 48214.

Simply presented facts about the problems of consumers.

Let the Seller Beware! James Bishop, Jr., and Henry W. Hubbard, 1969. 195 p. $6.95. *Newsweek Magazine,* 1750 Pennsylvania Avenue, N.W., Washington, D.C.

Traces the growth of the consumer movement and protective legislation and discusses the personalities involved in "The Consumer Revolution."

Marketers Fiddle While Consumers Burn, by E. B. Weiss, *Harvard Business Review,* v. 46, July/Aug., 1968: 45–53.

A marketing man's view of consumerism, stressing the need for industry to work with the government to protect the consumer. By so doing, the industrialist will protect himself from excessive government regulation.

The Person Nobody Quite Understands, by Oscar Sussman. *Nation's Business,* v. 56, May 1968: 48–55.

Defense against government assistance to the consumer. The author contends that the consumer may be overprotected, preventing a flow of new goods to the marketplace.

The Poor Pay More, by David Caplovitz, 1967. 192 p. $6.95 Free Press, New York.

Survey of consumer habits of 464 households in low-cost housing projects in New York City. Provides facts and figures which show how and why poor people are victimized by high pressure salesmen, bait advertising, and "easy credit."

Poverty American Style, edited by Herman P. Miller, 1966. 304 p. $4.95 (paper). Wadsworth Pub. Co., Belmont, Calif.

Series of essays dealing with the problems of poverty, including consumer problems and patterns among low-income groups.

Rattles, Pings, Dents, Creaks and Costs. *Newsweek,* v. 72, Nov. 25, 1968: 92–93.

Enlightening article on the lack of quality control in consumer products.

Report of the National Advisory Commission on Civil Disorders, by the editors of *The New York Times,* 1968. 660 p. $1.25 (paper). Bantam Books, Inc., 271 Madison Ave., New York, N.Y. 10016.

One section of the Kerner Report deals with the exploitation of consumers in ghetto areas by retail merchants.

The Responsible Consumer, by Sidney Margolius, 1970. 20 p. 25¢ (Public Affairs Pamphlet no. 453). Public Affairs Committee,

381 Park Ave. South, New York, N.Y. 10016.

Reports on the various problems facing today's consumer. Discusses the advances made in protecting the consumer, and counsels the individual in spending his money wisely.

Safeguarding the Consumer; an Interview with Virginia Knauer. *Retired Officer Magazine,* Aug. 1970: 24+.

A question and answer review of the problems and prospects of consumer protection. A concise and lucid presentation.

Why Customers Complain. *U.S. News & World Report,* v. 67, Dec. 1, 1969: 50–52.

The breakdown in service or slipshod service at high prices in stores, hotels and garages are attributed to the demands of affluence and to workers' attitudes.

Agencies and Organizations

GOVERNMENT

Federal

The following section contains only a sampling of the agencies of the Federal government which provide services and sources of information for the consumer. For a broader listing consult *Guide to Federal Consumer Services.* For the most complete information contact each agency or department individually.

Guide to Federal Consumer Services, 1971. 51 p. $1 Office of Consumer Affairs, (cat. no. PR36.8: C76/SE6) Supt. of Documents, GPO, Washington, D.C. 20402.

Contains information on services to consumer provided by forty federal agencies and divisions. Information on each agency includes basic facts on its organization and origin, major laws administered, services for consumers, and how these services can be obtained. Also gives publications released by the agencies.

Consumer Alert. Monthly. Free. Federal Trade Commission, Washington, D.C. 20580.

Newsletter of consumer affairs and consumer protection. Items relate to the FTC.

Consumer Messages. Free as available. House Document Room, Room H226, The Capitol, Washington, D.C. 20510.

Transmitted by the President to the Congress. Each message comments on presidential consumer concerns. All consumer messages appear in the *Congressional Record.*

Consumer News. Monthly. 4 p. $1.00. Office of Consumer Affairs, (cat. no. PREX16.9:) Supt. of Documents, GPO, Washington, D.C. 20402.

Newsletter describing regulations, legal actions and continuing programs of Federal agencies in the field of consumer affairs.

Consumer Report/New Program Spotlights Government as Comparison Shopper, by Andrea F. Schoenfeld. *National Journal,* v. 2, Nov. 28, 1970: 2596–2603.

A review of the presidential order charging the General Services Administration, the President's Committee on Consumer Interests, and the Defense Department with making available to consumers information about the products that the government buys for its own use.

Consumer Services for Older Americans, by James J. Barry. *Vital Speeches,* v. 35, Aug. 15, 1969: 649–652.

An address made on May 24, 1969 by a representative of the Department of Health, Education and Welfare. Concerns the steps we must take to protect our older citizens.

Enforcing the FDC Act, 1966. 5 p. 10¢ (cat. no. FS 13. 122:6). Supt. of Documents, GPO, Washington, D.C. 20402.

This Food and Drug Administration Consumer Protection Student Reference Sheet gives information on enforcing the FDC Act. A description is given of the types of court procedures used to enforce the law.

Establish a Department of Consumer Affairs, 1969. 826 p. Free. Committee on Government Operations, U.S. Senate, Washington, D.C. 20510.

Reports of the hearings held during March, April and July, 1969 before the Committee on Government Operations, U.S. Senate, 91st Congress, first session. The report of "Nader's Raiders" concerning the Federal Trade Commission.

FDA Papers. Monthly, except combined July–Aug., Dec–Jan. $5.50. Supt. of Documents, GPO, Washington, D.C. 20402.

The official magazine of the Food and Drug Administration.

FTC Gets a Nader Needling. *Business Week,* Jan. 11, 1969: 34+.

The Federal Trade Commission is indicated by Ralph Nader for its incompetence, its too friendly attitude toward business and its lack of regard for the consumer.

Guide to OE-Administered Programs, Fiscal Year 1971, (published) Nov. 1970. 8 p. Single copies free. The Editor, *American Education,* U.S. Office of Education, Washington, D.C. 20202. Quantity reprints available from Supt. of Documents, GPO, Washington, D.C. 20402. (cat. no. OE–11015–71).

Reprinted from *American Education,* Nov. 1970. A listing of U.S. Office of Education funds allotted to various educational programs. Many of these are adaptable to consumer education programs.

How the FDA Works for You, 1968. 16 p. Free. (FDA publication no. 1) Food and Drug Administration, Washington, D.C. 20204.

Discusses the organization and work of the Food and Drug Administration. Of interest to some teenagers.

Instructions for Updating the Catalog of HEW Assistance, 1970. 204 p. $1.75 (cat. no. HE-1.6/6.:969/Supp.970) Supt. of Documents, GPO, Washington, D.C. 20402.

Basic information about more than two hundred separate programs. Some of these are specifically directed to the consumer.

Le Conseiller du President des USA pour les Interets des Consommateurs, by Virginia H. Knauer. *Consommateurs Actualite,* no. 27, Feb. 1971: 55–57.

A description of the duties of the President's Committee on Consumer Interests. Text in French.

Mrs. Knauer, Consumer Envoy —Both for and to the White House, by Andrea F. Schoenfeld. *National Journal,* v. 2, Jan. 10, 1970: 90–98.

A review of the operations and activities of Virginia H. Knauer, special assistant to President Nixon for consumer affairs.

"The Nader Report" on the Federal Trade Commission, by Edward F. Cox and others, 1969. 241 p. $5.95. Richard Baron Publishing Co., distributed by E. P. Dutton, New York.

Investigation of the Federal Trade Commission's structure, policies, and operations, by a task force of young law students in the summer of 1968. This very critical report was supervised by Ralph Nader. Of interest to some teenagers.

New Help for Shoppers, Tighter Rules for Business. *U.S. News & World Report,* v. 70, Mar. 8, 1971: 68–69.

A review of possible changes in the government's relations with consumers and business.

Organization and Functions of the President's Committee on Consumer Interests and the Consumer Advisory Council. *Federal Register,* v. 32, Sept. 7, 1967: 12813–12814.

A concise statement of the functions and structure of these two government organizations.

Producer Versus Consumer, by Benjamin S. Rosenthal, *Economic and Business Bulletin, Temple University,* v. 22, winter, 1970: 37–40.

How government can help solve the purchaser's problems in the marketplace.

Publications of the Bureau of Labor Statistics. Semi-annual. Free. U.S. Dept. of Labor, Bureau of Labor Statistics, Washington, D.C. 20210.

Provides an annotated bibliography of the Bureau's publications, including periodical articles. Many are of value to consumer specialists. Entries are arranged under broad subject fields. (January—June 1970 issue [published 1971] contains 56 pages).

The Question of a Federal Consumer Protection Agency. *Congressional Digest,* v. 50, Feb. 1971: 33–64.

A "pro and con" debate featuring views by such authorities as Senator Montoya, Representative Rosenthal, Louis Lefkowitz, Ralph Nader, James L. Goddard, and Joseph A. Califano.

Raiders Report Finds FDA Ineffectual in Guarding Food. *Advertising Age,* v. 41, Apr. 13, 1970: 2+.

Summarizes the main points of *The Chemical Feast,* an indictment of the Food and Drug Administration.

Recent Developments in the Federal Trade Commission's Consumer Protection Program, 1970. 12 p. Free. Federal Trade Commission, Washington, D.C. 20580.

A brief outline of current activity in the FTC's program to educate the American consumer.

The Regulators Can't Go on This Way. *Business Week,* Feb. 28, 1970: 60–61+.

Discusses the various reforms needed in regulatory agencies.

The Regulators: Watchdog Agencies and the Public Interest, by L. M. Kohlmeier, 1969. 339 p. $8.95. Harper & Row, New York.

Charges regulatory agencies represent, rather than regulate, industries in their charge. Conflicts among agencies result in subordination of consumer interests. The author suggests that these agencies be abolished and their powers be reapportioned among the traditional branches of government.

Report of the ABA Commission to Study the FTC, 1969. 63 p. $2.00. Bureau of National Affairs, Inc., Washington, D.C. 20037.

Special supplement to the Antitrust and Trade Regulation Report, which presents the American Bar Association's very critical analysis of the Federal Trade Commission. President Nixon requested this report.

Science and Consumers, 1967. 16 p. 25¢ (Agricultural Information Bulletin no. 322, cat. no. A1.75:322) Supt. of Documents, GPO, Washington, D.C. 20402.

Sub-title: "The story of how agricultural research serves you." A profile of the Department of Agriculture's contributions to consumer welfare.

Service: USDA's Report to Consumers. Monthly. Free to media and organizations and teachers only. USDA, Office of Information, Washington, D.C. 20250.

A monthly four-page newsletter of consumer interest. A typical issue contains several short paragraphs on a wide range of topics.

Services for You from USDA's Consumer and Marketing Service, 1966. 12 p. 10¢ (cat. no. A1. 68:570/2). Supt. of Documents, GPO, Washington, D.C. 20402.

Subject Guide to Major United States Government Publications, 1968. 175 p. $5.50. American Library Association, 50 E. Huron St., Chicago, Ill. 60611.

A comprehensive guide covering titles of permanent importance issued from the earliest period to the present. Many of the subjects covered are of current and historical interest to consumers and consumer specialists.

Virginia Knauer Likes Action, and She's an Expert at Getting It. *Washington Post,* Aug. 8, 1970, *The Potomac* (Sunday supplement) : 1–5.

An intimate description of the President's Special Assistant for Consumer Affairs.

Virginia Knauer: What She Tells the President, by Robert T. Gray. *Nation's Business,* v. 58, July 1970: 35–38.

Reviews the work of Mrs. Knauer during her first year as head of the Office of Consumer Affairs.

The Weights and Measures Men, 1969. 6 p. Free. National Conference on Weights and Measures, National Bureau of Standards, Washington, D.C. 20234.

Brief and elementary information for the consumer.

Where the FTC's New Chairman Stands. *Nation's Business,* v. 58, Apr. 1970: 28–30.

Caspar Weinberger gives his philosophy on the Federal Trade Commission's relations with business.

State

Many States, some counties and cities, now have some form of specifically designated consumer office, or offices, although the responsibilities and powers of these offices vary. Consumers with questions or problems may consult the offices listed, asking referral of their letters to the appropriate State agency in the event the office itself does not have jurisdiction, information, or educational materials on the specific issue.

Free and inexpensive consumer educational materials are, in many cases, available from these offices or other States offices such as Department of Agriculture, Agriculture Extension Service, Office of the Attorney General, or Division of Weights and Measures to assist residents of the specific State.

ALASKA
Attorney General of Alaska
Pouch "K", State Capitol
Juneau, Alaska 99801

ARIZONA
Consumer Fraud Division
Office of Attorney General
159 State Capitol Building
Phoenix, Arizona 85007

ARKANSAS
Consumer Protection Division
Office of Attorney General
Justice Building
Little Rock, Arkansas 72201

CALIFORNIA
Consumer Fraud Section
Office of Attorney General
600 State Building
Los Angeles, California 90012

Director
Department of Consumer Affairs
1020 N Street
Sacramento, California 95814

COLORADO
Office of Consumer Affairs
Attorney General of Colorado
503 Farmers Union Building
1575 Sherman Street
Denver, Colorado 80203

CONNECTICUT
Commissioner, Department of
  Consumer Protection
State Office Building
Hartford, Connecticut 06115

DELAWARE
Consumer Protection Division
Office of Attorney General
1206 King Street
Wilmington, Delaware 19801

FLORIDA
Attorney General of Florida
State Capitol
Tallahassee, Florida 32304

Division of Consumer Affairs
Florida Department of Agriculture and Consumer Services
The Capitol
Tallahassee, Florida 32304

GEORGIA
Georgia Consumer Services Program
Department of Family and
  Children Services
15 Peachtree Street, Room 909
Atlanta, Georgia 30303

HAWAII
Director of Consumer Protection
Office of the Governor
602 Kamamalu Bldg.
250 South King Street
P. O. Box 3767
Honolulu, Hawaii 96811

IDAHO
Consumer Protection Division
Office of Attorney General
State Capitol
Boise, Idaho 83707

ILLINOIS
Consumer Fraud Section
Office of Attorney General
134 N. LaSalle Street
Chicago, Illinois 60602

INDIANA
Attorney General of Indiana
219 State House
Indianapolis, Indiana 46204

Consumer Advisory Council
c/o Indiana Dept. of Commerce
336 State House
Indianapolis, Indiana 46204

IOWA
Consumer Fraud Division
Office of Attorney General
1223 E. Court
Des Moines, Iowa 50319

KANSAS
Consumer Protection Division
Office of Attorney General
The Capitol
Topeka, Kansas 66612

KENTUCKY
Consumer Protection Division
Office of Attorney General
The Capitol
Frankfort, Kentucky 40601

Executive Director
Citizen's Commission for Consumer Protection
State Capitol
Frankfort, Kentucky 40601

MAINE
Consumer Protection Division
Office of Attorney General
State House
Augusta, Maine 04330

MARYLAND
Consumer Protection Division
Office of Attorney General
1200 One Charles Center
Baltimore, Maryland 21201

MASSACHUSETTS
Consumer Protection Division
Office of Attorney General
State House
Boston, Massachusetts 02133

Executive Secretary
Mass. Consumers' Council
State Office Bldg., Gov't. Center
100 Cambridge Street
Boston, Massachusetts 02202

MICHIGAN
Consumer Protection Division
Office of Attorney General
Law Building
Lansing, Michigan 48902

Special Assistant to the Governor
for Consumer Affairs
1033 South Washington Street
Lansing, Michigan

Executive Director
Michigan Consumer Council
525 Hollister Building
Lansing, Michigan 48933

MINNESOTA
Special Assistant Attorney
General for Cons. Protection
Attorney General of Minnesota
102 State Capitol
St. Paul, Minnesota 55101

Office of Consumer Services
Dept. of Commerce, Room 230
State Office Building
St. Paul, Minnesota 55101

MISSISSIPPI
Assistant Attorney General
for Consumer Protection
Attorney General of Mississippi
State Capitol
Jackson, Mississippi 39201

Consumer Protection Division
Dept. of Agriculture & Commerce
Jackson, Mississippi 39205

MISSOURI
Consumer Protection Division
Office of Attorney General
Supreme Court Bldg.
Jefferson City, Missouri 65101

NEW HAMPSHIRE
Assistant Attorney General
for Consumer Protection
Office of Attorney General
State House Annex
Concord, New Hampshire 03301

NEW JERSEY
Office of Consumer Protection
1100 Raymond Boulevard
Newark, New Jersey 07102

NEW MEXICO
Consumer Protection Division
Office of Attorney General
Supreme Court Bldg., Box 2246
Santa Fe New Mexico 87501

NEW YORK
Consumer Frauds and Protection
Bureau
Office of Attorney General
80 Centre Street
New York, New York 10013

Chairman and Executive Director
Consumer Protection Board
380 Madison Avenue
New York, New York 10017

NORTH CAROLINA
Consumer Protection and Antitrust Division
Office of Attorney General
P. O. Box 629
Raleigh, North Carolina 27602

NORTH DAKOTA
Consumer Protection Division
Office of Attorney General
The Capitol
Bismarck, North Dakota 58501

OHIO
Consumer Frauds and Crimes
Section

Office of Attorney General
State House Annex
Columbus, Ohio 43215

OKLAHOMA
Administrator
Department of Consumer Affairs
Lincoln Office Plaza, Suite 74
4545 Lincoln Boulevard
Oklahoma City, Oklahoma 73105

OREGON
Assistant Attorney General for
Antitrust and Consumer Protection
Office of Attorney General
322 State Office Building
Salem, Oregon 97310

Assistant to the Governor for
Economic Development &
Consumer Services
State Capitol Bldg.
Salem, Oregon 97301

PENNSYLVANIA
Bureau of Consumer Protection
Pennsylvania Dept. of Justice
2–4 N. Market Square (Durbin
Bldg.)
Harrisburg, Pennsylvania 17101

RHODE ISLAND
Special Assistant Attorney
General for Consumer Protection
Office of Attorney General
Providence County Court House
Providence, Rhode Island 02903

Executive Director
Rhode Island Consumers' Council
365 Broadway
Providence, Rhode Island 02902

SOUTH DAKOTA
Office of Consumer Affairs
Attorney General of South
  Dakota
State Capitol
Pierre, South Dakota 57501

TEXAS
Antitrust and Consumer Protection Division
Office of Attorney General
Capitol Station, P. O. Box 12548
Austin, Texas 78711

Office of Consumer Credit
1011 Jan Jacinto Boulevard
P. O. Box 2107
Austin, Texas 78767

UTAH
Assistant Attorney General for
  Consumer Protection
Office of Attorney General
State Capitol
Salt Lake City, Utah

Administrator of Consumer
  Credit
403 State Capitol
Salt Lake City, Utah 84114

VERMONT
Consumer Protection Bureau
Office of Attorney General
94 Church Street
Burlington, Vermont 05401

Family Economics and Home
  Management Specialist
Room 210, Terrill Hall
University of Vermont
Burlington, Vermont 05401

VIRGINIA
Assistant Attorney General for
  Consumer Protection

Office of Attorney General
Supreme Court—Library Building
Richmond, Virginia 23219

Special Assistant to the Governor on Minority Groups and
  Consumer Affairs
Office of the Governor
Richmond, Virginia 23219

Administrator, Consumer Affairs
Department of Agriculture and
  Commerce
8th Street Office Building
Richmond, Virginia 23219

WASHINGTON
Consumer Protection and Antitrust Division
Office of Attorney General
1266 Dexter Horton Building
Seattle, Washington 98104

WEST VIRGINIA
Assistant Attorney General
  for Consumer Protection
Office of Attorney General
The Capitol
Charleston, West Virginia 25305

Consumer Protection Division
West Va. Dept. of Labor
1900 Washington St. E.
Charleston, W. Va. 25305

WISCONSIN
Assistant Attorney General
  For Consumer Protection
Office of Attorney General
Department of Justice
Madison, Wisconsin 53702

Bureau of Consumer Protection,
  Trade Division
Department of Agriculture
801 W. Badger Road
Madison, Wisconsin 53713

WYOMING
State Examiner and Administrator Consumer Credit Code
State Supreme Court Building
Cheyenne, Wyoming

COMMONWEALTH OF PUERTO RICO AND THE VIRGIN ISLANDS
Attorney General of Puerto Rico
P. O. Box 192
San Juan, Puerto Rico 00902

Consumer Services Administration
P. O. Box 13934
Santurce, Puerto Rico 00908

Executive Director
Public Services Commission
Charlotte Amalie
St. Thomas, Virgin Islands 00801

Local

LOS ANGELES, CALIFORNIA
Secretary
Los Angeles Consumer
  Protection Committee
107 S. Broadway
Los Angeles, Calif. 90012

SAN FRANCISCO, CALIFORNIA
Secretary
Bay Area Consumer Protection
  Coordinating Committee
450 Golden Gate Avenue
Box 36005
San Francisco, Calif. 94102

SANTA CLARA COUNTY, CALIFORNIA
Director
Santa Clara County Dept. of

Weights & Measures
& Consumer Affairs
Division of Consumer Affairs
409 Matthew Street
Santa Clara, California 95050

DADE COUNTY, FLORIDA
Director
Consumer Protection Division
1351 N.W. 12th Street
Miami, Florida 33125

JACKSONVILLE, FLORIDA
Consumer Affairs Officer
Division of Consumer Affairs
Department of Public Safety
220 East Bay Street
Jacksonville, Florida 32202

ST. PETERSBURG, FLORIDA
Director of Consumer Affairs
264 First Ave. N.
St. Petersburg, Fla. 33701

CHICAGO, ILLINOIS
Commissioner
Department of Consumer Sales
  and Weights & Measures
City Hall
121 N. LaSalle St.
Chicago, Illinois 60602

CHICAGO, ILLINOIS
Secretary
Chicago Consumer Protection
  Committee
Room 486
U.S. Court House and Federal
  Office Bldg.
219 South Dearborn Street
Chicago, Ill. 60604

LOUISVILLE, KENTUCKY
Supervisor
Division of Weights & Measures
  & Consumer Affairs

Metropolitan Sewer District
Building, Second Floor
Louisville, Kentucky 40202

NEW ORLEANS, LOUISIANA
Secretary
Consumer Protection Committee
of New Orleans
1000 Masonic Temple Building
333 St. Charles Street
New Orleans, Louisiana 70130

PRINCE GEORGES COUNTY, MARYLAND
Consumer Protection Division
Prince Georges County Court
House
Upper Marlboro, Maryland 20870

BOSTON, MASSACHUSETTS
Chairman
Boston Consumer's Council
Office of the Mayor, Boston
City Hall
Boston, Massachusetts 02201

BOSTON, MASSACHUSETTS
Secretary
Boston Metropolitan Consumer
Protection Committee
% Federal Trade Commission
John Fitzgerald Kennedy
Federal Bldg.
Government Center
Boston, Mass. 02203

DETROIT, MICHIGAN
Secretary
Detroit Consumer Protection
Coordinating Committee
Immigration and Naturalization
Bldg.
333 Mt. Elliott Avenue
Detroit, Michigan 48207

ST. LOUIS, MISSOURI
Chairman
Citizens Consumer Advisory
Committee
7701 Forsyth Boulevard
Clayton, Missouri 63105

CAMDEN COUNTY, NEW JERSEY
Director
Camden County Office of
Consumer Affairs, Room 606
Commerce Building
#1 Broadway
Camden, New Jersey 08101

LONG BEACH, LONG ISLAND, NEW YORK
Director, Consumer Affairs
City Hall
Long Beach, Long Island, New
York 11561

NASSAU COUNTY, NEW YORK
Commissioner
Office of Consumer Affairs
160 Old Country Road
Mineola, New York 11501

NEW YORK CITY, NEW YORK
Commissioner
City of New York Department
of Consumer Affairs
80 Lafayette Street
New York, New York 10013

COLUMBUS, OHIO
City Sealer of Weights and
Measures
City Hall
Columbus, Ohio 43215

MULTNOMAH COUNTY, OREGON

Deputy District Attorney in Charge of Consumer Protection
600 County Court House
Portland, Oregon 97204

PHILADELPHIA, PENNSYLVANIA

Secretary
Philadelphia Consumer Protection Committee
53 Long Lane
Upper Darby, Pa. 19082

PHILADELPHIA, PENNSYLVANIA

Consumer Protection Office
City Hall, Room 121
Philadelphia, Pennsylvania 19107

PRIVATE

Canadian Consumer Council— First Annual Report, 1969. 29 p. Free. The Council, P. O. Box 94, Ottawa 2, Canada.

Report of the government appointed, but independent, council for its first year of operation, 1969.

Catalogue of Caveats. *Time,* v. 96, Aug. 24, 1970: 38.

Discusses the activities of Consumers Union.

The Consumer Interest, by John Martin and George W. Smith, 1968. 280 p. 45 s. ($6.30) Pall Mall Press, London.

Describes consumer organizations, both local and national, in Great Britain; assesses their effectiveness in responding to the problems and complexities of the consumer market; and compares development in Britain with other countries.

Consumer Rights: a World Review, 1968. 123 p. $3.50. (Proceedings of the 5th Biennial Conference of the International Organization of Consumers Unions held in Bronxville, New York from June 26 to July 1, 1968.) International Organization of Consumers Unions, 81 Sweelinchplein, The Hague, Holland.

Discussions of the roles of governments and independent consumer organizations in the fields of consumer representation, safety, information and production. Emphasized were safety standards for foods, medicines, and other consumer goods; and product listing, labeling, packaging and evaluation.

Consumers Review. 6 per year. $50.00. International Organization of Consumers Unions (IOCU) Information Center, 9 Emmastraat. The Hague, Holland.

A listing of the contents and articles of all major international consumer publications and standard publications throughout the world. A free list is available upon request of publications issued by IOCU members.

The Consumer's Right to Know. *Consumer Reports,* v. 33, Oct. 1968: 551–553.

An account of part of the Consumers Union's testimony in its suit to force the Veteran's Administration to make public results of tests made on hearing aids. The issue is the consumer's right of "access to information in federal agencies' files about the quality of consumer goods and services."

Consumers Union Puts on Muscle. *Business Week,* Dec. 23, 1967: 84–86.

Overview and a brief history of Consumers Union, the publisher of *Consumer Reports.* Suggested reading for all concerned with consumer interests and the part of Consumers Union in protecting consumer welfare.

44

Empire of the Consumer Crusader Blossoms Bringing Him New Challenges and Problems, by Ronald G. Shafer. *Wall Street Journal,* v. 175. Nov. 19, 1970: 40+.

Detailed breakdown of the operations and organizations that constitute Ralph Nader's Raiders.

Facts You Should Know about Your Better Business Bureau, n.d. 16 p. 15¢. Council of Better Business Bureaus, 1101 17th St., N.W., Washington, D.C. 20036.

"Public service of private business in the public interest;" a discussion of the work and organization of the B.B.B.

Forming Consumer Organizations, 1971. 27 p. Free. Office of Consumer Affairs, Director of Field Operations, New Executive Office Building, Washington, D.C. 20506.

Manual to help consumers organize for greater effectiveness.

Industry Nips at Consumers' Watchdog, by John D. Drummond and Frederick Corey. *Electronics,* v. 41, Aug. 5, 1968: 170–173+.

Critical article concerning the Consumers Union's subjective approach to product testing and limited sampling basis.

International Consumer. Quarterly. $10.00. IOCU, 9 Emmastraat, The Hague, Holland.

The official organ of the International Organization of Consumers Unions. Text in English and French.

International Organization of Consumer Unions, 1969. 32 p. Free. American Council on Consumer Interests, 238 Stanley Hall, University of Missouri, Columbia, Mo. 65201.

The function of the American Council on Consumer Interests is explained in four languages—English, French, German and Spanish.

Let the Buyer Not Despair, by Virginia H. Knauer. *AAUW Journal,* v. 64 no. 5, April 1971. 2 p.

An appeal for citizen involvement in the search for consumer justice.

Meet Ralph Nader, *Newsweek,* v. 71, Jan. 22, 1968: 65–67+.

Interesting discussion of "everyman's lobbyist and his consumer crusade."

Nader's Raiders: Older and Bolder. *Sales Management,* v. 104, Mar. 15, 1970: 27–28.

Considers the scope and objectives of the Center for the Study of Responsive Law.

Nader's Raiders: the Lone Ranger Gets a Posse, by Jack Newfield. *Life,* v. 67, Oct. 3, 1969: 56–63.

Interesting and perceptive analysis of consumer advocate, Ralph Nader. An addition to an explanation of Nader's raiders, this issue carries an editorial "The consumers and the regulators." Of interest to some teenagers.

National Consumers League Bulletin. Bi-monthly. Available to members only. National Consumers League, 1029 Vermont Ave., N.W. Washington, D.C. 20005.

Reports on social legislation of interest to the League. Membership in the League is a minimum of $7.50 per year.

Ralph Nader: Consumer Protection or Lobbyist's Gadfly.

Consumer Bulletin, v. 51, Apr. 1968: 25–27.

"The . . . ordinary consumer will not find groceries any cheaper . . . or new family auto any more convenient or comfortable to drive as a result of the current flood of legislation in the name of the consumer." A critical examination of Nader's role as consumer advocate.

Ralph Nader, Crusader, by Patrick Anderson. *New York Times Magazine,* v. 55, Oct. 29, 1967: 25+.

Brief but interesting biographical sketch of a "self-appointed lobbyist" for the public and consumer interest.

Ralph Nader: Playboy Interview. *Playboy,* v. 15, Oct. 1968: 73+.

Lengthy and fascinating interview with the leading exponent of consumer democracy. Nader discusses his current activities, the philosophy which guides him, and his views about the relations between consumers, business and government.

Report on Local British Groups, 1967. 10 p. Free. Consumers Union of U.S., 256 Washington St., Mount Vernon, N.Y. 10550.

Prepared by Consumers Union. Discusses activities of local British consumer groups and lists their projects.

The U.S.'s Toughest Customer. *Time,* v. 94, Dec. 12, 1969: 89–96.

A detailed discussion of present day consumer activity as personified in the work of Ralph Nader.

Who Speaks for the Consumer, by Ralph Nader, 1968. 12 p. 35¢. League for Industrial Democracy, 112 E. 19th St., New York, N.Y. 10003.

A reprint of a speech by Nader outlining his crusade for consumer protection.

Who Speaks for the Consumer Now? *Changing Times,* July 1967: 41–44.

A discussion of national, state and local consumer organizations. Includes a list of organizations with addresses.

Which? Monthly. 30s ($4.00). Consumers' Association, 14 Buckingham, Street, London WC2N6DS.

An English consumer periodical devoted to testing and rating consumer products.

REGISTERING COMPLAINTS

Associations Answer Consumerism Challenge. *Association Management,* v. 23, Jan. 1971: 24–27.

How trade associations have met the challenge of Virginia Knauer in the resolution of consumer complaints.

Buckpassing Blues: Lo! the Complaining Consumer Put in the Run-around Mill, by Ronald G. Shafer. *Wall Street Journal,* v. 174, Nov. 3, 1969: 18.

Details consumer complaints concerning malfunctioning products, faulty repairs, and misdeliveries.

The Concern for Quality, 1970. 6 p. Free. National Association of Manufacturers, 277 Park Ave., New York, N.Y. 10017.

"Got a complaint . . . be a good complainer! Tell your story directly to the seller or manufacturer. Here are a few simple hints."

Consumer Complaints: How Marketers Listen. *Sales Management,* v. 104, Apr. 15, 1970: 29–31.

Discusses the ways in which some major companies handle their consumer complaints.

Got a Gripe? Here's Where to Complain. *Changing Times,* v. 24, Mar. 1970: 31–34.

Includes the names and addresses of one hundred and eleven agencies and organizations ready to help the consumer.

Information Directory, 1970. 26 p. 25¢. World Council of Credit Unions, P. O. Box 431, Madison, Wis. 53701.

A "complaint" directory which tells you how to file a complaint and where. Lists addresses of federal and state agencies, state consumer organizations, and names and addresses of major consumer products manufacturers in the United States and Canada.

Nice People to Do Business With. *Consumer Reports,* v. 32, June 1967: 332–333.

Descriptions of the methods used by some companies to satisfy consumer complaints.

Nothing Works Anymore, by D. Sanford. *New Republic,* Feb. 14, 1970: 21–24.

"And you can't fix it." A discussion of breakdowns, with a report on some of the complaints received by Virginia Knauer, the President's Special Assistant for Consumer Affairs.

When Consumers Complain, by C. Merle Crawford. *Sales Management,* v. 105, Nov. 15, 1970: 29–31.

Studies the handling of consumer complaints by ten corporations. The article details a study made by the university of Michigan's Graduate Business School.

Consumer and the Environment

Advances in Environmental Sciences and Technology, edited by James N. Pitts, Jr. and Robert L. Metcalf, 1969. 356 p. $15.95. Wiley, New York.

Nine authorities consider the causes and side effects of various forms of environmental pollution.

Chemical Fallout, edited by Morton W. Miller and George G. Berg, 1969. 560 p. $22.50. Charles C. Thomas Publishing Co., Springfield, Ill.

Current, highly technical research on persistent pesticides. Proceedings of the Rochester Conferences on Toxicity.

The Chemical Feast. by Ralph Nader and Summer Study Group, 1970. 256 p. $6.95. Grossman, New York.

A report on our failure to control our chemical environment. Of interest to some teenagers.

Consumer Beware! by Beatrice Trum Hunter, 1971. 442 p. $8.95. Simon and Schuster, New York.

"Your food and what's been done to it." A survey of the deterioration of our basic foods and its impact on the nation's health.

Directory of Government Agencies Safeguarding the Consumer and Environment. $4.95. 90 p. Serina Press, 70 Kennedy St. Alexandria, Va. 22305.

Lists the federal and state offices of such areas as meat and poultry surveillance, weights and measures, and air pollution.

The Economy of Cities, by Jane Jacobs, 1969. 268 p. $5.95. Random House, New York.

How the processes of production and consumption contribute to the cycle of growth and decay in the city structure.

Ecotactics, edited by John G. Mitchell with Constance L. Stallings, 1970. 288 p. 95¢ (paper) Pocket Books, 1 W. 39th St., New York, N.Y. 10018.

"The Sierra Club handbook for environmental activists." Introduction by Ralph Nader. Of interest to some teenagers.

The Environment, by the Editors of *Fortune*, 1970. 220 p. $1.25. Harper & Row, New York.

Thirteen articles on various economic aspects of environmental pollution reprinted from the October 1969 and February 1970 issues of *Fortune*.

Environment: a Challenge for Modern Society, by Lynton Caldwell, 1970. 312 p. $7.95. Doubleday, Garden City, N.Y.

Published for the American Museum of Natural History. A political scientist considers the critical problems of maintaining an environment in which a life of quality is possible.

Everyman's Guide to Ecological Living, by Greg Cailliet and others. 119 p. 95¢ (paper) Macmillan, 866 Third Ave., New York, N.Y. 10022.

Provides advice and suggestions about activities that concerned people can undertake to relieve the impending environmental crisis. Has a section on proposed consumer activities. Of interest to some teenagers.

The Facts about Today's Detergents, n.d. 8 p. Free. Soap and Detergent Association, 475 Park Ave., South, New York, N.Y. 10016.

"Answers to frequently asked questions about biodegradability, phosphates, enzymes."

Facts for Consumers, Pesticide Residues, rev. 1964. 12 p. 15¢ (cat. no. FS13.111:18/2) Supt. of Documents, GPO, Washington, D.C. 20402.

Summary of safety control through the Federal Insecticide, Fungicide, and Rodenticide Act, and Food, Drug and Cosmetics Act. Reports on safe tolerances and other safety requirements.

The Fight for Quiet, by Theodore Berland, 1970. 370 p. $8.95. Prentice-Hall, Englewood Cliffs, N.J.

Surveys the hazards of noise pollution.

Garbage as You Like It, by Jerome Goldstein, 1970. 243 p. $6.95. Rodale, Emmaus, Pa.

How to dispose of wastes—sewage, organic solids, paper, cans, bottles, junk. Considers recycling, composting and other less orthodox means of disposal. Of interest to some teenagers.

Geotechnics, by William A. Niering. *Choice,* v. 6, Jan. 1970: 1529–1536.

Bibliographic essay surveying many aspects of environmental literature. Included are books on natural resources, conservation, ecology, pollution, marine ecosystems, and population problems.

God's Own Junkyard, by Peter Blake, 1964. 144 p. $2.95. Holt, Rinehart and Winston, New York.

Describes the deterioration in contemporary design and the destruction of natural beauty caused by public apathy, commercial interests, and our materialistic national goals. Illustrated by numerous photographs. Of special interest to teenagers.

Guide to Organic Foods Shopping and Organic Living, compiled by *Organic Gardening and Farming and Prevention, The Magazine for Better Living,* edited by Jerome Goldstein and M. C. Goldman, 1970. 119 p. $1.00.

Rodale Press, Emmaus, Pa., distributed by David McKay, New York.

Guide to *How to Live Better With Less Conveniences*. Contents include: how to read a label and what "ingredients" (additives) to avoid; a list of products which are "extra good" from an environmental standpoint; a list of safe detergents; directories of organic food sources (growers, shops and stands offering a wide selection of naturally raised food products), ecology action groups, ecology researchers, legislators, teachers and students; and a listing of natural resources, wildlife conservation and health organizations. Also gives examples of people who have organized to fight environmental problems and to promote better, safer and healthier products. Of interest to some teenagers.

Home Insecticides, Part II. *Consumer Reports*, v. 28, Aug. 1963: 392–397.

Advice on how to solve specific insect problems. Tells what to do when you must hire an exterminator.

Household Insecticides, Part I. *Consumer Reports*, v. 28, July 1963: 321–327.

How to select a product for safety and effectiveness, why the public needs to be alarmed, safety precautions in the war on insects and a guide to the most hazardous chemicals.

In Quest of Quiet, by Henry Still, 1970. 224 p. $6.95. Stackpole, Harrisburg, Pa.

Examines such contributions to noise pollution as automobiles and aircraft and appeals to government and industry to establish standards for noise control.

The Politics of Pollution, by Clarence J. Davies, Jr., 1970. 231 p. $6.00. Scribners, New York.

A comprehensive study of government's response to the need for pollution control.

Report of the Secretary's Commission on Pesticides and Their Relationship to Environmental Health, 1969. 677 p. $3.00 set (cat. no. HE 1.2:P43/Part I, II) Supt. of Documents, GPO, Washington, D.C. 20402.

Part I details recommendations on hazards of pesticides to the environment and man's health. Part II includes subcommittee reports, including carcinogenesis, interaction, mutagenesis and teratogenesis.

Since Silent Spring, by Frank Graham, Jr., 1970. 333 p. $6.95. Houghton Mifflin, Boston. Also available in paperback: $2.00, Consumers Union, Mount Vernon, N.Y. 10550.

An epilogue to Rachel Carson's *Silent Spring*. A report of what has and has not been done in understanding and controlling pesticides since 1962. Of interest to some teenagers.

So Human an Animal, by René Dubos, 1968. 267 p. $6.95. Scribner's, New York.

Discusses how man responds to his physical and social surroundings and questions whether or not man is thoughtlessly creating conditions which will thwart his pursuit of human freedom.

The State of Siege, by C. P. Snow, 1969. 50 p. $2.95. Scribner's, New York.

A plea for a world-wide social policy to avoid a food consumption-population collision in the near future.

The Third Pollution, by William E. Small, 1971. 120 p. $6.50. Praeger, New York.

A definitive picture of the costs and problems of solid waste disposal.

The User's Guide to the Protection of the Environment, by Paul

Swatik, 1970. 312 p. $1.25 (paper). Ballantine Books, Inc., 101 Fifth Ave., New York, N.Y. 10003.

A commonsense approach to the contributions each citizen can make in protecting our environment. Of interest to some teenagers.

The Vanishing Air, by John Esposito, 1970. 348 p. 95¢ (paper) Grossman Publishers, New York.

Ralph Nader summer study group report on air pollution sources, such as the automobile industry, manufacturing industries, power plants, and current programs to curb pollution.

Money Management

PLANNING AND CONSUMER DECISION MAKING

Answers to Your Everyday Money Questions, by Lorraine L. Blair, 1968. 200 p. $4.95. Regnery, Chicago, Ill.

A careful, philosophical discussion of the principles of good money management.

Business Week's Guide to Personal Business, by Joseph L. Wiltsee, 1970. 334 p. $9.95. McGraw-Hill, New York.

"Designed for the man who wants to manage his personal business as competently as he manages his company business. Written for the man who earns more than $15,000 a year."

Champagne Living on a Beer Budget, by Mike and Marilyn Ferguson, 1968. 271 p. $5.95. Putnam, New York.

An encyclopedic practical guide to getting the "best for less" in everything from motel rooms to prime chopped beef and cruises by sea and air.

Consumer Buying Guide, by Better Business Bureau, 1969. 206 p. $1.25 (paper). Universal Publishing and Distributing Corporation, 235 E. 45th St., New York, N.Y. 10017.

Sub-title: "How to get your money's worth." The only guide authorized to carry the name of Better Business Bureau. Written by those involved with the problems brought to the BBB's attention.

Consumers All, 1965. 496 p. $2.75 (cat. no. A 1.10:965) Supt. of Documents, GPO, Washington, D.C. 20402.

The *Yearbook of Agriculture,* 1965. Practical handbook of information for everyone who has a part in the management and care of a house, home and family. Chapters deal with houses, home furnishings, finances, clothing, food and nutrition.

The Consumer's Handbook, by *National Observer* Editors, 1969. 162 p. $1.85. Dow Jones Books, Box 300, Princeton, New Jersey 08540.

A manual essaying the wise use of money.

A Discussion of Family Money, How Budgets Work and What They Do, 1970. 24 p. Free. Women's Division, Institute of Life Insurance, 277 Park Ave., New York, N.Y. 10017.

A discussion of basic money management for the growing family.

The Dollar Squeeze and How to Beat It, by George Sullivan, 1970. 213 p. $5.95. Macmillan, New York.

Hints to assist the consumer in his battle to defeat inflation. One half of the book treats of credit and debt, the other with buymanship and budgeting.

Financial Self-Defense, by John L. Springer, 1969. 201 p. $5.95. McGraw Hill, New York.

A general guide to the financial pitfalls which await the modern American—inflation, taxes, credit problems, frauds, and the necessity for careful planning.

Getting By on $20,000 a Year, by Ann Bayer. *Life,* v. 65, Dec. 20, 1968: 58–60.

Sub-title: "Almost all of them end up in the red." Spending patterns of six families.

Guide to Record Retention Requirements, 1970. 89 p. $1.00 (cat. no. GS4.107/a:R245/970). Supt. of Documents, GPO, Washington, D.C. 20402.

What records must be kept under federal laws and regulations, who must keep them, and how long they must be kept.

Head of Household, 1968. 32 p. 92¢. Follett Educational Corporation, 1010 W. Washington Blvd., Chicago, Ill. 60607.

How a young black girl learns to handle the financial responsibilities of her household during the illness of her mother who is receiving welfare assistance. Includes a teacher's manual for $1.50. Fifth and sixth grade reading levels, designed for the high school and young adult level consumer with poor reading skills.

Helpful Hints for Homemakers: a Variety of Booklets on Home Economics, 1970. 2 p. Free. Supt. of Documents, GPO, Washington, D.C. 20402.

An annotated listing of thirty-seven leaflets published by the Government Printing Office from 1963 to 1970.

Helping Families Manage Their Finances, rev. 1968. 51 p. 40¢ (U.S. Dept. of Agriculture, Home Economics Research Report No. 21, cat. no. A1.87:21/2) Supt. of Documents, GPO, Washington, D.C. 20402.

A guide to the basic practices of family financial management.

How Do Those Joneses Do It? *Changing Times,* v. 22, Apr. 1968: 7–11.

A discussion of family differences and how they are reflected in varying lifestyles.

How to Get Twenty to Ninety Percent Off on Everything You Buy, by J. and C. Kinney, 1966. 255 p. $6.95; $1.95 (paper) Prentice-Hall, Englewood Cliffs, N.J.

General advice, specific ways to save and cut back expenses, along with useful suggestions on wise buying.

How to Live Better and Spend Twenty Percent Less, by Merle E. Dowd, 1967. 237 p. $6.95. Prentice-Hall, Englewood Cliffs, N.J.

Suggested savings on a variety of goods and services. Designed for the inexperienced buyer.

How to Live on Nothing, by Joan Ransom Shortney, 1968. 75¢ (paper) Pocket Books, 1 W. 39th St., New York, N.Y. 10018.

"A thousand and more ways you can use wit and imagination to live very well on very little." Of interest to some teenagers.

How to Make the Most of Your Money, by Sidney Margolius, rev. 1969. 148 p. $6.95; $3.95 (paper) Hawthorn Books, New York.

A guide to money management. Aimed especially at the young-married.

How to Manage Your Money, by John Kirk, 1967. 144 p. $1.00 (paper) Essandess Special Editions, 1 W. 39th Street, New York, N.Y. 10018.

An elementary guide to family finance. Contains thirty-two pages of worksheets for recording income and expenses.

How to S–t–r–e–t–c–h Your M–o–n–e–y, by Sidney Margolius, 1968. 28 p. 25¢ (Public Affairs Pamphlets no. 302) Public Affairs Committee, 381 Park Ave. South, New York, N.Y. 10016.

Useful guide to the art of mastering money.

How You Can Beat Inflation, by David L. Marlestein, 1970. 226 p. $7.95. McGraw-Hill, New York.

Specific information in the areas of food, shelter, services and investment.

The Macmillan Guide to Finance. by Rex Wilder, 1967. 235 p. $6.95. Macmillan, New York.

Basically a primer on personal finance. Approximately one quarter of the text is devoted to insurance.

Managing Your Family Finances, by J. K. Lasser Tax Institute, 1968. 278 p. $6.50. Doubleday, New York.

A basic money management handbook.

Managing Your Money, 1964. 12 p. 15¢ (cat. no. A43.16/2:M74). Supt. of Documents, GPO, Washington, D.C. 20402.

"A family plan" for establishing financial security.

Measuring Retired Couple's Living Costs in Urban Areas, by Mary H. Hawes. *Monthly Labor Review,* v. 92, Nov. 1969: 3–16.

Analysis of cost of living for a retired couple on a moderate budget. The Bureau of Labor statistics are designed to permit comparisons with budgets for younger families in urban areas. Many tables are included.

Mind Your Money—When You Spend, When You Shop, and When You Use Credit, 1968. 15 p. each. 15¢ per set. Household Finance Corporation, Money Management Institute, Prudential Plaza, Chicago, Ill. 60601.

Simple instructions for good money management. This set of pamphlets has been developed for use with groups of limited income, reading ability and experience. Of interest to some teenagers.

Moment of Truth for Consumer Credit, by George C. Cochran, III. *Business Review* (Federal Reserve Bank of Dallas, Texas). Apr. 1969: 3–12.

Discusses the federal truth in lending program, particularly in its advertising aspects.

Money and Your Marriage, by Roy A. Burkhart and others, 1963. 32 p. 35¢ National Consumer Finance Association, 1000 Sixteenth St., N.W., Washington, D.C. 20402.

Discusses "planning together" as the basis for sound family finance.

The Money Book, by Anthony Scaduto. *Ladies' Home Journal,* v. 87, Mar. 1970: 147–150.

A brief summary of the ideas contained in the author's book: *Getting the Most for Your Money.* Many helpful hints are included.

Money in Your Life, 1970. 40 p. Free. Women's Division, Institute of Life Insurance, 277 Park Ave., New York, N.Y. 10017.

"Financial planning for the woman on her own." An elementary but practical guide.

Money Management: Children's Spending, 1968. 36 p. 25¢. Money Management Institute, Household Finance Corp., Prudential Plaza, Chicago, Ill. 60601.

Presents ideas on children's allowances, earnings, savings and borrowing.

Money Management: Your Shopping Dollar, 1969. 36 p. 25¢. Household Finance Corporation, Money Management Institute, Prudential Plaza, Chicago, Ill. 60601.

Hints for effective shopping and dollar-stretching. Others in series:

Money Management: Your Automobile Dollar, 1969. 36 p. 25¢

Money Management: Your Equipment Dollar, 1969. 36 p. 25¢

Money Management: Your Home Furnishings Dollar, 1969. 40 p. 25¢

Money, Money, Money, by John Kuenster, 1969. 63 p. 50¢. Claretian Publishers, 221 W. Madison St., Chicago, Ill. 60606.

A readable psychological, sociological, and economic study of money. An analysis from those different points of view of what it is, what it does for us, and what we do for it.

New Adult Guide to Independent Living, by Sidney Margolius, 1968. 213 p. O. P. Macmillan, New York.

"What you need to know at 21 about: your legal rights, your money, your place in the sun." Simple discussion of many areas vital to the "new adults" which should prove of benefit.

The New York Times Guide to Personal Finance, by Sal Nuccio, 1968. 240 p. $4.95. Harper and Row, New York.

Covers the entire field of personal finance. Brief but lucid and helpful.

Present Value of Estimated Lifetime Earnings, by Herman P. Miller and Richard A. Hornseth, 1967. 54 p. Free. Bureau of the Census, Washington, D.C. 20233.

Includes forty-six pages of charts showing the lifetime earnings of people in various age groups and in various occupations.

Rich Man, Poor Man, by Herman P. Miller, 1964. 260 p. O. P. Thomas Y. Crowell, New York.

Statistical analysis of the distribution of income in America, based on United States census information.

Save Money and Grow Rich, by John W. King, 1968. 288 p. $4.95. Lyle Stuart, New York.

Popular approach to the art of saving money by cutting corners. This dictionary guide has entries from "abstracts" to "zoos."

Sense with Dollars, by Charles V. Neal, rev. ed. 1967. 380 p. $1.45 (Dolphin C456, paper). Doubleday, New York.

A money management counselor discusses several aspects of personal finance.

The Spender Syndrome, by Brenda Dervin, 1965. 212 p. O. P. Center for Consumer Affairs, University of Wisconsin, University Extension, 432 N. Lake St., Madison, Wis. 53706.

Sub-title: "Case studies of sixty-eight families and their consumer problems." Cases are drawn from all ages, occupational levels, and from all types of consumer problems. Bound into the book is a 6 1/2 minute record on which three cases have been recorded.

Three Standards of Living for an Urban Family of Four Persons, spring 1967. 92 p. $1.00 (cat. no. L2.3:1570–5) Supt. of Documents, GPO, Washington, D.C. 20402.

This Department of Labor study gives data for a carefully defined family of four in different financial circumstances in 39 areas, in answer to the question: "How much does it cost to live?"

The Time-Life Book of Family Finance, by Carlton Smith and Richard P. Pratt, 1970. 415 p. $11.95. Time-Life Books. Order from Little, Brown, Boston.

An exceptionally effective guide to personal finance. Contains many worthwhile charts and graphs.

What a Young Family Should Do with Its Money. *Changing Times,* v. 21, Dec. 1967: 17–21.

The advice of five financial experts is given on housing, life and medical insurance, savings and investments, estate planning, and other matters of special interest to the youthful family.

What Every Young Wife Should Know about Money, by Martin Cohen. *Redbook,* v. 131, Sept. 1968: 70–72.

Summarizes many points on managing money. For reprints send twenty-five cents and a stamped, business size, self addressed envelope. Of interest to some teenagers.

Women's Wealth ... How Much? 1968. folder. Free Women's Division, Institute of Life Insurance, 277 Park Ave., New York, N.Y. 10017.

Facts about women's incomes and their importance to the financial structure.

Young Teens and Money, by Mary Beery, 1971. 159 p. $3.83. McGraw-Hill, New York.

How much allowance should I get? What should it cover? Should I get more as I get older? I'm fourteen now. If I go to a discount store, am I going to end up with a junky product? Are all checking accounts alike? If not, which is best? The author answers these and hundreds of other questions asked by actual teenagers in matters relating to earning, saving and spending money in this informal, easy-to-read book for the younger teens. Especially valuable are the long list of suggestions on how teenagers can earn money, the guide to tipping and a long bibliography of books and pamphlets and list of source materials (pp. 150–154). Of special interest to younger teens.

BUDGETING

Annual Price Survey: Family Budget Costs, 13th ed., 1970. 57 p. $2.50. Community Council of Greater New York, 225 Park Ave. South, New York, N.Y. 10003.

For New York City, this pamphlet lists costs for the family and the retired couple, weekly costs for individuals, retail price lists.

Family Budget Standard, 1970. 76 p. $4.00. Community Council of Greater New York, 225 Park Ave. South, New York, N.Y. 10003.

Prepared for the use of social and health agencies in New York City. Presents detailed information on a family budget standard, quantity standards for major categories of expenditures, and a general cost summation.

Family Budgeting, Don't Wonder Where the Money Went, by Thelma Vivian Winder, 1960. 9 p. Free. Family Services Program, Baltimore Urban League, 2404 Pennsylvania Ave., Baltimore, Md. 21217.

A basic introduction to the principles of family finance. Other resources for use with low-income consumers are available from this organization.

Family Economics Review.

Quarterly. Free to professional workers. Consumer and Food Economics Research Division. U.S. Department of Agriculture, Federal Center Bldg., Hyattsville, Md. 20782.

A report of current developments in family and food economics and the economic aspects of home management. Gives costs of food under various budgets.

Family Money Problems, by Sidney Margolius, 1967. 20 p. 25¢ (Public Affairs Pamphlet no. 412) Public Affairs Committee, 381 Park Ave. South, New York, N.Y. 10016.

A simple, down-to-earth discussion of family money problems.

Food For the Young Couple, rev. 1967. 16 p. 10¢ (cat. no. A1.77: 85/2). Supt. of Documents, GPO, Washington, D.C. 20402.

Describes a weekly food plan and gives sample menus. Tells how to cut food costs. An additional feature: how to purchase kitchen tools and utensils. Of interest to older teenagers.

A Guide to Budgeting For the Family, 1970. 14 p. 10¢ (U.S. Dept. of Agriculture, Home and Garden Bulletin no. 108, cat. no. A1.77:108/3). Supt. of Documents, GPO, Washington, D.C. 20402.

Elementary guide on setting up a budget and following its limits.

A Guide to Budgeting for the Young Couple, 1968. 16 p. 10¢ (cat. no. A1.77:98/3) Supt. of Documents, GPO, Washington, D.C. 20402.

Elementary but useful little guide, giving hints on why budgets are necessary and steps in developing a family plan. Of interest to older teenagers.

Methodology of Consumer Expenditures Surveys, 1968. 80 p. $1.00. Working paper no. 27. Bureau of the Census Publications Division, Washington, D.C. 20233.

Exploration in depth of the experience with family budget surveys both here and abroad. These insights should prove helpful in formulating a design for a continuing government program in the United States.

Retired Couple's Budget For a Moderate Living Standards, Autumn 1966, 1969. 36 p. 35¢ (cat no. L2.3:1570–4) Supt. of Documents, GPO, Washington, D.C. 20402.

Presents comparative data on how much it will cost a retired couple, covered by medicare, to live on a moderate level in a metropolitan area. Estimates for non-urban areas are also given.

Spring 1970 Cost Estimates For Urban Family Budgets, [published] Dec. 21, 1970. [14 p] Free. U.S. Dept. of Labor, Bureau of Labor Statistics, Washington, D.C. 20210.

Updates the final spring 1969 cost estimates. Also available free, together with the 1969 cost estimates, from Bureau of Labor Statistics Regional Offices and the Office of Prices and Living Conditions.

Three Budgets For a Retired Couple in Urban Areas of the United States, 1967–68, [published] 1970. 74 p. 70¢. (U.S. Dept. of Labor, Bureau of Labor Statistics, Bulletin 1570–6. cat. no. L2.3:1570–4) Supt. of Documents, GPO, Washington, D.C. 2402.

Provides budgets at three levels of income: lower, intermediate, and higher.

Three Budgets For an Urban Family of Four Persons, Final Spring 1969 Cost Estimates, [published] Dec. 1970. [16 p.] Free. U.S. Dept. of Labor, Bureau of Labor Statistics, Washington, D.C. 20212.

Sample budgets in three income levels: lower, intermediate, and higher. Based on a family consisting of husband, wife, thirteen year old boy, and eight year old girl. An analytical report on these budgets "will be published shortly as a supplement to Bulletin 1570–5." Copies of the spring 1969 budgets, and estimates for spring 1970 are also available free upon request from the Regional Offices of Bureau of Labor Statistics and the Office of Prices and Living Conditions.

Young Couples Make Money Work, 1971. 16 p. Free. Institute of Life Insurance, 277 Park Ave., New York, N.Y. 10017.

How the new family can budget its income.

CREDIT

Using Credit

AHEA's Workshop on Consumer Credit in Family Financial Management. *Journal of Home Economics*, v. 60, Jan. 1968: 12.

Editorial introduction to an issue devoted to the workshop's activities. Excerpts are included within the issue from all of the papers presented during the four-day session.

Borrower's Handbook of Annual Percentage Rates for Installment Credit, by George A. Peirce, 1967. 26 p. 50¢. Consumers League of New Jersey, 20 Church St., Montclair, N.J. 07042.

Instructions, examples and tables are given to find the true annual rates of interest. The discussion on revolving credit is of particular interest.

Buy Now, Pay Later, by Hillel Black, 1961. 240 p. $5.95. Morrow, New York. Also available in paperback: 50¢. Pocket Books, 1 W. 39th St., New York, N.Y. 10018.

Examines the uses and abuses of credit in the U.S. Describes the work of collection agencies and the growing use of teen-age credit.

Buy Now, Pay Never, by Liz R. Gallese. *Wall Street Journal*, v. 175, Nov. 18, 1970: 1+.

In depth discussion of the many problems created by the theft of credit cards, from the viewpoints of the consumer and business.

Buying on Time?, 1967. 19 p. Free. State of New York Banking Dept., 100 Church St., New York, N.Y. 10007.

Clear explanation of installment buying. Emphasis is on buyers' rights and responsibilities.

Cash or Credit, by Carl F. Christ, 1970. 33 p. Free. Family Services Program, Baltimore Urban League, 2406 Pennsylvania Ave., Baltimore, Md. 21217.

An explanation of the various kinds of credit available to the consumer. Emphasizes the advantages of saving and the advantages of paying in cash.

Common Sense Credit, by Charles Morrow Wilson, 1962. 180 p. $4.95. Devin-Adair, Greenwich, Conn.

Sub-title: "Credit unions come of age." How millions of Americans have escaped from loan sharks, high interest rates and extravagant installment buying through a unique institution called the credit union.

Consumer and Commercial Credit Management, by Robert H. Cole, 3d ed. 1968. 615 p. $14.00 (text ed. $10.50) Richard D. Irwin, Homewood, Ill.

Gives the reader an appreciation of the economic and social implications of credit and defines types of credit available.

Consumer, Beware! rev. 1968, 22 p. 15¢ AFL-CIO Department of Publications, 815 16th St., N.W., Washington, D.C. 20006. ($13.50 per 100 copies).

Guide to installment buying. Includes tables of the statutory maximum small loan rates for all states, and the laws regulating installment sales contract for the states which have them. Shows various types of credit available.

Consumer Conference Guide: Credit, n.d. 16 p. 1–9 copies: $1.00 each; 10–99 copies: 75¢. Chamber of Commerce of the United States, 1615 H St., N.W., Washington, D.C. 20006.

Guidelines for local chambers of commerce planning consumer conference programs on credit. Presents a model agenda, suggests publicity, gives ideas about follow-up activities, and provides a resource list.

Consumer Credit, by Elsie Fetterman, n.d. 23 p. 20¢. Publications Room, University of Connecticut, Box U–35, Storrs, Conn. 06268.

Facts one should know about consumer credit—types available, advantages and disadvantages, interest rates, precautions and sales contracts.

Consumer Credit and the Low Income Consumer, 1969. 105 p. Free up to 10 copies, 11 or more 50¢ each. Urban Coalition, 2100 M St., N.W., Washington, D.C. 20037.

Study of selected activities by commercial banks, credit unions and retailers to make consumer credit, consumer counseling and consumer education available to low income persons.

Consumer Credit and Wealth, by Reavis Cox, 1965. 47 p. $1.00. National Foundation for Consumer Credit, 1819 H Street, N.W., Washington, D.C. 20006.

This study in consumer credit has been published by a trade association of manufacturers, distributors and financing agencies. It is a technical, but popularized, presentation on the use of credit—its accumulation, maintenance, and growth.

Consumer Credit Annual, 1969. 38 p. $3.75. National Foundation for Consumer Credit, Inc., 1819 H St., N.W., Washington, D.C. 20006.

Compilation of statistical reference material and data related to consumer credit.

A Consumer Credit Bibliography, *Journal of Home Economics,* v. 60, Jan. 1968: 53–54.

A wide variety of books, articles, booklets, leaflets and other printed materials selected by the planning committee for display at the AHEA Workshop on Consumer Credit.

Consumer Credit Finance Charges, by Wallace P. Mors, 1965. 133 p. $5.00. National Bureau of Economic Research; order from Columbia University Press, New York.

Concerned with the problem of providing finance charge information to consumers. The methods financing agents and sellers use in computing finance charges are analyzed and the consumers' degrees of comprehension of this information have been surveyed and conclusions drawn.

Consumer Credit in Family Financial Management, 1968. 183 p. $2.00. American Home Economics Association, 2010 Massachusetts Ave., N.W., Washington, D.C. 20036.

Proceedings of the AHEA national workshop held fall 1967. Contains an extensive bibliography on consumer credit.

Consumer Finance, by Irving S. Michelman, 2d ed. 1970. 336 p. $10.00. Augustus M. Kelley, New York.

Sub-title: "A case history in American business." Includes the history and development of credit unions, auto finance companies and the entry of banks into the consumer credit field.

Consumer Finance Industry, edited by John M. Chapman and Robert A. Shay, 1967. 183 p. $6.00. Columbia University Press, New York.

An evaluation of loan service rendered by regulated consumer finance companies. Standards are suggested for the control of interest rates and loan ceilings.

The Consumer Finance Industry, by the National Consumer Finance Association, 1962. 187 p. $5.75. Prentice-Hall, Englewood Cliffs, N.J.

Outlines development of the regulated consumer finance industry. Includes problems involved in the effort of the industry to achieve and maintain a position of maximum service and usefulness to the consumers of America.

Consumer's Quick Credit Guide, 1964. 2 p. 5¢ (cat. no. A1.11/3: C86) Supt. of Documents, GPO, Washington, D.C. 20402.

Capsule information on typical credit charges, buying on the installment plan, and borrowing money.

Credit and Collections, by Richard P. Ettinger and David E. Golieb, 5th ed. 1962. 388 p. $11.95. Prentice-Hall, Englewood Cliffs, N.J.

Contains material on personal loans: who uses them, how they are obtained, from whom they are borrowed.

Credit Cards, by Elsie Fetterman, 1970. 20 p. 15¢. Agricultural Publications Dept., Box U–35, University of Connecticut, Storrs, Conn. 06268.

A description of the advantages and disadvantages of credit cards. Subtitled: "Thirty days to reality."

Credit Counselor Training Handbook, 1970. 87 p. Apply for price. Credit Counseling Centers, Inc., 17000 West Eight Mile Rd., Southfield, Mich. 48075.

A handbook compiled by experienced credit counselors. Recommended to those working with the poor and indebted.

Credit, Master or Servant? 1966. 52 p. 25¢ (cat. no. D2.14:PA–10) Supt. of Documents, GPO, Washington, D.C. 20402.

Official Department of Defense pamphlet offering information on lenders, credit, finance charges and rates, contracts. Explains things you should know before taking on debts, what to do to protect yourself, how to use your knowledge to save money. Also offers suggestions for financial relief if you are in credit trouble.

Credit Unions, by Jack Dublin, 1966. 179 p. $4.95; $1.95 (paper) Wayne State University, Detroit, Mich.

Discusses the basic philosophy of credit unions, and shows how a credit union should and should not operate.

Economic Report on Installment Credit and Retail Sales Practices of District of Columbia Retail-

ers, Mar. 1968. 52 p. 35¢ (Federal Trade Commission, cat. no. FT1.2:IN7) Supt. of Documents, GPO, Washington, D.C. 20402.

The results of a survey of installment credit and sales practices of ninety-six furniture, appliance and department stores having 85 percent of the sales in the District of Columbia. The results show that the poor do pay more.

Facts You Should Know about Your Credit, 1962. 16 p. 15¢ each to non-members. National Consumer Finance Association, 1000 16th St., N.W., Washington, D.C. 20036. (1–10 copies free to members, 11–1000, 15¢ each).

Prepared by the Better Business Bureau of Boston for the NCFA.

Family Credit Counseling, by Perry B. Hall, 1968. 127 p. $8.75. Family Service Association of America, 44 E. 23rd St., New York, N.Y. 10010.

A national study evaluating family credit counseling as provided through non-profit community-based programs. A summary is also available for $1.00.

Finance Facts Yearbook, 1970. 72 p. Free (limited distribution). National Consumer Finance Association, 1000 16th St., N.W., Washington, D.C. 20036.

A fact book about consumer financial behavior and the consumer finance business. Information about the American consumer is included—his employment, income, spending, saving, money management and his use of credit. Tables, charts and maps.

A Financial Checkup on the Use of Credit, by Gwen J. Bymers, rev. 1968. 6 p. 10¢. Cooperative Extension, Cornell University, Ithaca, N.Y. 14850.

An aid to assist the individual in assessing his personal financial condition.

A Guide to Consumer Credit, by Sidney Margolius, 1967. 20 p. 25¢ (Public Affairs Pamphlet no. 348) Public Affairs Committee, 381 Park Ave. South, New York, N.Y. 10016.

Provides basic information about the wise uses of credit. Explains interest and the problems of debt. Compares sources and costs of credit, and suggests how much debt a family can safely carry.

Hi! I'm Mr. Moneywise. I'd Like to Tell You Why I'm a Credit Union Member, 1966. 12 p. 10¢ (cat. no. FS3.302:M74/2) Supt. of Documents, GPO, Washington, D.C. 20402.

Illustrated in cartoon style, this booklet points out the advantages of being a credit union member in saving and borrowing money.

Hidden Costs of Credit Cards, by M. S. Schlossberg and L. M. Andrews. *Nation*, v. 210, Mar. 2, 1970: 240–242.

A discussion of the growing phenomenon of bank credit cards.

How and Where to Borrow Money, by Ira U. Cobleigh, 1964. 160 p. 60¢ (paper) Avon Books, 959 Eighth Ave., New York, N.Y. 10019.

An elementary discussion of borrowing. Included are chapters on lending institutions, borrowing for specific purposes and from specific places.

How Much Credit Can You Afford? by M. Feeley, *American Home*, v. 71, Oct. 1968: 20–21.

"Demarcation line between using credit and being in debt gets blurred." Discussion on how far you can go before you are in trouble. Includes use of credit cards, open-end credit, and guides for credit control.

How to Shake the Money Tree, by Robert Metz, 1966. 277 p. $5.95. Putnam's, New York.

Intelligent man's guide to borrowing and credit buying. Information provided is from prosaic to bizarre.

Hows and Whys of Credit Unions. *Changing Times,* v. 22, Dec. 1968: 33–37.

A simple but complete article on what a credit union is, the advantages of joining one and practical advice on how to organize such a group.

International Credit Union Yearbook. Annual. CUNA Inc., 1617 Sherman Ave., P.O. Box 431, Madison, Wis. 53701.

A source for world wide credit union information. Basic and summary statistics of savings, assets and reserves.

It's Not Just Money, edited by John R. Prindle, 1967. 145 p. CUNA, Inc., 1617 Sherman Ave., P.O. Box 431, Madison, Wis. 53701.

Basic information about the goals, purposes and activities of a credit union.

It's Your Credit: Manage It Wisely, 1970. 43 p. 50¢. Household Finance Corporation, Money Management Institute, Prudential Plaza, Chicago, Ill. 60601.

Basic advice on borrowing, interest and other credit problems.

The Mammon Madness, by Daniel Manesse, 1970. 173 p. $5.95. Community Credit Bureau, 475 Fifth Ave., New York, N.Y. 10017.

An unusual adult novel based on the inner workings of the personal finance business. The plot serves as a vehicle for exposing the abuses and describing the mechanics of credit collection.

Money Worries? A Credit Union Can Help, rev. 1969. 10 p. 10¢ (cat. no. HE3.3021M74/969) Supt. of Documents, GPO, Washington, D.C. 20402.

Explains the organization and functions of a federal credit union.

The Quality of Consumer Installment Credit, by Geoffrey H. Moore and Philip A. Klein, 1967. 260 p. $8.50. Columbia University Press, New York.

Shows that since the 1920's consumer installment credit has grown spectacularly accompanied by a reduction in down payment requirements, and an increase in the number of monthly payments.

Revision of Consumer Credit Statistics. *Federal Reserve Bulletin,* v. 54, Dec. 1968: 983–1003.

Estimates of consumer credit have been revised for the period since 1960. Four pages discuss the revisions, and the remaining seventeen pages are tables on consumer credit.

Screen Test Your Credit Risks, by William P. Boggess. *Harvard Business Review,* v. 45, Nov./Dec. 1967: 113–122.

"Use of advanced techniques and computers in consumer credit can reduce defaults" thus ultimately lowering credit costs and making consumer credit a more attractive risk to lenders.

Those Charge Anything Anywhere Cards. *Changing Times,* v. 24, Mar. 1970: 6–10.

A survey of the history, use, and dangers of the credit card.

The U.S. Takes Off on Credit Cards: a Little Gift from Your Friendly Banker, by Paul O'Neil. *Life,* v. 68, Mar. 27, 1970: 48–58.

An interesting and many-faceted discussion of the millions of credit cards that offer "instant cash, crime, and chaos."

The four major headings are: "Credit —Possible Repercussions," "Revolving Credit," "Contract Credit" and "Activities and Questions."

Using Our Credit Intelligently, 1970. 54 p. Apply for price. National Foundation for Consumer Credit, Inc., 1819 H St., N.W., Washington, D.C. 20006.

A description of consumer credit: what it is, what it can accomplish if used correctly, how it can be best utilized.

What the Farm Wife Should Know about Credit, by E. A. Anderson. *Successful Farming* (Eastern Edition), v. 66, Dec. 1968: 58–59.

What Young Farm Families Should Know about Credit, 1965. 20 p. 10¢ (cat. no. A 1.9:2135/2) Supt. of Documents, GPO, Washington, D.C. 20402.

Credit problems and solutions in a rural area.

When You Use Credit for the Family, 1965. 12 p. 10¢ (cat. no. A43:2:C86) Supt. of Documents, GPO, Washington, D.C. 20402.

How to understand your credit contract, how credit costs are figured, and the kinds of credit available to the consumer.

Why the Worry about Credit Cards? *U.S. News & World Report*, v. 67, Nov. 24, 1969: 62–65.

"Complaints about credit cards are heard daily—jumbled accounts, computer errors, slow response; result— issuers are concerned; so is Congress; both promise action."

A Workbook on Consumer Credit, by Richard L. D. Morse. *Journal of Home Economics*, v. 60, Jan. 1968: 47–52.

Consumer Credit Protection

Annual Report to Congress on Truth in Lending, 1970. 54 p. Free. Board of Governors, Federal Reserve System, Washington D.C. 20551.

Contains a study entitled *Survey of consumer awareness of finance charges and interest rates.*

Consumer Credit Protection Act. 139 p. 40¢ (cat. no. 90–1:H.rp. 1040) Supt. of Documents, GPO, Washington, D.C. 20402.

"Report of the Committee on Banking and Currency, to accompany H. R. 11601, together with supplemental and minority views."

Consumer Credit Protection Act . . . Approved May 29, 1968. 15¢ (cat. no. 90–2:Public Law 321). Supt of Documents, GPO, Washington, D.C. 20402.

"An act to safeguard the consumer in connection with the utilization of credit by requiring full disclosure of the terms and conditions of finance charges in credit transactions or in offers to extend credit; by restricting the garnishment of wages; and by creating the National Commission on Consumer Finance to study and make recommendations on the need for further regulation of the consumer finance industry; and for other purposes. Approved May 29, 1968."

Consumer Credit Code . . . for Lenders. *Consumer Reports*, v. 34, Mar. 1969: 121–126.

Discussion of the pros and cons of the Uniform Consumer Credit Code promulgated by the National Conference of Commissioners on Uniform State Laws. Includes sources of additional information.

Consumer Credit Reform. *Law and Contemporary Problems,* v. 33, autumn 1968: 641–785.

Entire issue devoted to a symposium on consumer credit articles include: "Consumer credit in the affluent society," "revolving credit and credit cards," "regulation of consumer credit insurance," and "federal attack on loan shark problems".

Consumer Viewpoints: a Critique of the Uniform Consumer Credit Code, 1969. Vol. I, 286 p. $15.00. Vol. II, 376 p. $20.00 (set for $30.00) Consumer Research Foundation, P. O. Box 9034, Berkeley, Calif. 94709.

Collection of pointed comments by noted consumer representatives and lawyers. Indexed with complete tables of reference to the final draft of the proposed credit code.

Credit and Installment Buying, by Richard L. D. Morse, 1969. 18 p. 25¢. Department of Family Economics, Justin Hall, Kansas State University, Kan. 66502.

Discusses possible state legislation to supplement the Truth in Lending Act.

Customer Reactions to Truth in Lending, by John W. Riday. *Banking,* v. 62, Jan. 1970: 53.

A poll of two-hundred and forty-two bank executives eliciting from them their opinions of public reaction to the law. 55% of those polled felt negative reactions from their customers; 39% indicated their customers were apathetic; only 6% said they had received favorable reactions from their customers.

Don't Get Garnisheed!, by Daniel R. Fusfeld, n.d. 21 p. 25¢. Labor and Industrial Relations Center, Michigan State University, East Lansing, Mich. 48823.

Guidance for the worker about a growing American credit practice and its abuses.

The Impact of Truth-in-Lending Legislation: the Massachusetts Experience, by Robert W. Pullen, 1968. 65 p. Free. Federal Reserve Bank, 30 Pearl St., Boston, Mass. 02106.

Considers the impact of the law on consumers and rate advertising. A twenty-two item bibliography is included.

Like the Debtors' Jail . . . The Case against Wage Garnishment, 1968. 1 p. Free. Consumer Federation of America, P. O. Box 19345, 20th St. Station, Washington, D.C. 20036.

Explains the practice of garnishment and the federal and state laws concerning it.

New Key to Credit Shopping: Truth-in-Lending Act. *Consumer Reports,* v. 34, July 1969: 360–366.

Explanation, by practical example, of finance charges and true interest rate. Points out loopholes in the law. Lists those federal agencies which have enforcement responsibilities.

New Rules on . . . Consumer Credit Protection, 1969. 439 p. $7.00 (paper) Commerce Clearing House, Chicago.

The full-text draft of the Uniform Commercial Credit Code and the official commissioners' comments. Basically a technical analysis, this guide outlines pertinent federal laws and regulations.

Regulation Z. *Federal Reserve Bulletin* v. 55, Feb. 1969: 126–145.

Final regulations which the nation's creditors must follow in carrying out provisions of the Truth in Lending Act. Itemized contents listed on p. 126.

Securing the Guarantee of Consumer Credit Legislation, by Peter J. Driscoll. *Notre Dame*

Lawyer, v. 44, Apr. 1969: 574–602.

Outlines the Uniform Consumer Credit Code and the Federal Consumer Credit Protection Act.

Shopping for Credit/Truth in Lending, 1969. 19 p. 30¢. Carter H. Golembe Associates, Inc., Suite 905, 270 Madison Avenue, New York, N.Y. 10016.

An overview of the truth in lending law and its effects on users and extenders of credit.

A Summary of the Uniform Consumer Credit Code, by Nathaniel Butler, 1969. 8 p. Free. National Conference of Commissioners on Uniform State Laws, 1155 E. 60th St., Chicago, Ill. 60637.

A summary of the final draft of the code.

Those One-sided Credit Laws. *Consumer Reports,* v. 31, Mar. 1966: 108–112.

Discusses the easy payment deals which give sellers far more rights to your property than you may realize, and the need for changes.

Truth about Credit, by Robert W. Johnson, 1969. 21 p. $1.00. Truth About Credit Committee, P.O. Box 239, Carmel, Ind. 46032.

A review of the protections extended consumers by the Consumer Credit Protection Act.

The Truth about Credit Is Coming. *Consumer Reports,* v. 33, Aug. 1968: 428–431.

Precise information about the Consumer Credit Protection Act. Includes history, analysis, strengths and weaknesses, as well as the actual provisions of the act.

The Truth about Truth-in-Lending, by Paul A. Khan and Patricia P. Douglas. *Montana Business Quarterly,* v. 7, autumn 1969: 9–15.

Despite creditors' skepticism and debtors' apathy, the new credit rules offer the public a yardstick for comparison of rates and services.

Truth-in-Lending. *Federal Reserve Bulletin,* v. 55, Feb. 1969: 98–102.

Detailed discussion of the provisions of the Truth in Lending Act. Includes sample table which may be used by lenders to determine the annual percentage rate for a transaction.

Truth-in-Lending, 1968. 88 p. $2.00 International Consumer Credit Association, 375 Jackson Avenue, St. Louis, Mo. 63130.

Prepared by Commerce Clearing House. Includes the complete text of the Consumer Credit Protection Act of May 29, 1968, P.L. 90–321.

Truth in Lending, by Frederick Solomon. *Banking,* v. 61, July 1968, 41–42+.

The salient features of the Truth in Lending Act are discussed as they will affect banks. The author headed the Federal Reserve's task force in implementing the act.

Truth in Lending, Draft of Proposed Regulation Z, 1968. 69 p. Free. Publications Services, Division of Administrative Services, Federal Reserve Bank, Washington, D.C. 20551.

New proposed regulations to emplement the Truth in Lending Act, are published here for public comment.

Truth in Lending Law. *U.S. News & World Report,* v. 66, June 23, 1969: 100–102.

Describes the ways in which the new law will affect credit situations.

Truth in Lending: Regulation Z, 1969. 85 p. Free. Publications Services, Division of Administrative Services, Federal Reserve System, Washington, D.C. 20551.

A description of the creditor's responsibilities under the Truth in Lending Act.

Truth in Lending: What It Means for Consumer Credit, 1970. 12 p. Free. Public Information Dept., Federal Reserve Bank, Philadelphia, Pa. 19101.

A non-technical introduction to the Truth in Lending Law.

Uniform Code for Consumer Credit, by R. W. Johnson. *Harvard Business Review,* v. 46, July/Aug. 1968: 119–125.

A discussion of the basic rationale underlying proposed changes (in 1968) of credit practices.

Uniform Consumer Credit Code, by R. D. L. Morse and W. R. Fasse, 1970. 80 p. $6.00. Dept. of Farm Economics, Kansas State University, Manhattan, Kans. 66502.

Statements and position papers prepared for a Kansas Legislative Study Committee. They constitute an article by article critique of UCCC.

The Uniform Consumer Credit Code, by Clarence L. James, Jr. and others. *Georgetown Law Journal,* v. 57, May 1969: 923–954.

Legislation concerning the uniform consumer credit code is discussed, focusing on the inadequate remedies under articles V and VI.

The Unsolicited Mailing of Credit Cards, 1970. 30 p. Free. Federal Trade Commission, Washington, D.C. 20580.

The FTC has adopted a trade regulation effective May 18, 1970, which states that the unsolicited mailing of credit cards constitutes an unfair trade practice.

What the New Truth-in-Lending Law Does for You. *Changing Times,* v. 23, June 1969: 7–12.

Detailed explanation of the provisions of the law which requires full disclosure, in understandable terms, of the annual percentage rate and other charges for credit. Included is a list of enforcement agencies.

What Truth in Lending Means to You, 1969. 6 p. Free. Federal Reserve System, Washington, D.C. 20551.

Simple, brief explanation of the Truth in Lending Act with a list of the Federal agencies responsible for enforcing it.

What You Must Tell Your Customers; Questions and Answers. *Nation's Business,* v. 57, June 1969: 42–44.

Questions and answers on the Truth in Lending Law.

What You Ought to Know about Federal Reserve Regulation Z—Truth-in-Lending Consumer Credit Cost Disclosure, 1969. 63 p. Free. Division of Administrative Services, Federal Reserve System, Washington, D.C. 20551.

Includes a list of Federal enforcement agencies, questions and answers, model forms, and a complete text of the law.

Where Is the Consumer in the Uniform Consumer Credit Code? by Richard L. D. Morse and William R. Fasse. *Journal of Home Economics,* v. 62, Jan. 1970: 30–33.

A detailed analysis of the UCCC. The authors conclude that there are other alternatives to its adoption. Contains a nineteen item selective bibliography.

Why Not Pay Cash? *Consumer Bulletin,* v. 52, July 1969: 13–14.

Discusses the Consumer Credit Protection Act of 1968 (Truth in Lending) and the Uniform Credit Code.

Will Your State Pass This Model Credit Law? *Changing Times,* v. 23, Mar. 1969: 39–41.

Discussion of Uniform Consumer Credit Code.

Debtor's Remedies

An Analysis of Economic and Personal Factors Leading to Consumer Bankruptcy, by Robert D. Dolphin, Jr., 1965. 138 p. $1.00. Michigan State University Press, East Lansing, Mich.

Discusses the legal environment, personal and economic characteristics of the bankrupt. Presents conclusions and recommendations.

Bankruptcy Laws of the United States, 1968. 393 p. $1.50 (cat. no. Y1.2:B22/2/968) Supt. of Documents, GPO, Washington, D.C. 20402.

Complete texts of all the ninety-nine bankruptcy acts passed from the first in 1898 through the act of November 28, 1967. No comment or explanation is included.

The Boom Is Going Bust, by George Sullivan, 1968. 215 p. $5.95. Macmillan, New York.

Subtitled: *"The Growing Scandal in Personal Bankruptcy".* An exploration of this national problem from all angles in terms consumers should understand.

Consumer Bankruptcy, by Elizabeth Hanford. *Personal Finance Law Quarterly Report,* v. 23, winter 1968: 25–28.

The author considers such "underlying and triggering causes" of bankruptcy as wage garnishment, "confession of judgment," debt adjustment, excessive credit extension, and consumer extravagance.

Debt Counseling, 1967. 2 p. Free. AFL-CIO Community Service Activities, 815 16th St., N.W., Washington, D.C. 20006.

A concise discussion of the intricacies of debt counseling.

Debtor Clinics—Rx for the Poor, by Jack Pollock. *Nation's Business,* v. 55, Dec. 1967: 75–77.

Analyzes some of the non-profit credit counseling clinics which have been established in sixty-four communities by business and sparked by the National Foundation for Consumer Credit, a lenders' association.

Debtors' and Creditors': Rights and Remedies, by Sidney Sherwin, 1969. 236 p. $12.95. Attorneys' Aid Publications, 169–12 Hillside Ave., Jamaica, N.Y. 11432.

This "how-to-do-it" is a guide to the legal rights of debtors and creditors. It is designed for attorneys, credit collectors, and credit managers as well as the individual creditor and debtor. Twenty-eight legal forms are included.

Debtors' Dilemma: Critics Charge Laws on Bankruptcies Fail to Protect Individuals, by Richard A. Shaffer. *Wall Street Journal,* v. 176, Nov. 5, 1970: 1, col. 1.

Lengthy and informative article on the procedures and pitfalls of personal bankruptcy.

The Excessively Indebted, by Mary E. Ryan and E. Scott Maynes. *Journal of Consumer Affairs,* v. 3, winter 1969: 107–126.

Based on data from the 1960 survey of consumer finances conducted by the Consumer Research Center, University of Michigan. Focuses on short-run consumer installment debt.

The Federal Wage Garnishment Law—Basic Information, Jan. 1970, 6 p. Free. (Wage, Hour and Public Contracts Publication 1279) Wage and Labor Studies Administration, U.S. Dept. of Labor, Washington, D.C. 20210.

A brief discussion of the federal wage garnishment law.

Guide to Wage Earner Plans Under Chapter 13 of the Bankruptcy Act, 1968. 67 p. $1.00. Section of Corporation Banking and Business Law, American Bar Association, 1155 E. 60th Street, Chicago, Ill. 60637.

Contains suggested forms and a practical outline of practice and procedure under Chapter Thirteen of the Bankruptcy Act.

How to Keep from Drowning in Debt. *Changing Times*, v. 23, Feb. 1969: 7–10.

Five symptoms that give warning of impending financial problems, four steps to pinpoint the amount of debt one can safely carry, and six practical rules for using credit wisely.

SAVINGS AND INVESTMENTS

Advice for Persons Who Are Considering an Investment in a Franchise Business, 1970. 11 p. 10¢ (cat. no. FT1.3/2:4) Supt. of Documents, GPO, Washington, D.C. 20402.

Alerts the consumer to pitfalls in the market place and how to protect himself as a prospective franchisee, while considering an investment in a franchise business.

All about Stocks, by Ira U. Cobleigh, 1970. 243 p. $6.95. Weybright and Talley, New York.

Sub-title: *"A Guide to Profitable Investing in the '70's."*

The Grim Truth about Mutual Funds, by Ralph Lee Smith, 1963. 122 p. O. P. Putnam's, New York.

Describes the operation of funds, interlocking arrangements, favored insiders, excessive management fees, excessive sales charges by inexperienced and unqualified salesmen, and excessive turnover of portfolio. Recommends reform.

How to Buy Stocks, by Louis Engel, 4th ed. rev. 1967. 339 p. $5.95. Little, Brown, Boston.

"A guide to making more money in the market." The author assumes the continuing decline in the purchasing value of the dollar, and views the market as a hedge against inflation. Describes the operation of the stock exchange and gives advice on dealing with brokers.

How to Gain Financial Independence, by Edward T. O'Toole, 1969. 142 p. $1.00, or 70¢ in quantities of 100. Benjamin Company, 485 Madison Ave., New York, N.Y. 10022.

An analysis of money management techniques. It highlights the financial services and special savings plans offered by mutual savings banks.

How to Invest in Stocks and Bonds, 1967. 30 p. Free. Merrill Lynch, Pierce, Fenner and Smith, Inc., 70 Pine St., New York, N.Y. 10005.

Provides information on the various kinds of stocks and bonds available to the potential investor.

How to Make Money with Mutual Funds, by David L. Markstein, 1969. 258 p. $7.95. McGraw-Hill, New York.

What the beginning investor should know about mutual funds and how the professional can use mutual funds more effectively. Included is a ninety-eight question programmed instruction section with a glossary.

How to Read a Financial Report, 1968. 34 p. Free. Merrill Lynch, Pierce, Fenner and Smith, Inc., 70 Pine St., New York, N.Y. 10005.

Introduction to Investments, by John C. Clendenin, 5th ed. 1969. 691 p. $9.95 (text ed.) McGraw-Hill, New York.

Lucid description of the art and science of investing.

Investment Facts, 1968. 23 p. Free. Merrill Lynch, Pierce, Fenner and Smith, Inc., 70 Pine St., New York, N.Y. 10005.

Information about common stocks, growth dividends, and market value in relation to the increased cost of living.

Investment Trusts and Funds from the Investor's Point of View, 1967. 96 p. $1.00. American Institute for Economic Research, Great Barrington, Mass. 01230.

The Kiplinger Book on Investing for the Years Ahead, by John W. Hazard and Lewis G. Coit, 1962. 285 p. O. P. Doubleday, Garden City, New York.

Recommends that securities be purchased only after careful thought, thorough investigation, and advice from competent advisors.

Some Legal Aspects of United States Savings Bonds . . . 1966. 12 p. 15¢ (cat. no. T66.6/2:L52) Supt. of Documents, GPO, Washington, D.C. 20402.

Aspects discussed include income taxes, estate taxes, gift taxes, change in ownership, rights of survivors, judicial proceedings.

Stock Market A B C, by Joanne K. Friedlander and Jean Neal, 1969. 96 p. $2.95. Follett Publishing Co., New York.

A short and relatively simple "first" book on the subject written specifically for young people.

Successful Investing through Mutual Funds, by Robert Frank, 1969. 222 p. $5.95; $2.45 (paper) Hart Publishing Co., New York.

A well organized, clearly written discussion of mutual funds.

Understanding the Stock Market: a Guide for Young Investors, by Janet Low, 1968. 210 p. $4.95. Little, Brown, Boston. Also available in paperback: 75¢ (cat. no. S4741) Bantam Books, Inc., 666 Fifth Ave., New York, N.Y. 10019.

Basic and practical information, attractively presented, for teen-agers interested in the stock market. Discusses things to consider before buying stock, how to read the stock market report in the daily newspaper and what goes on at the Exchange.

U.S. Savings Bonds—Build Your Own Retirement Program; Freedom Shares; Information about Series E Savings Bonds; Current Income Series H Savings Bonds; Investment Advantages of the Series E; and Savings Bonds for Education. Free. Supt. of Documents, GPO, Washington, D.C. 20402.

A selection of pamphlets available singly or in quantity for classroom use.

What Every Woman Should Know about Investing Her Money, by Herta H. Levy, 1968. 222 p. $6.95. Dartnell Corp., Chicago. Also available in paperback: 95¢, Pocket Books, 1 W. 39th St. New York, N.Y. 10018.

Practical advice not necessarily limited by gender. Includes a discussion of investment terminology.

What Everybody Ought to Know about This Stock and Bond Business. n.d. 29 p. Free. Merrill Lynch, Pierce, Fenner and Smith, Inc., 70 Pine St., New York, N.Y. 10005.

Defines such market terms as stocks, bonds, price changes, Bulls and Bears, and speculation. Outlines the operation of the New York Stock Exchange.

What Shall I Do with My Money? by Eliot Janeway, 1970. 209 p. $5.95. David McKay, New York.

A brief discussion of current economic problems is followed by investment counseling advice about property, mutual funds, stocks and bonds.

You and the Investment World, 1967. 48 p. Free. New York Stock Exchange, 11 Wall St., New York, N.Y. 10005.

Explains types of business organizations, stocks and bonds, and investment. Each chapter contains a short test and an individual problem-solving activity. A glossary is included.

Your Savings and Investment Dollar, rev. 1968. 40 p. 25¢. Household Finance Corp., Prudential Plaza, Chicago, Ill. 60601.

One of the "Money Management Series"; this covers the basic areas of savings and investments.

INSURANCE

The Consumer's Guide to Insurance Buying, by Vladimir P. Chernik, 1970. 288 p. $6.50. Sherbourne Press, Los Angeles, Calif.

A consumer-oriented presentation of life, health, automobile and property insurance.

Decade of Decision, by Jerome B. Cohen, rev. 1966. 56 p. Free. Educational Division, Institute of Life Insurance, 277 Park Ave., New York, N.Y. 10017.

Considers the financial and insurance needs of the young family.

How to Find Out about Insurance, by Oswald William Pendleton, 1967. 196 p. $6.50; $4.00 (paper) Pergamon Press, New York.

A guide to sources of insurance information. Includes encyclopedias, dictionaries, documents, research reports, lectures, periodicals, directories, statistical annuals, associations and books.

How to Settle Your Own Insurance Claim, by Daniel G. Baldyga, 1968. 159 p. $4.95. Macmillan, New York.

The author contends that one can save money by settling some insurance claims without a lawyer.

Insurance Facts for Farmers, rev. 1967. 23 p. 15¢ (cat. no. A1.9:2137/5) Supt. of Documents, GPO, Washington, D.C. 20402.

A discussion of insurance information for rural consumers.

The Law of Insurance, by Irwin M. Taylor, 2d ed. rev. 1968. (Legal Almanac series no. 37) 116 p. $3.00. Oceana, Dobbs Ferry, N.Y. 10522.

Basic theoretical information about insurance. Covers life, accident, fire, casualty, and marine policies.

Pitfalls to Watch for in Mail Order Insurance Policies, 1969. 5 p. 10¢ (Federal Trade Commission Reports, cat. no. FT1. 3/2:1) Supt. of Documents, GPO, Washington, D.C. 20402.

Stop Wasting Your Insurance Dollars, by Dave Goodwin, 1969. 153 p. $1.50. Simon and Schuster, New York.

A new and provocative approach to guide the buyer of all types of insurance.

Life

The Consumers Union Report on Life Insurance, 1967. 128 p. $3.95; $1.95 (paper) Consumers Union of U.S., Mount Vernon, N.Y.

An expansion of the "How to buy life insurance" series which appeared in the Jan., Feb., Mar. 1967 issues of *Consumer Reports.*

The Farm Family Looks at Life Insurance, 1966. 30 p. Free. Women's Division, Institute of Life Insurance, 277 Park Ave., New York, N.Y. 10017.

Basic information designed specifically for the rural person, but also of use to others.

Getting the Most for Your Family's Life Insurance Dollar, by Chester C. Nash, 1966. 26 p. 75¢. Association Press, 291 Broadway, New York, N.Y. 10007.

An elementary discussion of life insurance—what it is, what it costs, how it works, and how to decide what is needed.

How to Get a Dollar's Value for a Dollar Spent, by Arthur Milton, 1964. 190 p. O. P. Citadel Press, New York.

Elementary advice on buying life insurance.

How to Get the Most Life Insurance Protection at the Lowest Cost, by J. K. Lasser Tax Institute, 1968. 210 p. $12.50. Business Reports, Inc., 2 East Ave., Larchmont, N.Y. 10538.

An extensive discussion of the kinds of variations in life insurance policies. The tax aspects of life insurance are discussed in detail.

Insurance in the Age of the Consumer, by Herbert S. Denenberg. *Best's Review, Life/Health Insurance Edition,* v. 70, Apr. 1970: 32–40.

A critique of the life insurance industry by a professor of insurance at the Wharton School of Finance and Commerce.

Interview with Mrs. Virginia H. Knauer, Special Assistant to the President for Consumer Affairs. *Spectator,* v. 178, June 1970: 20–27+.

Mrs. Knauer and Mr. Otto C. Lee discuss the insurance industry's relationship and response to American consumers. Mr. Lee is president of Harleysville Insurance Companies.

Life and Health Insurance Handbook, edited by Davis W. Gregg, 2d ed., 1966. 1348 p. $16.00 (text ed. $12.00) Dow-Jones-Irwin, Homewood, Ill.

Designed primarily for insurance agents, executives, accountants and others concerned with life and health insurance.

Life Insurance, by S. S. Huebner and Kenneth Black, Jr., 7th ed.,

1969. 875 p. $8.50. Appleton-Century-Crofts, New York.

A standard textbook in insurance. Deals primarily with life and health insurance. Bibliographies are included.

Life Insurance and Annuities from the Buyer's Point of View, 1969. 34 p. $1.00. American Institute for Economic Research, Great Barrington, Mass. 01230.

An analysis for the potential buyer; costs for life insurance and annuities are discussed.

Life Insurance—Dollars and Sense; The Family Money Manager; You and Your Family's Life Insurance, 1967–1968. Paging varies. Free. Canadian Life Insurance Association, 44 King St. West, Toronto, Ontario, Canada.

Three leaflets issued by an insurance association, presenting the savings and protection point-of-view in buying insurance.

Life Insurance Fact Book 1970. 128 p. Free. Institute of Life Insurance, 277 Park Ave., New York, N.Y. 10017.

Includes a wealth of statistical data, a history of all the state life insurance commissions, and a four-page glossary.

Life Insurance: How to Get Your Money's Worth, by Arnold Geier, 1965. 95¢ (paper) Collier Books, 60 Fifth Ave., New York, N.Y. 10003.

Comprehensive guide to life, retirement, and health insurance for the layman.

Life Insurance: the Immaculate Deception, by G. Scott Reynolds. *Nation,* v. 207, Sept. 30, 1968: 304–305.

A strong criticism of the life insurance industry.

The Little Gem Life Chart, Annual. $6.00. National Underwriter Co., 420 Fourth St., Cincinnati, Ohio 45202.

Presentation of life insurance facts and figures. By using this buying guide to life insurance, a prospective buyer can shop more than two hundred companies.

The Mortality Merchants, by G. Scott Reynolds, 1968. 242 p. $4.95. David McKay, New York.

"The legalized racket of life insurance and what you can do about it."

Pay Now, Die Later, by James Gollin, 1966. 276 p. $7.95. Random House, New York. Also available in paperback: $1.25, Penguin Books, Inc., 39 W. 55th St., New York, N.Y. 10019.

"What's wrong with life insurance: a report on our biggest and most wasteful industry."

A Report on Life Insurance, by Joseph M. Belth, 1967. 192 p. $3.00. Bureau of Business Research, Indiana University, Bloomington, Ind. 47401.

Written from the viewpoint of the buyer. One chapter discusses life insurance prices and includes specific recommendations regarding companies that showed up well in the author's price analysis.

The Tired Tirade, by Halsey D. Josephson, 1968. 155 p. $3.75. Farnsworth Publishing Co. Lynbrook, N.Y.

A certified life underwriter attempts to refute the major criticisms made of life insurance, particularly the *Consumers Union Report on Life Insurance.*

70

Understanding Life Insurance for the Family, 1964. 12 p. Free. Division of Home Economics, Federal Extension Services, U.S. Dept. of Agriculture, Washington, D.C 20515.

Explains the basic kinds of life insurance policies including combination policies and special clauses. Discusses group insurance and other protection plans.

What Every Young Couple Should Know about Life Insurance, by A. M. Watkins. *Redbook Magazine,* v. 130, Feb. 1968: 53–60.

A forthright discussion of life insurance. Of interest to older teenagers.

What's Wrong with Your Life Insurance?, by Norman F. Dacey, 1966. 445 p. $6.95; $1.50 (paper) Macmillan, New York.

A critique of the life insurance industry.

You and Your Family's Life Insurance, 1971. 28 p. Free. Women's Division, Institute of Life Insurance, 277 Park Ave., New York, N.Y. 10017.

An explanation of life insurance designed specifically for women.

Liability and casualty

Automobile

After Cars Crash, by Robert E. Keeton and Jeffrey O'Connell, 1967. 145 p. $11.95. Dow-Jones-Irwin, Homewood, Ill.

A concise discussion of automobile insurance as it exists now, including its many defects. Outlines a "Basic Protection Insurance," a much improved form of automobile insurance.

Auto Insurance. *Consumer Reports,* v. 35, June; July 1970.

A two-part article which discusses the ramifications of price shopping for automobile insurance. Twenty-five leading companies are rated.

Auto Insurance and Compensation Study, 1970. 17 v. Dept. of Transportation, Supt. of Documents, GPO, Washington, D.C. 20402.

A comprehensive study of motor vehicle insurance and compensation systems as directed by Public Law 90–313. The seventeen volumes have various catalog numbers and prices.

Auto Insurance: No Risks Preferred, by James Ridgeway. *New Republic,* v. 160, Feb. 22, 1969: 18–21.

How automobile insurance policy holders are selected and why many people are turned down.

Auto Insurance Reform. *Consumer Reports,* v. 33, Jan. 1968: 9–15.

Discussion of the "Basic Protection Plan" which partially replaces negligence liability insurance with direct loss insurance, payable without regard to fault. CU finds the Basic Protection Plan the best solution yet devised for reform within limits of private enterprise.

Auto Insurance; the Need for Reform, by Sidney Margolius. *American Federationist,* v. 74, Dec. 1967: 5–9.

Comprehensive discussion of the problems of auto insurance and the need for change.

Automobile Insurance Study, 1967. 183 p. 60¢ (cat. no. 90–1: H rp 815). Supt. of Documents, GPO, Washington, D.C. 20402.

"Report by the staff of the Antitrust Subcommittee (subcommittee no. 5) of the Committee on the Judiciary, House, 90th Cong., 1st sess., pursuant to H. Res. 40, Oct. 24, 1967."

Car Insurance and Consumer Desires, by Jeffrey O'Connell and Wallace H. Wilson, 1969. 115 p. $6.50. University of Illinois Press, Urbana, Ill.

Two thousand Illinois families are surveyed to discern their preferences between a "fault" and "no fault" form of automobile insurance.

Crisis in Car Insurance, edited by Robert E. Keeton and others, 1968. 279 p. $6.95. University of Illinois Press, Urbana, Ill.

Details the needs for reforms in the automobile insurance industry.

Hit from Both Sides, by Robert R. Lewiston, 1967. 224 p. $5.00. Abelard-Schuman, New York. Also available in paperback: $1.00, Essandess Special Editions, 1 W. 39th St., New York, N.Y. 10018.

"An exposé of our auto insurance system." Criticizes the U.S.'s "archaic" negligence laws.

Insurance Industry, Hearings Before the Subcommittee on Antitrust and Monopoly of the Committee on the Judiciary, Senate, 90th Cong. 2d. Sess. and 91st Cong., 1st. sess: Pt. 13. Automobile liability insurance, June 25–28, 1968. p. 7389–8244, $3.50 (cat. no. Y4.J89/2: In 7/3pt.13). Pt. 14. Automobile liability insurance, July 9–24, 1968. p. 8245–8808 $2.50 (cat. no. Y 4.J89/2:In7/3/pt.14). Supt. of Documents, GPO, Washington, D.C. 20402.

A New Road for Auto Insurance, by Robert Sheehan. *Fortune,* v. 76, Nov. 1967: 170–172, 218–222.

An interesting discussion of the problems of auto insurance and a suggested replacement: non-fault insurance.

Public Attitude toward Auto Insurance, 1970. 266 p. $1.25 (cat. no. TD 1.2:Au 8). Supt. of Documents, GPO, Washington, D.C. 20402.

Report of Survey Research Center Institute for Social Research, University of Michigan, to Department of Transportation staff. Analysis of consumer complaint letters concerning auto insurance.

Why Young Drivers Pay High Insurance Rates and **What's Causing the Increase In Your Auto Insurance Bill,** 1970. Free. American Mutual Insurance Alliance, 20 N. Wacker Dr., Chicago, Ill. 60606.

Short leaflets available in quantity for classes and study groups. Of special interest to teenagers.

Property

All-in-One Insurance for Householders. *Changing Times,* v. 23, Apr. 1969: 24–28.

Detailed discussion of the "homeowners" policy.

A Family Guide to Property and Liability Insurance. 4th ed., 1967. 24 p. Free. Educational Division, Insurance Information Institute, 110 William St., New York, N.Y. 10038.

Covers property insurance for the homeowner or renter. Explains liability insurance for the family, automobile and household insurance.

Home Mortgage Insurance, 1969. 14 p. Free. U.S. Dept. of Housing and Urban Development, Washington, D.C. 20410.

A discussion of the principles of home mortgage insurance.

TAXES

Farmer's Tax Guide. 47 p. Free. (Publication 225), Internal Revenue Service, Department of the Treasury, Washington, D.C. 20224, or local Internal Revenue Office.

Explains the tax laws as they apply to farming and contains information to assist in filing Federal income tax returns.

German Added Value Tax—Two Years After, by Rudolf J. Niehus. *Taxes,* v. 47, Sept. 1969: 554–566.

Surveys the methods of introducing and operating the value added tax in West Germany. The author concludes that the tax entails considerable additional administrative burden on the taxpayer.

Halfway to Tax Reform, by Joseph A. Ruskay and Richard Osserman, 1970. 320 p. $8.95. Indiana University Press, Bloomington, Ind.

A review of recent achievements in tax reform, and an analysis of areas in which additional revisions are needed.

A Primer on Government Spending, by Robert L. Heilbroner and Peter L. Bernstein, 1963. 120 p. $4.95; $1.95 (paper) Random House, New York.

A searching analysis of public budgeting and financial systems, and a consideration of the government's role in balancing the national economy.

Replacement of the Income Tax. *Nation's Business,* v. 57, Apr. 1969: 38–41.

A short, popularly written introduction to the principles of the value added tax. The article is an interview with Dan Throop Smith, professor of finance at Harvard's Graduate School of Business Administration.

A Report on the Better Homes and Gardens Tax Questionnaire, Jan. 1971. 95 p. 1—10 copies, $1.00 each; 11–25 copies, 80¢; 26–50 copies, 65¢; over 50 copies, 55¢. Better Homes and Gardens, Box 374, Department 2Q0, Des Moines, Iowa 50302.

Complete report of answers submitted to a tax opinion questionnaire printed in the June 1970 issue of *Better Homes and Gardens.* The opinions of 70,000 respondents are reported.

Revenue Sharing, by Henry S. Reuss, 1970. 160 p. $5.95. Praeger, New York.

Outlines and defines revenue sharing as a system of revitalizing state and local governments.

Revenue Sharing and the City, edited by Harvey S. Perloff and Richard P. Nathan, 1968. 128 p. $6.00; $2.50 (paper) Johns Hopkins Press, Baltimore, Md.

Discusses various systems of sharing federal tax revenues with city governments.

70,000 Taxpayers Speak Out, edited by Peter Lindberg. *Better Homes and Gardens,* v. 49, Mar. 1971: 58–59 +.

A summary of replies to a tax questionnaire printed in the June 1970 issue of this periodical.

Should Churches Be Taxed? by D. B. Robertson, 1968. 288 p. $6.50. Westminster, Philadelphia, Pa.

Surveys the intensifying controversy over continuing tax exemptions for churches.

Some Problems in Implementing a Tax on Value Added, by W. Missorten. *National Tax Journal*, v. 21, Dec. 1968: 396–411.

Examines the mechanism of collecting the value added tax. The author considers EEC experience in drawing his conclusions.

The Tax on Value Added, by Clara Sullivan, 1965. 340 p. $10.00. Columbia University Press, New York.

A definitive study of the theory, techniques, and presumed effects of the value added tax. Bibliography: pp. 313–327.

A Value-Added Tax—Is It Coming to the U.S.? by Gilbert Simonetti. *Journal of Accountancy.* v. 129, Feb. 1970: 75–77.

Surveys the arguments, pro and con, for adopting the VAT as a new revenue measure.

The Value Added Tax: the Case For, by Dan Throop Smith. Value Added Tax: the Case Against, by Stanley S. Surrey. *Harvard Business Review*, v. 48, Nov./Dec. 1970: 77–85, 86–94.

Two noted authorities debate the VAT question. A basic periodical resource.

Where's the Money Coming From? *Forbes*, v. 105, Feb. 15, 1970: 20–21.

A brief discussion of the VAT and its effects on pricing. Popular in tone.

Will the Value Added Tax Solve our Foreign Trade Problems? by Joseph W. Barr. *Banking*, v. 61, May 1969: 43–44.

"The former Secretary of the Treasury says the answer is 'No'," and outlines the reasons for his beliefs.

Your Federal Income Tax. 160 p. 75¢ (Publication 17, Internal Revenue Service, Department of the Treasury). Obtainable from the Supt. of Documents, GPO, Washington, D.C. 20402 or local Internal Revenue Office.

Annual guide designed to assist in preparing Federal income tax returns for individuals.

Your Income Tax, by J. K. Lasser. Annual. Simon and Schuster, New York.

A guide to preparing returns.

RETIREMENT PLANNING

Are You Planning on Living the Rest of Your Life? 1969. 72 p. 30¢ (cat. no. HE17.302:L62) Supt. of Documents, GPO, Washington, D.C. 20402.

A "do-it-yourself" planner to be used at home, this book is designed for the hard-to-reach in pre-retirement planning.

Part-time Employment for Older People, 1965. 19 p. 15¢ (cat. no. FS14.11:K41/2). Supt. of Documents, GPO, Washington, D.C. 20402.

Ideas for retired people who are anxious to supplement their retirement incomes.

Personal Finance for Ministers, by John C. Banker, 1969. 127 p. $1.65 (paper) Westminster, Philadelphia, Pa.

This guide will be of assistance to anyone who needs basic knowledge of personal finance.

Planning for the Later Years, 1969. 51 p. 35¢ (cat. no.

FS3.2:P69/969) Supt. of Documents, GPO, Washington, D.C. 20402.

A program for financial security for the senior citizen. Covers housing, income, social security and medicare.

The Truth about Probate and Family Financial Planning, by William J. Casey, 1967. 193 p. $6.95. Institute for Business Planning, Inc., 2 W. 13th St., New York, N.Y. 10011.

Subtitle: "How to build and preserve your wealth." Declaration of principles adopted by a Committee of American Associations and a Committee of Publishers' Associations geared to provide accurate and authoritative information in regard to probate and family financial planning.

Your Personal Guide to Successful Retirement, by Sidney Margolius, 1969. 160 p. $6.95; $3.95 (paper) Random House, New York.

"As complete and authoritative a book on the subject of retirement as one could conceive." Emphasizes financial aspects of retirement.

Your Retirement, 1970. 20 p. Free. Women's Division, Institute of Life Insurance, 277 Park Ave., New York, N.Y. 10017.

"A discussion of your financial resources and how you might use them."

Estates, wills and trusts

Complete Estate Planning Guide, by Robert Brosterman, rev. ed. 1970. 352 p. $1.50 (paper). New American Library, 1301 Avenue of the Americas, New York, N.Y. 10019.

An investment book for business and professional men and women which

features a personal estate planning workbook. The two broad areas covered are: "Creating your estate," and "Conserving and transferring your estate." Comprehensive; particularly addressed to those earning $20,000 or more, and building large estates, such as $500,000.

A Guide to Federal Estate and Gift Taxation, 1967. 32 p. 25¢ (cat. no. T22.19/2:ES8/967) Supt. of Documents, GPO, Washington, D.C. 20402.

A summary of the more important provisions of the estate and gift tax laws. Material is derived from the laws and regulations in force on December 1, 1967.

How to Save Estate and Gift Taxes, by the J. K. Lasser Tax Institute and Ralph Wallace, rev. ed. 1969. 266 p. $5.95. Doubleday, New York.

Covers federal estate and gift taxes and what you can do about them. Presents twenty-five tax-saving ideas.

J. K. Lasser's 53 New Plans for Saving Estate and Gift Taxes. 5th ed., rev. 1969. 204 p. $5.95. Doubleday, New York.

Fifty-three specific practical plans to protect your estate. In addition, a summary of the fifty states' inheritance law are included.

Social Security

Social Security Cash Benefits, 1970. 14 p. 15¢ (cat. no. HE3.52: 47/3) Supt. of Documents, GPO, Washington, D.C. 10402.

How you earn your social security benefits, how to estimate the amount and how much credit you need.

Social Security Cash Benefits for Students 18–22, 1968. 6 p. Free. Obtain from local Social Security Office.

Explains the requirements and procedures for applying for available aid.

Social Security Handbook, 4th ed., 1969. 477 p. $2.25 (cat. no. FS3.52:135) Supt. of Documents, GPO, Washington, D.C. 20402.

An exhaustive reference guide to the various social security programs. This edition reflects the provisions of the social security act as amended through January 2, 1968. Subject index: p. 449–477.

Social Security Information for Young Families, 1968. 19 p. 15¢ (cat. no. HE3.52:35b/3) Supt. of Documents, GPO, Washington, D.C. 20402.

Basic information on benefits, disability and other aspects of social security.

Social Security Programs in the United States, 1968. 120 p. 55¢ (cat. no. FS3.2:SO13/21/968) Supt. of Documents, GPO, Washington, D.C. 20402.

Contains information on the historical development of major income maintenance programs in the United States.

What You Need to Know about Social Security. *Changing Times*, v. 22, Nov. 1968: 7–12.

Describes the social security system—law—how you qualify, what you pay and what you get.

Your Social Security, 1970. 47 p. 15¢ (cat. no. HE3.52:35/6.) Supt of Documents, GPO, Washington, D.C. 20402.

Retirement, survivor benefits, disability insurance, and medicare are outlined.

Your Social Security Earnings Record, 1970. 32 p. 20¢ (cat. no. HE3.52:44/4) Supt. of Documents, GPO, Washington, D.C. 20402.

How social security records are kept and how benefits are computed. How to obtain a copy of your record to check for accuracy in your earnings.

Funerals

The American Funeral, by Leroy Bowman, 1959. 181 p. O. P. Public Affairs Press, Washington, D.C.

Sub-title: "A study in guilt, extravagance and sublimity." Introduction by Harry A. Overstreet. Covers group behavior at funerals, the funeral business, and changes in cultural forms.

The American Way of Death, by Jessica Mitford, 1963. 333 p. $4.95. Simon and Schuster, New York. Also available in paperback: 95¢, Crest Books, 67 W. 44th St., New York, N.Y. 10036.

Comments on the American funeral industry. Included in the appendices are a "Directory of Memorial Societies and Related Organizations," and "How to Organize a Memorial Society." Lively and provocative presentation.

Death, Here Is Thy Sting, by Cariolis, pseudonym for Robert Forrest, 1967. 139 p. Canadian $5.00. McClelland and Stewart, 25 Hollinger Road, Toronto 16, Canada.

A candid commentary on undertaking practices.

Funeral Costs and Death Benefits, by Sidney Margolius, 1967. 20 p. 25¢ (Public Affairs Pamphlet no. 409) Public Affairs Committee, 381 Park Ave. South, New York, N.Y. 10016.

Concerned primarily with expenses involved and the various financial benefits available to a family to meet these expenses. Includes a section on insurance plans.

Funeral Service Facts and Figures, 1968. 42 p. $5.00 (paper) National Funeral Directors Association, 135 Wells St., Milwaukee, Wis. 53203.

Details the findings of a survey of 1967 funeral service income and expense data.

The High Cost of Dying, by Ruth Mulvey Harmer, 1963. 256 p. O. P. Crowell-Collier, New York.

Traces the evolution of funeral rites from earliest times and chronicles the rise of the American funeral industry to its present "flamboyance." Includes a description and list of non-profit burial societies.

A Reading List on Funerals, 1963. n.p. 25¢. University Book Stores, University of Wisconsin, 3203 N. Downer Ave., Milwaukee, Wis. 53211.

Annotated list of publications on funeral costs, funeral customs, and the burial industry, compiled by the Center for Consumer Affairs.

What About Funeral Costs?, 1967. 4 p. 10¢. National Funeral Directors Association, 135 W. Wells St., Milwaukee, Wis. 53203.

A discussion of costs and suggestions for families after death occurs.

Consumer Goods and Services

GENERAL PRINCIPLES

Be a Better Shopper, by Heinz B. Biesdorf and Mary Ellen Burris, 1968. 42 p. $1.00. Cornell University, Mailing Room, Bldg. 7, Research Park, Ithaca, N.Y. 14850.

A self-contained teaching unit for individuals or groups.

Be a Good Shopper, 1965. 8 p. 5¢ (cat. no. A43.2:SL7) Supt. of Documents, GPO, Washington, D.C. 20402.

Simple basic steps to consider before buying a product. Compares prices and quality; discusses various kinds of sales; and describes protective agencies that help the consumer get what he paid for. Of interest to some teenagers.

Be Sure Before You Sign, 1970. 4 p. 10¢ (cat. no. Pr36.8:C76/Si2) Supt. of Documents, GPO, Washington, D.C. 20402.

Hints to be remembered before signing a contract.

Beware the Pitfalls in Fine Print, by Jean Carper. *Reader's Digest,* v. 98, Feb. 1971: 123–126.

"Innocent sounding phrases tucked away on the back of a ticket or credit card, or in a contract, can carry a load of grief. Here are the major problem makers to watch out for." Article condensed from *Family Weekly,* Apr. 12, 1970.

Buyer, Be Wary, by Sidney Margolius, rev. 1968. 28 p. 25¢ (Public Affairs Pamphlet no. 382) Public Affairs Committee, 381 Park Ave. South, New York, N.Y. 10016.

Points out major shopping difficulties and gives standards for buying foods, clothing, and other consumer goods. Of interest to some teenagers.

The Buying Guide Issue, Consumer Reports, 1970. 448 p. $2.65. Consumers Union of U.S., 256 Washington St., Mount Vernon, N.Y. 10550.

Revised and published annually as the December issue of *Consumer Reports.*

Summarizes many of the tests made on consumer products over the previous few years, and includes much additional information. May be purchased separately or as part of a subscription to *Consumer Reports.* Of interest to some teenagers.

The Chaos of Competition Indicated by *Consumer Reports,* by Ruby Turner Morris and Claire S. Bronson. *Journal of Marketing,* v. 33, July 1969: 26–34.

Summaries of forty-eight product rating studies issued during 1958–1967. Emphasis is on price-quality correlation.

Consumer Bulletin. Monthly. $8.00. Consumers' Research Inc., Washington, N.J. 07882.

A non-profit, consumer-supported testing agency reporting laboratory tests on a wide range of consumer goods and services. Products are rated. Of interest to some teenagers.

Consumer Reports. Monthly. $8.00. Consumers Union of U.S., 256 Washington St., Mount Vernon, N.Y. 10550.

Reports the results of tests of products, ranking them as best buy, acceptable, not acceptable. Financed entirely by the sale of its publications. Of interest to some teenagers.

$$$ and Sense, by Ella Gale, 1965. 283 p. $5.95. Fleet, New York.

Practical tips on saving money by stretching the food budget, cutting clothing costs, and a variety of other saving devices.

Family Circle. Monthly. 15¢ per copy. Family Circle, 488 Madison Ave., New York, N.Y. 10022.

A magazine distributed through chain and independent grocery stores and newsstands in the U.S. and Canada. Contains consumer advice for the housewife.

Getting the Most for Your Money, by Anthony Scaduto, 1970. 241 p. $6.95. David McKay, New York.

Sub-title: "How to beat the high cost of living." A handy reference book on how, where and when to buy.

Important "Seals of Approval" and What They Mean to the Consumer. *Consumer Bulletin,* v. 46, July 7, 1963: 24–25.

Discusses the "seals of approval" of eight important American organizations.

Interagency Committee on Product Information: Report to the White House, 1970. 124 p. Free. Office of Consumer Affairs, New Executive Office Building, Washington, D.C. 20506.

Study conducted by twenty-two government agencies. Information is given about methods by which government consumer product testing studies could be made useful to the public.

Knock, Knock. 1970. 4 p. 10¢ (cat. no. Pr36.8:C76/K75) Supt. of Documents, GPO, Washington, D.C. 20402.

Hints to remember before buying from a door-to-door salesman.

Know Your Merchandise, by Isabel B. Wingate and others, 3rd ed., 1964. 672 p. $7.20. McGraw-Hill, New York.

A textbook, written chiefly from the merchandising viewpoint. Covers textile and non-textile merchandise usually found in a well-stocked department store.

Knowing What You're Buying, by David Sanford. *New Republic,* v. 162, Jan. 24, 1970: 11–13.

A brief recapitulation of the past history and future potential of the Fair Packaging and Labeling Act.

Let the Buyer Beware, by A. R. Roalman. *Today's Health,* v. 48, Mar. 1970: 66–67.

Discusses the hazards one must face in today's marketplace.

Metric Association Newsletter. 4 p. $1.00. Metric Association, Inc., 2004 Ash St., Waukegan, Ill. 60085.

Published three times a year. General information concerning the metric system. A subscription includes a 12-page pamphlet, *Metric Units of Measurements.*

$1.20 Divided by 14 Ounces Is What?" *Forbes,* v. 105, Apr. 1, 1970: 55.

"Unit pricing, the consumer gimmick that has the food chains in an uproar and the politicians drooling."

Recent Purchases of Cars, Houses, and Other Durables and Expectations to Buy During the Months Ahead, 1970. 18 p. 20¢ (Consumer buying indicators—current population reports, Series P–65, no. 34, Nov. 19, 1970) Supt. of Documents, GPO, Washington, D.C. 20402.

Statistical presentation of consumer actions and intentions derived from a survey conducted in October, 1970.

Report of the 53rd National Conference on Weights and Measures, 1968. 175 p. $1.25 (cat. no. C13.10:311) Supt. of Documents, GPO, Washington, D.C. 20402.

A valuable source of information on weights and measures.

The Story of Standards, by John Perry, 1955. 260 p. $5.00. Funk & Wagnalls, New York.

The evolution of weights and measures. The author has succeeded in making difficult technical data interesting.

20 Ways to Save Money at the Supermarket, by Robert O'Brien. *Reader's Digest,* v. 96, May 1970: 68–70.

Helpful hints on everyday shopping.

Unit Prices Move onto the Shelf, *Business Week,* June 6, 1970: 23.

"Benner Tea Company of Burlington, Iowa has become the first chain to take up the idea" of unit pricing.

Weights and Measures and the Consumer, by Leland J. Gordon, 1970. 252 p. $3.00. Consumers Union of U.S., 256 Washington St., Mount Vernon, N.Y. 10550.

A comprehensive and broadly based study. Discusses virtually all aspects of the problem of weights and measures legislation. A basic resource in the field.

Weights and Measures and Your Money's Worth. *Changing Times,* v. 22, Mar. 1968: 37–40.

Discussion of weights and measures problems and how the consumer can protect himself by greater knowledge of scales, meters and labels.

Weights and Measures: Protection for Consumers, n.d. 3 p. Free. State of New York, Department of Agriculture and Markets, State Office Building, Albany, N.Y. 12225.

A consumer tool. Contains a table illustrating conversion from decimal pounds to ounces.

What Consumers Need—Show Biz or Hard Facts, by A. Q. Mowbray. *Nation,* v. 209, Sept. 15, 1969: 245–248.

A plea for standards to assist consumers in making intelligent choices.

What's Happened to Truth-in-Packaging? *Consumer Reports,* v. 34, Jan. 1969: 40–43.

A discussion of the problems faced by the consumer who is trying to compare prices.

Whole Earth Catalog. 6 per yr. $8.00. Portola Institute, Whole Earth Catalog, 558 Santa Cruz Ave., Menlo Park, Calif. 94025.

"The *Whole Earth Catalog* functions as an evaluative and access device," presenting the reader with a mind-boggling array of unusual consumer items. A popular publication for curious young consumers. Apply for price for single issues.

PRODUCT SAFETY AND TESTING

Accident Research, 1968–1969. 2 vols. Free. (Bibliographical Series. Medical and Allied Literature) Accident Control Graduate Program, Dept. of Public Health Administration, School of Public Health, University of North Carolina, Chapel Hill, N.C. 27514.

V. 1, *Fire and burn injury,* 1968. 185 p.; v. 2, *Falls,* 1969. 321 p. Editors: Darla Fishbein Stone and Janice R. Westaby.

An annotated resource bibliography in the various fields of safety. Basic to collections in this field for academic, medical, and large public libraries.

Consumer Product Safety Index, 1970. 3 vols. $10.00 each. National Technical Information Center, Springfield, Va. 22151.

This three-thousand page commission computer information system printout may be ordered in full-size page copy in three volumes by designating documents PB–193 425, PB–193 426, and PB–193 427 and enclosing $30.00. It may also be ordered in 16mm microfilm by designating document PB–193 148 and enclosing $10.00.

Contains references to household products; commission hearings; private and government testing laboratories, key excerpts of consumer letters, and technical articles. A basic resource in its field.

Federal Consumer Safety Legislation, 1970. 213 p. $1.25. (cat. no. Y3.N21/25:2C76) Supt. of Documents, GPO, Washington, D.C. 20402.

"A study of the scope and adequacy of the automobile safety, flammable fabrics and hazardous substances programs."

Federal Hazardous Substance Act, hearings before the Consumer Subcommittee of the Committee on Commerce, Senate 91st Congress, 1st sess., on S. 2162, to amend the Federal Hazardous Substance Act, to provide for child-resistant packaging to protect children from serious personal injury or serious illness resulting from handling, using, or ingesting any hazardous substance, and for other purposes, Oct. 1 and 2, 1969. [published] 1969. 261 p. $1.00. (cat. no. Y4.C73/2:91–35) Supt. of Documents, GPO, Washington, D.C. 20402.

Final Report of the National Commission on Product Safety, 1970. 197 p. $1.75 (cat. no. Y3.N21/25:1/970) Supt. of Documents, GPO, Washington, D.C. 20402.

Makes a strong plea for comprehensive federal safety legislation and urges a permanent separate agency to deal exclusively with product safety.

Highway Safety Literature: Annual Cumulation 1969 Vehicle Safety Bibliography, 1970. 214 p.

U.S. Department of Transportation, National Safety Bureau, Washington, D.C. 20590.

Bibliography of scientific and technical information covering all phases of motor vehicle safety.

How Safe Are Our Drugs, rev. 1968. 12 p. 15¢ (cat. no. FS13.-111:44/2) Supt. of Documents, GPO, Washington, D.C. 20402.

Outlines the processes of FDA's premarketing approval of a new drug, and the preparation of essential labeling information. Also defines areas of responsibility for the pharmacist and the physician in providing safe drugs for effective consumer use.

How Safe Is Our Food?, 1968. 12 p. 20¢ (cat. no. FS13.111:41/2) Supt. of Documents, GPO, Washington, D.C. 20402.

A pamphlet in the Food and Drug Administration's "Life Protection Series." A basic and brief description of the laws which protect our food supply.

Inspection For Your Protection, 1968. 2 p. 5¢ (cat. no. PA 877) Supt. of Documents, GPO. Washington, D.C. 20402.

Provides an introduction to the Federal Meat Inspection Program and explains how it protects the consumer.

Meat and Poultry: Wholesome For You, 1969. 8 p. 10¢ (cat. no. A1.77:170) Supt. of Documents, GPO, Washington, D.C. 20402.

A brief discussion of meat inspection combined with a statement of "protection you can provide" when buying meats and poultry.

Meat Inspection, by Nick Kotz. *Nation,* v. 205, Sept. 18, 1967: 230–233.

"The new jungle." An informative article on the need for federal meat inspection.

Nader: From Auto Safety To A Permanent Crusade, by Marti Mueller. *Science,* v. 166. Nov. 21, 1969: 979–983.

Detailed discussion of the consumer protection activities of Ralph Nader and his "raiders." Of interest to some teenagers.

New Law's Dangerous Deceit, by Oscar Sussman. *Nation's Business,* v. 56, May 1968: 34–37.

A health expert presents the other side of the Wholesale Meat Act and condemns consumer advocates who worked for its passage.

The Overweight Society, by Peter Wyden, 1965. 338 p. $5.95. Morrow, New York. Also available in paperback: 75¢, Pocket Books, 1 W. 39th St., New York, N.Y. 10018.

"An authoritative, entertaining investigation into the facts and follies of girth control." Includes many accounts of medical quackery in selling diet programs and "medicines." Also a twenty-page bibliography.

Pesticides, 1967. 9 p. 25¢ (cat. no. FS13:128/a:P439) Supt. of Documents, GPO, Washington, D.C. 20402.

Reprint from *FDA Papers,* June 1967. A report on residues in food.

Poisons and Cosmetics, by Toni Stabile. *Nation,* v. 206, Jan. 1, 1968: 16–19.

Emphasizes that the many thousands of products that have been classified as cosmetics escape the more stringent controls provided for foods and drugs.

Poisons in Your Food, by Ruth Winter, 1969. 248 p. $5.95. Crown, New York.

Alarming report on the distribution of dangerous foods and drugs. Of interest to some teenagers.

Product Safety in Household Goods, edited by F. Reed Dickerson, 1969. 190 p. $7.50. Bobbs, Merrill, Indianapolis, Ind.

Prepared by the seminar on legislation of the Indiana University School of Law.

Product Safety: Nobody's Business, by Tom Stanton. *Nation,* v. 211, Sept. 28, 1970: 270–272.

Indictment of some of American industries' callous attitudes toward product safety.

Stop, Look, Investigate Says the Federal Trade Commission, 1969. 10 p. 15¢ (Federal Trade Commission Reports, cat. no. FT1.2: 1n8) Supt. of Documents, GPO, Washington, D.C. 20402.

Alerts the elderly to join forces with relatives and friends in stiffening their defense against medical quackery or high speed mail order "bargain" cures for disease.

Textile Flammability and Consumer Safety, 1969. 206 p. $5.00. Gottlieb Duttweiler Institute for Economic and Social Studies, CH–8803 Ruschlikon, Zurich, Switzerland.

Proceedings of an international conference on textile inflammability and consumer safety organized by the Duttweiler Institute, Jan. 23–24, 1969. An extensive bibliography is included.

USDA Poultry Inspection, Consumer's Safeguard, rev. 1965. [6 p.] 5¢ (cat. no. 1.68:299/3) Supt. of Documents, GPO, Washington, D.C. 20402.

Use of Radium in Consumer Products, 1968. [published 1969]. 25 p. 40¢ (cat. no. FS2.314:68–5) Supt. of Documents, GPO, Washington, D.C. 20402.

What Can Be Done about Product Hazards? *Consumer Reports,* v. 35, Sept. 1970: 559–564.

Discusses the *Final Report of the National Commission on Product Safety* and includes an abridged version of Chapter 1 of the report, "Perspective on product safety."

Wholesome Meat Act . . . Approved Dec. 15, 1967. 15¢ (cat. no. 90–1: Public Law 201) Supt. of Documents, GPO, Washington, D.C. 20402.

"An act to clarify and otherwise amend the Meat Inspection Act, to provide for cooperation with appropriate State agencies with respect to State meat inspection programs, and for other purposes."

FOOD AND NUTRITION

Acceptance of New Food Products by Supermarkets, by Neil H. Bordon, Jr., 1968. 227 p. $5.50. Division of Research, Harvard Business School, Soldiers Field, Boston, Mass. 02163.

Examines a number of case studies on the introduction of new products into supermarkets by food manufacturers.

Additives in Our Food, 1968. 8 p. 15¢ (cat. no. FS13.111:43/2) Supt. of Documents, GPO, Washington, D.C. 20402.

Basic and brief introduction to the problems of food additives. One in the FDA's "Life Protection Series." Of interest to some teenagers.

Answers to Questions Customers Ask about Meat and Poultry, 1969, 20 p. 75¢. Home Economists in Business, P.O. Box 178, Western Spring, Ill. 60558.

Answers 108 commonly asked consumer questions on meat and poultry.

Of value to the teacher, student, and marketing specialist.

Are Meats on Sale Really a Bargain? *Consumer Reports*, v. 35, Aug. 1970: 472–476.

The mystery and intrigue in the meat market is discussed and, as an example, one hundred and fifty names are given for the basic nine meat cuts.

Bargain? Freezer Meats, There May Be a Catch to It, 1970, 14 p. 10¢ (cat. no. FT1.3/2.5) Supt. of Documents, GPO, Washington, D.C. 20402.

Warns consumers against the "bait and switch" operators and unscrupulous advertisers who falsely promise to provide freezer meat at a fraction of its normal cost.

Blind Dates in the Supermarket, by Jennifer Cross. *Nation*, v. 211, Nov. 2, 1970: 434–436.

A pointed article favoring the open dating of food products.

Box Score on New Imitation Foods, by Robert O. Herrmann and Rex H. Warland, 1970. 4 p. Free. Farm Economics, Room 6, Weaver Building, Pennsylvania State University, University Park, Pa. 16802.

A brief discussion of reactions to synthetic and imitation foods.

This is USDA's Consumer and Marketing Service, 1968. 31 p. 30¢. (cat. no. A1.68:661/2) Supt. of Documents, GPO, Washington, D.C. 20402.

Explains the mission of the Consumer and Marketing Service—to service, regulate, improve and protect the marketing system. This service also helps in giving force to the principle that our supply of food and other farm products shall move from producer to consumer quickly, efficiently, safely, and with fairness to all.

Calories and Weight, the USDA Pocket Guide, 1968. 76 p. 25¢ (cat. no. A1.77:153) Supt. of Documents, GPO, Washington, D.C. 20402.

How to lose weight, how to choose food for weight control, and how to cut down on calories. Contains a listing of calorie tables and a guide for estimating serving sizes of meat. Of interest to some teenagers.

The Chemical Breakfast, by David Sanford. *New Republic*, v. 163, Aug. 22, 1970: 12–15.

Questions the addition of food additives to breakfast foods.

Consumer Conference Guide: Foods, n.d. 16 p. 1–9 copies: $1.00 each; 10–99 copies: 75¢ each. Chamber of Commerce of the United States, 1615 H St., N.W., Washington, D.C. 20006.

Guidelines for local chambers of commerce planning consumer conference programs on foods. Presents a model agenda, suggests publicity, gives ideas about follow-up activities, and provides a resource list.

Consumers' Knowledge and Use of Government Grades for Selected Food Items, by T. Q. Hutchinson, 1970. 38 p. 40¢ (U.S. Dept. of Agriculture, Economic Research Service, Marketing Research Report no. 876, cat. no. A1.82:876) Supt. of Documents, GPO, Washington, D.C. 20402.

Based on 3,014 telephone interviews in a national sample conducted to determine consumer awareness of grading standards used by the Department of Agriculture.

The Cost of Living, by Betty Furness. *McCall's*, v. 97, Feb. 1970: 28+; Mar: 36+.

A thorough article on the supermarket's bewildering array of sizes, shapes, and prices. Presents a strong argument for unit pricing.

Daily Food Guide, Some Choices for Thrifty Families, 1970. 28 in. x 22 in. poster. 15¢ (cat. no. A98.9:13) Supt. of Documents, GPO, Washington, D.C. 20402.

Reverse side of this poster contains a food guide to follow every day, listing milk, meat, vegetable, fruit and bread-cereal groups.

Dry Cereals, July-Aug. 1970. 284 p. $1.25 (cat. no. Y4.C73/2:91–72) Supt. of Documents, GPO. Washington, D.C. 20402.

Hearings before the Subcommittee of the Committee of Commerce, U.S. Senate, on the nutritional content of dry breakfast cereals. Includes a discussion of Robert B. Choate's nutritional rating chart.

Facts about Nutrition, rev. 1968. 24 p. 35¢ (cat. no. FS2.22:N95/968) Supt. of Documents, GPO, Washington, D.C. 20402.

Discusses important food elements, good sources of vitamins and minerals, infant nutrition, weight watching, nutrition in pregnancy and in old age. Gives sample menus.

Family Fare, rev. 1970. 91 p. 45¢ (cat. no. A1.77:1/6) Supt. of Documents, GPO, Washington, D.C. 20402.

A guide to good nutrition together with information on food management and preparation.

Family Food Budgeting for Good Meals and Good Nutrition, rev. 1969. 16 p. 15¢ (cat. no. A1.77:94/3) Supt. of Documents, GPO, Washington, D.C. 20402.

Contains workable guides to family food budgeting at different cost levels.

Family Food Buying, 1969. 60 p. 35¢ (cat. no. A1.87:37) Supt. of Documents, GPO, Washington, D.C. 20402.

"A guide for calculating amounts to buy, comparing costs."

Food, 1959. 736 p. $3.25 (cat. no. A1.10:959) Supt. of Documents, GPO, Washington, D.C. 20402.

The Yearbook of Agriculture, 1959. Tells how to eat better at less cost. Provides information on food buying, preserving, cooking, vitamins, and many other topics relating to food.

Food Consumption, Prices and Expenditures, by John J. Hiemstra, 1968. 193 p. $1.25 (cat. no. A93.28:138) Supt. of Documents, GPO, Washington, D.C. 20402.

A discussion of changes in food consumption patterns, trends in retail food prices, aggregate demands for food, and the relationship of food expenditures to income. Contains statistical information for the years 1909 through 1966. A supplement is also available for the same price, cat. no. A93.28:138/Supp.

Food Expenditures by Upper Income Families, by Marguerite C. Burk, 1969. 323 p. n.p. (Technical Bulletin 269) Minnesota Agricultural Experimental Station, St. Paul, Minn. 55101.

Published in cooperation with the U.S. Department of Agriculture, findings are based on a special study of upper-income families in Minneapolis and St. Paul. An analysis is also given of the importance of the findings to the U.S. food market.

Food for the Family with Young Children, 1970. 16 p. 10¢ (U.S. Dept. of Agriculture, cat. no. A1.77:5/10) Supt. of Documents, GPO, Washington, D.C. 20402.

Included are low cost weekly food plans, a sample week's market list and menus, and suggestions for the family with more money to spend on food.

Food for Us All, 1969. 360 p. $3.50 (cat. no. A1.10:969) Supt. of Documents, GPO, Washington, D.C. 20402.

The Yearbook of Agriculture, 1969. Arranged in three major sections: Food from farm to you; Buying and cooking food; Food and your life. Of interest to some teenagers.

Food from Farmer to Consumer, Report of the National Commission on Food Marketing, 1966. 203 p. $1.25 (cat. no. Y3N21/ 22:1/966) Supt. of Documents, GPO, Washington, D.C. 20402.

A report based on detailed studies of changes taking place in the industry and of conditions necessary for efficiency, appropriate services to consumers, and acceptable competitive alternatives of procurement and sale in all segments of the industry from producer to consumer.

Technical studies from above. cat no. Y3.N21/22:9/(no.)

Summarize data that, together with hearings and formal interviews, provided the background information on food marketing and other related subjects presented in the Commission's report.

1. *Organization and Competition in the Livestock and Meat Industry.* 1966. 189 p. Out of print.

2. *Organization and Competition in the Poultry and Egg Industries.* 1966. 118 p. Out of print.

3. *Organization and Competition in the Dairy Industry.* 1966. 409 p. il. Out of print.

4. *Organization and Competition in the Fruit and Vegetable Industry.* 1966. 392 p. $1.25.

5. *Organization and Competition in the Milling and Baking Industries.* 1966. 167 p. 50¢.

6. *Studies of Organization and Competition in Grocery Manufacturing.* 1966. 270 p. 75¢.

7. *Organization and Competition in Food Retailing.* 1966. 568 p. $1.50.

8. *The Structure of Food Manufacturing.* 1966. 292 p. $1.00.

9. *Cost Components of Farm-Retail Price Spreads for Foods.* 1966. 55 p. 25¢.

10. *Special Studies in Food Marketing —Private Label Products in Food Retailing, Retail Food Prices in Low and Higher Income Areas, Notes on Economic Regulation.* 1966. 229 p. Out of print.

Food Guide for Older Folks, rev. 1970. 16 p. 10¢ (cat. no. A.177: 17/9) Supt. of Documents, GPO, Washington, D.C. 20402.

Older people's food needs, and how to meet them.

Food Makes the Difference, 1969. 7 p. 10¢ (cat. no. A77.714:F73) Supt. of Documents, GPO, Washington, D.C. 20402.

A selected list of publications, slide sets, and other items which will be helpful to professional and volunteer workers in the nutrition field, especially those who work with low income groups.

Food Makes the Difference: Ideas for Economy Minded Families, n.d. 4 p. Free. U.S. Department of Agriculture, Washington, D.C. 20250.

A basic and colorful guide to the better use of the food budget.

Food Makes the Difference: Ideas for Families Using Donated Foods, n.d. 4 p. Free. U.S. Department of Agriculture, Washington, D.C. 20250.

Simple attractive guide to better diet for the low income family.

Food Product Dating, by Eileen F. Taylor. Nov. 1970. Free. Marketing and Transportation Situation, Economic Research Service, U.S. Department of Agriculture, Washington, D.C. 20250.

Industry practices on product dating and recommendations for further research.

The Great American Food Hoax, by Sidney Margolius, 1971. 216 p. $5.95. Walker, New York.

Analysis of modern convenience foods: shows the cost of modern food processing and includes guidelines for food shopping.

Homemakers' Opinion about Selected Meats, 1969. 156 p. $1.25 (cat. no. A1.82:854) Supt. of Documents, GPO, Washington, D.C. 20402.

One of a series of important consumer surveys related to agricultural products.

How Much Health is There in Health Foods? by Ronald M. Deutsch. *Reader's Digest,* v. 82, May 1963: 57–61.

Nutrition and health experts expose five popular fallacies which food faddists exploit.

How to Buy Beef Roasts, 1968. 16 p. 10¢ (cat. no. A1.77:146) Supt. of Documents, GPO, Washington, D.C. 20402.

How to Buy Beef Steaks. 1968. 16 p. 10¢ (cat. no. A1.77:145) Supt. of Documents, GPO, Washington, D.C. 20402.

How to Buy Eggs, 1968. 8 p. 10¢ (cat. no. A1.77:144) Supt. of Documents, GPO, Washington, D.C. 20402.

Tips on buying and storing eggs.

How to Buy Food, 1969. $1.25 (cat. no. A88.2:F73/5) Supt. of Documents, GPO, Washington, D.C. 20402.

Nine leaflets, fully illustrated, describe the basic principles of food shopping. Of interest to some teenagers.

How to Buy Fresh Fruits, 1968. 24 p. 15¢ (cat. no. A1.77:177:141) Supt. of Documents, GPO, Washington, D.C. 20402.

Tips on picking the best fruit for your money.

How to Buy Meat for Your Freezer, rev. 1969. 28 p. 20¢ (cat. no. A1.77:166/2) Supt. of Documents, GPO, Washington, D.C. 20402.

How to choose and prepare meat for your freezer.

How to Buy Poultry, 1968. 8 p. 10¢ (cat. no. A1.77:157) Supt. of Documents, GPO, Washington, D.C. 20402.

Tips on choosing the best in poultry for your family.

How to Use USDA Grades in Buying Food, Dairy Products, Poultry, Fruits and Vegetables, Eggs, Meat, rev. 1969. 12 p. 15¢ (cat. no. A1.68:708/3) Supt. of Documents, GPO, Washington, D.C. 20402.

An explanation of the various grade marks on food labels. A handy pocket-size booklet.

Keeping Food Safe to Eat, 1969. 12 p. 10¢ (cat. no. A1.77:162) Supt. of Documents, GPO, Washington, D.C. 20402.

A guide for homemakers on how to protect their families from illnesses caused by tainted food.

Labeling Requirements for Consumer Packages of Fresh Fruits and Vegetables, n.d. 21 p. $2.00. Produce Packaging and Marketing Association, Box 674, Newark, Del. 19711.

Contains the various federal and state regulations germane to packaging produce. Also has a directory of state officials who may be contacted for further information on state laws and regulations.

Mealtime Manual for the Aged and Handicapped, compiled by the Institute of Rehabilitation Medicine, New York University Medical Center, 1970. 242 p. $2.00 (spiral binding) Essandess Special Editions, 1 W. 39th St., New York, N.Y. 10018.

A well-illustrated guide to kitchen techniques and cooking equipment. Specific appliances are recommended and approximate prices are quoted.

Money Management: Your Food Dollar, rev. 1970. 40 p. 25¢. Money Management Institute, Household Finance Corp., Prudential Plaza, Chicago, Ill. 60601.

Broad spectrum of hints on saving money by proper shopping and planning. Has a section explaining the Fair Packaging and Labeling Act.

Monosodium Glutamate, *Consumer Bulletin,* v. 53, Mar. 1970: 16–19.

Urges that the Food and Drug Administration set up regulations on the use of this common flavor enhancer.

Nutrition at Work for You, 1968. 16 p. 10¢ (cat. no. A1.77/a:1/4) Supt. of Documents, GPO. Washington, D.C. 20402.

Research information on nutrition together with a daily food guide and hints on buying and storing food.

Nutritive Value of Foods, 1970. 41 p. 30¢. (cat. no. A1.77:72/3). Supt. of Documents, GPO, Washington, D.C. 20402.

Both calorie tables and food composition values are included.

The Nuts Among the Berries, by Ronald M. Deutsch, 1967. 320 p.

95¢ (paper) Ballantine Books, 101 Fifth Ave., New York, N.Y. 10003.

An informative and often entertaining survey of health food fads and food quackery.

Packet for the Bride, 1967. $1.50 per packet of 10 books. (cat. no. A1.2:B76/2) Supt. of Documents, GPO, Washington, D.C. 20402.

Although designed for the bride, these leaflets will be helpful to all consumers. Offers aid in preparing wholesome, attractive meals and in obtaining full value for every food dollar spent. Of interest to some teenagers.

A Pint's a Pound the World Around. *Chain Store Age,* v. 46, June 1970: 23–27.

A survey of the long-run implications of unit pricing.

Product Innovation in Food Processing, 1954–1964, by Robert D. Buzzell and Robert E. M. Nourse, 1967. 220 p. $6.00. Division of Research, Harvard Business School, Boston, Mass.

Examines the phenomenal growth of new products in the food industry, considers their sources and development and their economic effect on consumers, processors, grocers, and on market concentration.

Protecting Our Food, 1966. 386 p. $2.50. (cat. no. A1.10:966) Supt. of Documents, GPO, Washington, D.C. 20402.

The Yearbook of Agriculture, 1966. Covers government's and industry's roles in food protection, with a look at "The road ahead" in chemicals, regulation, research, and consumer responsibility.

The Seventeen Cookbook, by the Editors of *Seventeen,* 1964. 430 p. $6.95. Macmillan, New York.

Has tips on marketing, cooking, and meal planning as, for example, what to look for when buying each fresh vegetable and how to cook and serve it. Illustrations of how to prepare some of the recipes and colored photographs of many of the prepared dishes. Of special interest to teenagers.

Smell It, Then Sell It. *New Republic,* v. 162, Apr. 25, 1970 : 8–9.

A condemnation of the practice of placing coded dates on food products and the malpractice of selling such products after the expiration of the coded date.

Storing Perishable Foods in the Home, 1970, 12 p. 10¢ (cat. no. A1.77:78/3) Supt. of Documents, GPO, Washington, D.C. 20402.

Storing Vegetables and Fruits in Basements, Cellars, Outbuildings, and Pits, 1970. 18 p. 15¢ (cat. no. A1.77:119/2) Supt. of Documents, GPO, Washington, D.C. 20402.

The Supermarket Trap, by Jennifer Cross, 1970. 258 p. $6.95. Indiana University Press, Bloomington, Ind.

"The consumer and the food industry." Those who are concerned about what is going on at the supermarket and what the food manufacturers are doing will find this an interesting book. Includes twelve appendices and an extensive bibliography.

To Promote Honesty and Fair Dealing in the Interest of Consumers, 1964. 12 p. 15¢ (cat. no. FS13.111:813) Supt. of Documents, GPO, Washington, D.C. 20402.

Facts for consumers on food standards, weights and measures.

Toward the New, 1970. 61 p. $1.00 (cat. no. A1.75:341) Supt. of Documents, GPO, Washington, D.C. 20402.

"A report on better foods and nutrition from agricultural research."

Trade Secrets: Grocers' Arcane Codes Telling Products' Age Coming Under Attack, by James MacGregor. *Wall Street Journal,* v. 176, Aug. 3, 1970: 1, col. 6.

"How long are games of hide-and-seek going to be played in the supermarket? When is the consumer going to get the information to which he is entitled?"

Unfoods: Do You Know What You're Eating? by David Sanford. *New Republic,* v. 158, May 18, 1968: 13–15.

Criticism of the new "non-meat meats" such as beef stroganoff, made from soy beans.

Unit Pricing in Supermarkets, by Daniel I. Padberg and T. David McCullough. *Search,* v. 1, no. 6, Jan., 1971: 1–27. Cornell University, Agricultural Experiment Station, New York State College of Agriculture, Ithaca, N.Y. 14850.

A study by Consumer Research Institute, the research arm of the grocery industry.

Unmilk: Cowing the Consumer, by David Sanford. *New Republic,* v. 159, Aug. 10, 1968: 11–13.

A discussion of imitation milk. A survey showed that three out of four cats rejected it!

USDA Grade Names for Food and Farm Products, 1968. 34 p. Free. Consumer and Marketing Service, Department of Agriculture, Washington, D.C. 20250.

Includes such items as cotton, dairy products, fruits, grain, livestock, and tobacco.

Vegetables in Family Needs, 1970. 32 p. 20¢ (cat. no. A1.77: 105/4) Supt. of Documents, GPO, Washington, D.C. 20402.

Basic tips on buying, storing, and preparing vegetables. Includes recipes.

We'll Help You Make It, 1971. 18 p. 15¢ each; 3 different plans 35¢. Foods, Computer Meal Planning Center, Box 1368, Dayton, Ohio 45401.

A computer printout personalized to the needs of the individual family. In requesting, state number of children and adults in the family and the weekly food budget.

What About Beef Prices? by Herrell De Graff, 1969. 14 p. Free. Department of Public Relations, American Meat Institute, 59 E. Van Buren St., Chicago, Ill. 60605.

A booklet which includes the statement presented by the president of the American Meat Institute to the Special Studies Subcommittee of the House Committee on Government Operations.

What To Do When Your Home Freezer Stops, 1967. 8 p. 15¢ (cat. no. A1.35:321/3) Supt. of Documents, GPO, Washington, D.C. 20402.

White House Conference on Food Nutrition and Health, 1970. 341 p. $3.00 (cat. no. Y3.w58/16:1/970) Supt. of Documents, GPO, Washington, D.C. 20402.

Text of the final report submitted to the President. Includes all panel and task force reports, together with the task force action reports.

You're in Good Company, 1969. 12 p. 20¢ (cat. no. A1.68:922) Supt. of Documents, GPO, Washington, D.C. 20402.

"Millions of American's use USDA food stamps."

CLOTHING AND PERSONAL CARE

Buying Your Home Sewing Machine, rev. 1969. 12 p. 10¢ (cat. no. A1.77:38/3) Supt. of Documents, GPO, Washington, D.C. 20402.

Clothing Repair, 1969. 30 p. 25¢ (cat. no. A1.77:107) Supt. of Documents, GPO, Washington, D.C. 20402.

Information on repairs to clothing by sewing, darning, and patching. Useful to young homemakers, teachers, and extension clothing specialists.

Consumer Conference Guide: Clothing, n.d. 17 p. 1–9 copies: $1.00 each; 10–99 copies: 75¢ each. Chamber of Commerce, 1615 H St., N.W., Washington, DC 20006.

Guidelines for local chambers of commerce planning consumer conference programs on clothing. Presents a model agenda, suggests publicity, gives ideas about follow-up activities, and provides a resource list.

Deodorants & Antiperspirants, 1970. 12 p. 25¢. American Medical Association, 535 N. Dearborn St., Chicago, Ill. 60610.

Discusses the purposes, properties, and ingredients of deodorants.

Disposable Diapers. *Consumer Reports,* v. 36, Feb. 1971: 81–83.

Advantages and disadvantages of ten brands. Includes comparative costs and tells how to dispose of them.

Fibers and Fabrics, 1970. 28 p. 65¢ (Dept. of Commerce, cat. no.

C13.53;1) Supt. of Documents, GPO, Washington, D.C. 20402.

"Information about natural and man-made fibers and fabrics to meet your particular needs." Devotes one page to each kind of fabric covered. Provides, in outline form, information on the properties, care, and uses of the fabric.

Look for That Label, 1968. 8 p. 15¢ (cat. no. FT1.2:L11) Supt. of Documents, GPO, Washington, D.C. 20402.

Contains the plain facts about the furs and fabrics the consumer buys. Of interest to some teenagers.

National Fair Claims Guide for Consumer Textile Products, 1969. 22 p. Free. National Institute of Dry Cleaning, Silver Spring, Md. 20910.

Prepared as a guide to settling customer claims made against dry cleaners. Gives life expectancy estimation for various articles of clothing.

Removing Stains from Fabrics, 1968. 32 p. 20¢ (cat. no. A1.77: 62/5) Supt. of Documents, GPO, Washington, D.C. 20402.

Home methods for stain removal from clothing and household fabrics. Of interest to some teenagers.

Report of Board Committee on Certification and Labeling under Which USASI May License the Use of its Mark as Evidence of Compliance with USA Standards, 1968. 4 p. Free. USA Standards Institute, 10 E. 40th St., New York, N.Y. 10016.

Relates the planning that has gone into the establishment of this certification program. Work is now underway on a set of operating procedures.

The Seventeen Book of Fashion and Beauty, by editors of *Seven-teen,* rev. ed. 1970. 265 p. $7.95. Macmillan, New York.

Valuable information on how to stretch your clothing budget, how to care for clothes, buying a wardrobe, the cost of hairpieces and wigs, eyeglasses versus contact lenses, and safe exercises and diets.

Sew Simply, Sew Right, by Mini Rhea and Frances S. Leighton, 1969. 215 p. $5.50. Fleet, New York.

A basic, step-by step approach to sewing with many illustrations. Includes chapters on fabrics, how to pick out a pattern, how to adjust it to a special figure problem, and how to make a dress the easy way. Easy to use. Mini Rhea was formerly designer and dressmaker to Jacqueline Kennedy. Of special interest to teenagers.

Shoppers' Handbook, by Madeline C. Blum and Jean McLean, 1969. 29 p. Free. Cooperative Extension Service, Cornell University, Ithaca, N.Y. 14850.

"Labeling fabric facts—clothing care." A discussion of both mandatory and voluntary labeling of natural and synthetic fibers.

Standardization of Consumers' Goods, by Jessie V. Coles, 1932. 323 p. O. P. Ronald, Philadelphia, Pa.

Basic study by one of the leading authorities on labeling and standardization.

The Successful Teen-Age Girl, by Gladys Denny Shultz, 1968. 236 p. $4.95. Lippincott, New York.

Sensible advice and information on matters of concern to teenage girls such as how to treat skin and hair problems and problems of menstruation, how to lose or gain weight, how to dress to look slimmer or plumper. Contains calorie charts, weight charts, food groupings, diets for losing or gaining weight, exercises, and information on vitamins and minerals.

Textile Handbook, 1970. 115 p. $2.00. American Home Economics Association, 2010 Massachusetts Ave., N.W., Washington, D.C. 20036.

Provides information on man-made and natural fibres, yarns, fabrics, finishes, dyes. Includes a discussion of labeling, legislation, and standards.

Textile Topics. Free controlled distribution. Celanese Fibers Marketing Co., 522 Fifth Ave., New York, N.Y. 10036.

A Celanese Education Service, published in the spring and fall. Distribution limited to home economics teachers and other professionals in the consumer education field.

A Voluntary Industry Guide for Improved and Permanent Care Labeling of Consumer Textile Products, 1967. 29 p. Free. National Retail Merchants Association, 100 W. 31st St., New York, N.Y. 10010.

Guidelines developed by the Industry Advisory Committee on Textile Information in cooperation with the President's Special Assistant on Consumer Affairs.

The Why of Fashion, by Karlyne Anspach, 1967. 378 p. $9.50. Iowa State University Press, Ames, Iowa.

The patterns of consumer behavior as related to fashions in clothing are discussed as "A Social Need," "An Economic Good," "A Reflection of American Life."

HOUSING

Advice on the Purchase and Sale of a Home and Lease of Dwellings by Military Personnel, 1969. 167 p. 70¢ (cat. no. D302.-9:11/1) Supt. of Documents, GPO, Washington, D.C. 20402.

Developed for military personnel seeking guidance concerning the purchase and sale of a home, this should also prove to be of value to anyone interested in buying or selling a home.

Before You Buy a House, by Robert A. Marshall, 1964. 96 p. $1.95. Kiplinger Washington Editors, Inc., 1729 H St., N.W., Washington, D.C. 20006.

A practical guide to selecting and purchasing a home. Includes information on mortgaging.

Building or Buying the High-Quality House at Lowest Cost, by Arthur M. Watkins, 1962. 267 p. $4.95; $1.45 (paper) Doubleday, New York.

A practical handbook which outlines the various steps to follow in choosing your future home.

The Complete Real Estate Adviser, by Daniel J. De Benedictis, 1969. 352 p. $6.95. Simon and Schuster, New York.

A compilation, in five parts, of four of the author's paperback books: *The Family Real Estate Adviser; Practical Ways to Make Money in Real Estate; Laws Every Home Owner and Tenant Should Know; How to Become a Real Estate Broker and Turn Your License into Big Money.* Can be used for a quick reference to any of the specific problems or questions facing the average buyer, seller, or broker.

Condominiums and Cooperatives, by David Chirman and Edna L. Hebard, 1970. 395 p. $14.95. Wiley, New York.

A guide for purchasing condominiums and cooperatives. Nineteen chapters range from "basic legal structure" to financing, associations and "new towns." Sample regulations and forms are given in eight appendices.

Cooperatives and Condominiums. *Changing Times,* v. 23, Jan. 1969: 31–33.

Describes the advantages and disadvantages of each of these forms of housing.

Designs for Low-Cost Wood Homes, 1969. 28 p. 25¢ (cat. no. A13.2:H75/3) Supt. of Documents, GPO, Washington, D.C. 20402.

Contains eleven designs including floor plans, sketches, and a description of materials of construction. Detailed working plans for construction of each design also available from Supt. of Documents. For description of individual plans request *Price List 72: Homes.*

The Family Real Estate Adviser, by Daniel J. DeBenedictis, 1966–1967. 96 p. $1.00 (paper) Simon and Schuster, New York.

A guide to the real estate market for the potential home buyer.

Getting the Most for Your Money When You Buy a Home, by Betty Yarmon, 1966. 128 p. 75¢ (paper) Association Press, 291 Broadway, New York, N.Y. 10007.

How to look for, finance, and buy a home. Written in simple, down to earth language.

Helping Your Family Make a Better Move, by Helen Giamattei and Katherine Slaughter, 1968. 173 p. $1.25 (paper) Doubleday, New York.

Helpful hints on the short and the long haul and the overseas move. Discusses selling and then buying another house, working with the moving company, and financing a new home.

Home Buyer's Guide, 1967. 14 p. 10¢. American Bar Association, 1155 E. 60th St., Chicago, Ill. 60637.

Legal steps to follow and legal pitfalls to avoid in making a home purchase.

Home Mortgage Delinquency and Foreclosure, by John P. Herzog and James S. Earley, 1970. 170 p. $7.50. National Bureau of Economic Research, distributed by Columbia University Press, New York.

An analysis of various loan and borrower characteristics in order to determine their relationship to the risk of delinquency and foreclosure. Borrowing for refinancing and the presence of junior financing are the most important factors in serious loan delinquency. Many charts and tables are included. For the serious reader.

The House You Want, by Lila Perl, 1965. 210 p. $5.50. David McKay, New York. Also available in paperback: $1.50, Funk and Wagnalls, 380 Madison Ave., New York, N.Y. 10017.

Subtitle: How to find it—how to buy it. Detailed information on buying, building and selling a house. Illustrated.

Housekeeping Directions, n.d. 62 p. Single copy free; subsequent copies 20¢ each; 100 copies, $15.00 Soap and Detergent Association, 475 Park Ave. South, New York, N.Y. 10016.

How to perform twenty-six household jobs in an efficient manner. Prepared especially for use with low-income, low-reading level adults.

Housing the Cooperative Way: Selected Readings, edited by Jerome Liblit, 1964. 300 p. $6.00. Twayne, New York.

Reviews the background of cooperative housing, discusses the strengths and weaknesses of the cooperative system, and makes recommendations for making cooperatives work better.

How Much House Can You Afford? by Arthur M. Watkins, 1963. 30 p. Free. New York

Life Insurance Co., Box 10, Madison Square Station, New York, N.Y. 10010.

A brief, sensible analysis of a family's housing needs.

How to Avoid the Ten Biggest Home-Buying Traps, by Arthur M. Watkins, 1968. 138 p. $3.95 (paper) Hawthorn, New York.

Some of the traps are: The high-priced house; the unforeseen expenses; the no-design house; the old house lemon; the discomfort house; the gimmick house.

How to Buy a Home—How to Sell a Home, by Glenn Fowler, 1969. 144 p. $1.45. Rutledge Books, New York.

A comprehensive book which includes a checklist to use when buying a home, and an eight-page glossary.

How to Buy a House, by Byron Moger and Martin Burke, 1969. 204 p. $4.95. Lyle Stuart, New York.

A comprehensive book which will answer most questions home buyers ask.

How to Finance Your Home, by Sidney Margolius, 1964. 20 p. 25¢ (Public Affairs Pamphlet no. 360) Public Affairs Committee, 381 Park Ave. South, New York, N.Y. 10016.

Discusses the various forms of financing available to the would-be home-owner.

Mobile Homes, 1971. 16 p. Free. Council of Better Business Bureaus, 1101 17th St., N.W., Washington, D.C. 20036.

'How to choose, where to put, how to finance," prepared by the Council in cooperation with the Mobile Homes Manufacturers Association. Apply for quantity prices.

Tenants' Rights. 1967. 44 p. 25¢ (cat. no. J1.2:T25) Supt. of Documents, GPO, Washington, D.C. 20402.

Legal tools for better housing.

The Tenement Landlord, by George Sternlieb, 1969. 269 p. $6.00; $2.95 (paper) Rutgers University Press, New Brunswick, N.J.

A study conducted in the Newark, New Jersey area. The goal of the study was to determine the rewards landowners would require to upgrade present slum housing.

Your Housing Today: Should You Rent or Buy? *American Home,* v. 72, winter 1969: 48.

A brief presentation of the dilemma. Provides some information on cooperatives and condominiums.

Your Rights and Responsibilities as a Tenant, 1968. 18 p. Free. Community Legal Assistance Office, 235 Broadway, Cambridge, Mass. 02139.

Although specifically directed to the Massachusetts citizen, this pamphlet has material of value to others, particularly those working with low-income groups.

TRANSPORTATION

Behind the High Cost of Auto Repairs, by Ralph Kinney Bennett. *Reader's Digest,* v. 95, Sept. 1969: 57–62.

"In the face of abundant evidence of shoddy, often overpriced repair work, government and industry are taking a hard look at what's wrong with the business. Here are the problems—and suggested solutions."

Brakes, a Comparison of Braking Performance for 1971 Passenger

Cars, 1970. 31 p. 40¢ (cat. no. TD 8.14/2.1/Pt1) Supt. of Documents, GPO, Washington, D.C. 20402.

One of the "Consumer Aid and Information Series" sponsored by the National Highway Safety Bureau.

Care and Service of Passenger Car Tires, 1968. 23 p. 50¢. Rubber Manufacturers Association, 444 Madison Ave., New York, N.Y. 10022.

A brief introduction to the facts every motorist should know.

Cash in on Cars, by Marilyn Gunther, 1968. 5 booklet series totalling 48 p. 10¢ each. Cooperative Extension Service, Iowa State University, Ames, Iowa 50010.

Packet includes a leader's guide and four other titles—*Selecting your car, Paying for your car, Be safe—be insured, Keeping your car on the road.*

Consumer Reports. "Auto buying guide," annually, in the April issue of this magazine. Consumers Union of U.S., 256 Washington St., Mount Vernon, N.Y. 10550.

The April issue of each year contains the auto buying guide. It gives prices, warranties, safety features, mechanical specifications, and frequency of repair records. Other information provided where pertinent. A comprehensive evaluation. Of interest to some teenagers.

Cost of Car Operation Study, by Sidney S. Von Loesecke, 1970. 6 p. Free. Automobile Legal Association, 1047 Commonwealth Ave., Boston, Mass. 02215.

Federal Trade Commission Staff Report on Automobile Warranties, 1968. 260 p. $2.00 (cat. no. FT1.2:AU8) Supt. of Documents, GPO, Washington, D.C. 20402.

Key points: better assembly-line inspection and testing would eliminate many warranty problems before they begin; dealer performance in correcting warranty-covered defects would be improved if auto makers increased their payments to dealers for warranty work.

Get the Most for Your Money When You Buy a Car, by Val Moolman, 1967. 144 p. $1.00 (paper) Simon and Schuster, New York.

A brief but adequate discussion of the factors to consider in making a new or used automobile purchase. Includes advice on costs. Of interest to some teenagers.

Highway Robbery, by Sam Crowther and Irwin Winehouse, 1966. 189 p. $4.95. Stein and Day, New York. Also available in paperback: 60¢ Fawcett World Library 67 W. 44th St., New York, N.Y. 10036.

The problems in buying and caring for an automobile.

Highway Robbery, by Selwyn Raab. McCall's, v. 96, Jan. 1969: 62–63.

Considers the problems of making a move. Discusses the problems of damage, over-charge, pick up, and delivery.

How to Buy a Used Car, by Charles R. Jackson, 1967. 90 p. $2.75; $1.75 (paper) Chilton, Philadelphia, Pa.

A guide to help you get your money's worth. Of particular value to one who has never read any guides on the subject. Of special interest to teenagers.

The Interstate Commerce Omission, by Ralph Nader and Summer Study Group, 1970. 272 p. $8.95; $1.45 (paper) Grossman, New York.

Report on the Interstate Commerce Commission and transportation. An in-depth analysis of the ICC, which contends that "the Commission is overly solicitous of the transportation industry on a variety of specific issues."

Moving, by Edith Ruina, 1970. 238 p. $8.95. Funk and Wagnalls, New York.

"A commonsense guide to relocating your family." Covers every aspect of a move, from a reminder to return library books, mortgage problems, tax deductions allowed by the 1969 tax-reform law to advice on how to handle the psychological impact of moves on family members.

The Octane Numbers Game, by A. Q. Mowbray. *Nation,* v. 209, Dec. 12, 1969: 659–661.

Discussion of the controversy concerning the posting of octane ratings on gas pumps.

Performance Data for New 1971 Passenger Cars and Motorcycles, 1970. 256 p. $2.00 (cat. no. TD-8.14:2/1) Supt. of Documents, GPO, Washington, D.C. 20402.

Presents tables on acceleration and passing, on tire reserve loads, and stopping ability. Technical but understandable. Aimed at developing greater safety consciousness. *Performance data for new 1970 cars* was the first publication in the U.S. Department of Transportation Consumer Information Series. Of interest to some teenagers.

Prepurchase Information Seeking Behavior of New Car Purchasers, by Peter D. Bennett and Robert M. Mandell. *Journal of Marketing Research,* v. 6, Nov. 1969: 430–433.

A highly technical study which attempts to delineate the process of consumer prepurchase information gathering. Includes a bibliography.

Purchasing and Maintaining an Automobile, 1969. 25¢. Center for Economic Education, State University of New York, 135 Western Ave., Albany, N.Y. 12203.

One of the titles in a series correlated with New York State 12th grade syllabus on consumer education. Included in each are vocabulatory, activities, and bibliography. Other titles in the series: *Consumer credit and money management; Fraud; Quackery and deception; Investments; Life insurance; Security programs; Social security; Medicare; Medicaid;* and *Consumer law.*

Quality Control, Warranties and a Crisis of Confidence. *Consumer Reports,* v. 30, Apr. 4, 1965: 173–174.

Discusses the automobile industry's failure to produce sound warranties while producing a slipshod product.

Report on Automobile Warranties, 1970. 128 p. Free. Federal Trade Commission, Washington, D.C. 20580.

Findings of a four-year study of car warranties. This policy-setting report calls for the regulation of the automobile industry in areas such as safety, warranties, and durability.

Shifty Priorities. *Motor Age Magazine.* Vol. 90, Jan. 1971: 50–51.

Letter to the Managing Editor, by Virginia H. Knauer, Special Assistant to the President for Consumer Affairs, commenting on the "service dealer/consumer relationship" in the automotive service industry.

Speak Up When You Buy a Car, 1970. 4 p. 10¢ (cat. no. Pr 36.8:C-76/Sp3) Supt. of Documents, GPO, Washington, D.C. 20402.

Pamphlet with suggestions on buying a car and emphasizing the need to shop for credit as well as the price of the car. Available in Spanish.

A Teen-Ager's First Car, by Henry Gregor Felsen, 1966. 128 p. $3.25. Dodd, Mead, New York.

For the teenager thinking about buying a second-hand car or now owning one. It covers where to buy a used car, what to ask for, how to bargain, automobile financing, insurance, and what it costs.

Tires, a Comparison of Tire Reserve Load for 1971 Passenger Cars, 1970. 34 p. 40¢ (cat. no. TD8.14/2:1Pt.2) Supt. of Documents, GPO, Washington, D.C. 20402.

One of an information series issued by the National Highway Safety Bureau.

Tires; Their Selection and Care, 1970. 28 p. 65¢ (Dept. of Commerce, cat. no. C13.53;2) Supt. of Documents, GPO, Washington, D.C. 20402.

"Information to help you get the maximum safety, wear, and performance from your tires."

To Buy or Not To Buy, 1968. 6 p. Free. Office of Consumer Protection, 1100 Raymond Blvd., Newark, N.J. 07102.

A twenty-eight point checklist developed by Consumers Union to aid in buying a used car. Of special interest to teenagers.

What to Do with Your Bad Car, by Ralph Nader and others, 1971. $8.95; $2.95 (paper) Grossman New York.

"An action manual for lemon owners." Shows how to reduce your chances of buying a "lemon," and "what to do if you're stuck with one." Of special interest to teenagers.

What You Should Know about Motor Oils, by E. D. Fales, Jr. *Reader's Digest,* v. 95, Oct. 1969: 166–169.

A brief, general discussion of interest to the motorist.

What You Should Know before You Buy a Car, by Anthony Till, 1970. 156 p. 75¢ (paper) Universal Publishing & Distributing Corporation, 235 E. 45th St., New York, N.Y. 10017.

A "how-to" book—also labeled as an exposé—written by a new and used car salesman with over 25 years experience in the trade. Of special interest to teenagers.

What You Should Know Before You Have Your Car Repaired, by Anthony Till, 1970. 166 p. $4.95. Sherbourne Press, Los Angeles, Calif.

Includes a special "Flat-Rate Book" to show you how much you should pay for all major and minor repair jobs, and a fourteen page glossary of automotive terms. Of interest to some teenagers.

HEALTH CARE AND SERVICES
General

Cigarette Smoking, Chronic Bronchitis, and Emphysema, 1967. 6 p. 5¢ (Dept. of Health, Education and Welfare, cat. no. FS2.2:SM7/3/967) Supt. of Documents, GPO, Washington, D.C. 20402.

A brief warning pamphlet suitable for quantity purchase.

Danger! the Cancer Quacks, 1969. 12 p. Free. Research Information Branch, National

Cancer Institute, Bethesda, Md. 20014.

A warning against the fraudulent claims and treatments of cancer "curing" charlatans.

Facts on Quacks . . . What You Should Know about Health Quackery, 1967. n.p. 30¢. American Medical Association, Dept. of Investigation, 535 N. Dearborn St., Chicago, Ill. 60610.

Outlines the health quack's activities in areas from arthritis to rejuvenation. Includes organizations and agencies that helped prepare the pamphlet.

Family Health. Monthly. $4.00. *Family Health*, 1271 Avenue of the Americas, New York, N.Y. 10020.

Contains articles for family consumers on subjects relating to health, such as: choosing the right health insurance, labeling of processed foods, nutrition, dental health, and a column "Ask the Doctor", by Dr. Morris Fishbein.

Hearing Aids. *Consumer Bulletin*, v. 53, May 1970: 27–28.

"The Veterans' Administration's evaluations." The information to be utilized for 1970 was available on October 1, 1969. Tests were made of eighty-two different models of hearing aids from twenty-one manufacturers. The sixteen finally chosen are here rated.

Is Your Doctor a Profiteer? by Charles and Bonnie Remsburg. *Good Housekeeping* v. 167, Nov. 1968: 94–95+.

Eleven specific ways you can tell whether you are being "taken" by a doctor who puts his personal gain ahead of your welfare.

Medical Progress and the Law, edited by Clark C. Havighurst, 1969. 190 p. $7.50. Oceana, Dobbs Ferry, N.Y.

R. B. Ruge discusses regulations of prescription drugs, advertising, medical progress, and private enterprise on pages 90–113.

Nursing Homes, by Ruth and Edward Brecher. *Consumer Reports*, v. 29, Jan. 1964: 30–36, Feb. 1964: 87–92, Mar. 1964: 139–142.

Three parts of a report on nursing homes—the types of facilities available and alternatives to them; how to evaluate nursing homes; costs and charges and recommendations for the improvement of nursing home care.

Partial Victory in the Hearing-Aid Case. *Consumer Reports*, v. 34 Sept. 1969, p. 492.

"CU vs. VA on hearing-aid data" (under the Freedom of Information Act which went into effect in 1967). Court decided that the Veteran's Administration did not need to release complete information if the harm in releasing it would outweigh benefits.

The Plot against the Patient, by Fred J. Cook, 1967. 373 p. $5.95. Prentice-Hall, Englewood Cliffs, N.J.

Contends that hospital costs have risen phenomenally, but the service in hospitals has not borne much relationship to this great rise. The author feels that too often the hospital patient is the victim of bad practices.

Psychiatry, by Francine Klagsbrun, 1969. 119 p. $3.95. Franklin Watts, New York.

What psychiatry is, and how it can help young people who are disturbed. This book explains a complicated subject in very simple terms. The author explains clearly the causes of mental problems, the differences between neurosis and psychosis and the methods of treatment. It includes several case histories of troubled young people— their special problem and how it was solved or treated.

The Quality of Mercy, by Selig Greenberg, 1971. 385 p. $6.95. Atheneum, New York.

"A powerful indictment of the American way of health." A study of the nationwide neglect that has brought American medical practices to the chaos of too few doctors, too few hospitals, and too much expense. A plea for a total rethinking of our national medical resources.

Smoking and Health, 1964. 387 p. $1.25 (Dept. of Health, Education and Welfare, cat. no. FS-2.2:SM7/2) Supt. of Documents, Washington, D.C. 20402.

Report of the Advisory Committee to the Surgeon General of the Public Health Service. A distinguished group of ten medical doctors studied the available evidence and found that "cigarette smoking is a health hazard of sufficient importance in the United States to warrant appropriate remedial action."

Smoking and Health: a Quick Reference Guide to the Report, 1965. 13 p. 10¢ (Dept. of Health, Education and Welfare, cat. no. FS2.2:SM7/2/guide) Supt. of Documents, GPO, Washington, D.C. 20402.

The Truth about Contact Lenses, by Jeffrey Baker, 1970. 248 p. $5.95. Putnam, New York.

An evaluation of contact lenses as opposed to eyeglasses. Considers the advantages and disadvantages of contact lenses and provides tips for wearing them. Of special interest to teenagers.

VD: Facts You Should Know, by Dr. Andre Blanzaco, 1970. 63 p. $3.95. Lothrop, Lee and Shepard, New York.

Everything that young people need to know about syphilis and gonorrhea—their cause, affects on the body and mind, cure, and prevention—presented in a short, clear and relatively easy-to-read book. Each page has a question box to help the reader review the information immediately preceeding it for the purpose of helping him get the facts straight in his mind. Also includes a short history of VD and a glossary of relevant words and phrases.

What's New on Smoking in: Print, rev. 1969. 8 p. 10¢ (cat. no. FS2.24:Sm7/969) Supt. of Documents, GPO, Washington, D.C. 20402.

List of printed materials for young people and adults on the relationship of smoking and health.

What to Look for in a Nursing Home, 1966. 12 p. 15¢. American Medical Association, 535 N. Dearborn St., Chicago, Ill. 60610.

How to choose and evaluate the right nursing home for your needs.

Your Money and Your Life, 1967. 20 p. 10¢ (cat. no. FS 13:111:19) Supt. of Documents, GPO, Washington, D.C. 20402.

A catalog of fakes and swindles in the health field. Discusses health products which are falsely promoted, worthless, and even dangerous. Also warns the public to beware of secret remedies in addition to exposing a number of worthless devices for diagnosing and treating various diseases.

Health and Disability Insurance

A Brief Explanation of Medicare, 1971. 12 p. 10¢ each; 100 copies, $5.00 (cat. no. HE3.52: 43-6) Supt. of Documents, GPO, Washington D.C. 20402.

A folder describing the provision of Medicare. Suitable for use with adult groups.

Guide to Your Disability Income Insurance, 1968. 7 p. Free. Health

Insurance Institute, 277 Park Ave., New York, N.Y. 10017.

Covers the types of policies, length of coverage, policies that can or cannot be cancelled, and details on premiums.

Health Insurance for People 65 or Older, 1968. 14 p. 10¢ (cat. no. FS3.52:43) Supt. of Documents, GPO, Washington, D.C. 20402.

A brief explanation of Medicare is outlined, including the 1967 amendments.

If You Become Disabled, 1970. 31 p. 15¢ each; 100 copies, $10.00 (cat. no. HE3.52:29/2) Supt. of Documents, GPO, Washington, D.C. 20402.

A brief, general description of the disability insurance benefits available under social security.

Just about 65? n.d. 8 p. 10¢. (cat. no. 3.35:875/2) Supt. of Documents, GPO, Washington, D.C. 20402.

Outlines Medicare health benefits available to the senior citizen, including hospital and doctor bill insurance.

A List of Worthwhile Life and Health Insurance Books, 1970. 80 p. 25¢. Institute of Life Insurance, 277 Park Ave., New York, N.Y. 10017.

An annotated listing of a variety of resource materials.

Medicaid-Medicare: Which is Which? 1969. 28 p. Free (single copy) Social and Rehabilitation Service, Dept. of Health, Education, and Welfare, Washington, D.C., 20201.

Very brief and very simple explanations of the differences between Medicaid and Medicare.

Medical Plans and Health Care, by Jerome L. Schwartz, 1968. 384 p. $16.75. C. C. Thomas, Springfield, Ill.

A thorough appraisal of the policies, benefits, quality controls, staffing, and other important aspects of consumer cooperative and private physician prepaid health plans.

The New ABC's of Health Insurance, 1971. 24 p. Free. Women's Division, Institute of Life Insurance, 277 Park Ave., New York, N.Y. 10017.

Basic facts to help families understand their health insurance.

Report of the Task Force on Medicaid and Related Programs, 1970. 144 p. 60¢ (cat. no. HE1.2: M46/8) Supt. of Documents, GPO, Washington, D.C. 20402.

Recommendations to the Secretary of the Department of Health, Education, and Welfare concerning legislative proposals to improve health delivery system.

Source Book of Health Insurance Data, 1970 69 p. Free to teachers, schools and professionals in the consumer field. 25¢ to the public. Health Insurance Institute, 277 Park Avenue, New York, N.Y. 10017.

Provides information on five major forms of health insurance: hospital, surgical, regular medical, major medical, and disability income insurance. Also includes facts and figures on the frequency of illness and injury of Americans.

Your Medicare Handbook, Health Insurance under Social Security, 1970. 32 p. 40¢ (cat. no. HE3.52:50/3) Supt. of Documents, GPO, Washington, D.C. 20402.

A simple explanation of how Medicare works.

Drugs

Before Your Kid Tries Drugs, 1969. 13 p. 15¢ (cat. no. FS2.22: D84/10) Supt. of Documents, GPO, Washington, D.C. 20402.

Helpful guide for concerned parents.

Black Market Medicine, by Margaret Kreig, 1967. 304 p. O. P. Prentice-Hall, Englewood Cliffs, N.J.

Exposé of a multi-million dollar racket in drugs based on the author's firsthand observations of undercover investigations conducted by FDA inspectors.

By Prescription Only (original title: **The Therapeutic Nightmare**), by Morton Mintz, 2nd ed., 1967. 446 p. $6.95. Houghton, Mifflin, Boston. Also available in paperback: $3.95. Beacon Press, 25 Beacon Street, Boston, Mass. 02108.

A report on the roles of the FDA, the AMA, pharmaceutical manufacturers, and others in connection with the use of prescription drugs that may be worthless, injurious, or even lethal. Explores all aspects of the drug industry, especially drug testing. Of interest to some teenagers.

Consumer Protection FDA Packet B—Drugs and Cosmetics, 1965. 17 booklets, etc. $1.50. Supt. of Documents, Washington, D.C. 20402.

Contains literature on the FDC Act and on the approval of new drugs, use of drugs by the consumers, medical quackery, cosmetic laws, and related material.

Don't Guess about Drugs, 1970. 18 p. 20¢ (cat. no. HE20.2417: D84/3) Supt. of Documents, GPO, Washington, D.C. 20402.

Don't guess when you can have the facts. Of special interest to teenagers.

The Drug Establishment, by James L. Goddard. *Esquire*, v. 71, Mar. 1969: 117–121, 152–154.

The author was formerly commissioner of the Food and Drug Administration. Includes an extensive chart of names and organizations aiding, and taking advantage of the consumer.

Drugs and Youth, by Dr. Joseph H. Brenner, Dr. Robert Coles, and Dermot Meagher, 1970. 258 p. $5.95. Liveright, New York.

Written by two medical doctors and a former assistant district attorney, this is an authoritative presentation of the medical, psychiatric and legal facts regarding the use of drugs. Revealing and sometimes contradictory insights are provided by means of candid tape recorded interviews with users and non users. The appendix lists the penalties for drug offenses in each of the states and also includes a bibliography of books and articles that give a wide range of opinion on the subject of drugs. Of special interest to teenagers.

Drugs: Facts on Their Use and Abuse, by Norman Houser, 1969. 48 p. $3.75. Lothrop, Lee and Shepard Co., New York.

The effects of each type of drug on the body and mind are described in this clear and concise book. The author discusses the law and drug control and lists the federal laws for the control of drugs, giving the date of legislation and a summary of the coverage and intent of the legislation. His purpose is to discourage experimentation with drugs, but he writes about them with a minimum of preaching and agonizing, a fact which should make this book more appealing to teenagers.

Drugs from A to Z, by Richard R. Lingeman, 1969. 277 p. $6.95; $2.95 (paper) McGraw-Hill, New York.

An informative book about drugs in dictionary format for the layman. Slang and drug names are intermixed. It lists the origins, both psychological and etymological, of slang terms that are different from the common or medical terms. The explanations of words or phrases run anywhere from one word as in the case of "haircut" which means marijuana to a page or more as in the case of "hallucinogen" and Harrison Narcotics Act." Of special interest to teenagers.

Drugs of Abuse, 1970. 18 p. 20¢ (cat. no. J24.2:D84) Supt. of Documents, GPO, Washington, D.C. 20402.

A warning against the improper use of drugs.

The Drug Users: Task Force on Prescription Drugs, 1968. 145 p. $1.50 (cat. no. FS1.32:US2) Supt. of Documents, GPO, Washington, D.C. 20402.

A major portion of this volume is devoted to a detailed analysis of the drugs actually used by the elderly. Drug prices and generic versus brand names are among the many subjects investigated.

Federal Source Book (Drug Abuse), 1970. 30 p. 25¢ (cat. no. Pr 13.2: An 8) Supt. of Documents, GPO, Washington, D.C. 20402.

Answers to the most frequently asked questions about drug abuse.

Food and Drug Administration Approval of New Drugs; Facts for Consumers, rev. 1964. 8 p. 15¢ (Food and Drug Administration, cat. no. FS13.111:21/4) Supt. of Documents, GPO, Washington, D.C. 20402.

The Great Vitamin Hoax, by Daniel Takton, 1968. 212 p. $5.95. Macmillan, New York.

A journalistic exposé of "how vitamin hucksters are conning the American public into buying products it does not need."

Informed Consent, 1968. [4]p. 5¢ (cat. No. FS 13.128/a:In 3) Supt. of Documents, GPO, Washington, D.C. 20402.

Discussion of FDA's requirement that a physician obtain the informed consent of his patient before he uses an investigational drug on him. A reprint from: *FDA papers.*

LSD 25, 1970. 44 p. 30¢ (cat. no. J24.8:L99/rep.) Supt. of Documents, GPO, Washington, D.C. 20402.

"Factual account, layman's guide to pharmacology, physiology, psychology, and sociology of LSD." Of interest to some teenagers.

Marihuana, 1969. 10 p. 5¢ (cat. no. HE20.2402:M33/2) Supt. of Documents, GPO, Washington, D.C. 20402.

Questions and answers about the drug and its use. Of special interest to teenagers.

Maybe You Can Pay Less for Prescriptions. *Changing Times,* v. 23, Mar. 1969, p. 19–20.

Out of 400 drugs examined, sixty-three were found by HEW to be selling for less under their chemical names. The *Journal of the American Medical Association* cautions physicians, however, to be careful in prescribing such drugs as they are not always as effective as their brand-name counterparts.

The Medicine Show, by the Editors of *Consumer Reports,* rev. ed. 1970. 272 p. $2.00 (paper) Consumers Union of U.S. Inc., 256 Washington St., Mount Vernon, N.Y. 10550.

"Some plain truths about popular remedies for common ailments."

The Million Dollar Bugs, by Michael Pearson, 1969. 291 p. $6.95. Putnam's, New York.

"The explosive inside story of the huge drug business—an industry at bay, beset by government and civil actions—all because of the birth, 30 years ago, of mankind's greatest boon; the age of the wonder drug."

The New Handbook of Prescription Drugs, by Richard Burack, rev. ed. 1970. 362 p. $7.95. Pantheon Books, New York.

"Official names, prices and sources for patient and doctor." The physician author gives his answers to the question "Are you paying too much for your prescriptions?" Tells how to get your doctor to write the generic name instead of the brand name on prescriptions. Some teenage interest.

The Real Voice, by Richard Harris, 1964. 345 p. O. P. Macmillan, New York.

An account of an investigation of the drug industry by Senator Estes Kefauver's Subcommittee on Antitrust and Monopoly.

Sedatives: Some Questions and Answers, 1970. n.p. 10¢; $5.50 per 100 (cat. no. HE20.2402: SE2) Supt. of Documents, GPO, Washington, D.C. 20402.

Stimulants: Some Questions and Answers, 1970. n.p. 10¢; $6.50 per 100 (cat. no. HE20.2402: ST5) Supt. of Documents, GPO Washington, D.C. 20402.

Task Force on Prescription Drugs Final Report, Feb. 1969. 86 p. $1.25 (cat. no. FS1.32: R29/969) Supt. of Documents, GPO, Washington, D.C. 20402.

In addition to Task Force Report, four background papers are available: *The Drug Users, The Drug Makers and the Drug Distributors, The Drug Prescribers: Current American and Foreign Programs, and Approaches to Drug Insurance Design.*

Use and Misuse of Drugs, Rev. 1968. 15 p. 15¢ (cat. no. FS13.111:46/2) Supt. of Documents, GPO, Washington, D.C. 20402.

Describes the use and misuse of prescription and over-the-counter drugs, especially the stimulants and depressants. Outlines the power of the FDA to protect society from the abuse of these dangerous drugs.

What You Can Do about Drugs and Your Child, by Herman W. Land, 1969–70. 240 p. $7.50; $2.45 (paper) Hart Publishing Co., New York.

For the parent who is concerned about a potential or actual problem of teenage drug abuse.

What's the Price of an Rx Drug? *Consumer Reports,* v. 35, May 1970: 278–279.

A brief study of the actual variations in prices among sixty stores for one prescription. The prices ranged from 79¢ to $7.45.

Youthful Drug Use, 1970. 39 p. 30¢ (cat. no. HE17.802:D84) Supt. of Documents, GPO, Washington, D.C. 20402.

A study of the growing problem of drug abuse among the young. Of interest to some teenagers.

HOUSEHOLD FURNISHING, EQUIPMENT AND SERVICES

Adhesives for Everyday Use, 1970. 14 p. 40¢ (Dept. of Commerce, cat. no. C13.53:3) Supt. of Documents, GPO, Washington, D.C. 20402.

"Information you need in selecting and applying adhesives for use in the home and hobby shop."

Appliance Warranties and Service. *Changing Times,* v. 18, Jan. 1964: 42–45.

Thirty-four manufacturers' warranties are listed and analyzed.

Care of Aluminum, n.d. 22 p. Free. Aluminum Association, 750 Third Ave., New York, N.Y. 10017.

Describes the various kinds of aluminum finishes and the proper care and cleaning of each.

Consumer Conference Guide: Appliances, n.d. 14 p. 1–9 copies: $1.00 each; 10–99 copies 75¢ each. Chamber of Commerce of the United States, 1615 H St., N.W., Washington, D.C. 20006.

Guidelines for local chambers of commerce planning consumer conferences on appliances. Presents a model agenda, suggests publicity, gives ideas about follow-up activities, and provides a resource list.

Consumer Discontent With Warranties Presses Congress, Agencies for Action. *National Journal,* v. 2, June 13, 1970: 1242–1250.

A review of complaints and proposed action to combat the growing mass of consumer complaints about false or misleading warranties and guarantees.

Dictionary of Cleanliness Products, n.d. 8 p. Free, Soap and Detergent Association, 475 Park Ave. South, New York, N.Y. 10016.

A list of commonly used terms related to soaps and detergents. For each a definition is given; for many directions for use are also included.

Door Locks. *Consumer Reports,* v. 36, Feb. 1971: 93–103.

Ratings of various types of locks. Includes diagrams of some types, and provides general security precautions of value to everyone.

The Good Housekeeping Guide to Buying Mattresses and Bedding, 1962. 24 p. 15¢. Good Housekeeping Bulletin Service, 959 Eighth Ave., New York, N.Y. 10019.

How to buy and maintain mattresses, blankets, pillows, comforters, and quilts.

Guidelines for Warranty Service after Sale, by George Fisk. *Journal of Marketing,* v. 34, Jan. 1970: 63–67.

Offers guidelines for a positive and effective warranty program. Based on interviews with consumer, government, and trade representatives.

Handbook of Household Equipment Terminology, 3d ed., 1970. 50 p. Apply for price. American Home Economics Association, 2010 Massachusetts Ave., N.W., Washington, D.C. 20036.

Provides definitions of household terms in order to promote uniformity of product description. Terms are arranged under broad categories such as: air conditioning, home laundering, and gas range.

Home Freezers: Their Selection and Use, rev. 1964. 22 p. 15¢ (cat. no. A1.77:48/3) Supt. of Documents, GPO, Washington, D.C. 20402.

How to purchase and maintain a home freezer.

How Much Good is a Guarantee? *Changing Times,* v. 23, July 1969: 6–10.

How to protect yourself when you get a warranty or guarantee. Same article abridged in *Reader's Digest,* v. 95, Nov. 1969: 83–85.

How to Buy Lawn Seed, 1969. 6 p. 10¢ (cat. no. A1.77:51/7) Supt. of Documents, GPO, Washington, D.C. 20402.

A brief instruction booklet for the home gardener.

If It Doesn't Work, Read the Instructions, by Charles Klamkin, 1970. 191 p. $4.95. Stein and Day, New York.

"The electrical appliance jungle." This guide gives much information that some manufacturers and retailers would prefer you did not know. It assists in selecting models, judging best buys and "bargains," and tells what to do when the appliance breaks down.

Overcharge, by Senator Lee Metcalf and Vic Reinemer, 1967. 338 p. $5.95. David McKay, New York.

Well documented and researched attack on the excessive and uneven pricing imposed by electric utility companies. Information of how to remedy these practices is included also.

Portable Appliances: Their Selection, Use and Care, by Amber M. Ludwig, 1971. $2.50. Sears, Roebuck and Co., Consumer Information Services, Dept. 703-Public Relations, 303 E. Ohio Street, Chicago, Ill. 60611.

Non-commercial buymanship information about 35 important household and personal grooming appliances. Also discusses wiring, safety and storage requirements.

Redecorating Your Room for Practically Nothing, by Esther Hautzig, 1967. 203 p. $4.50. Thomas Y. Crowell, New York.

A how-to-do-it book for the teenage girl who has a limited budget but wants to express her own individuality in her bedroom. It is full of ideas with step-by-step instructions and illustrations on redoing old furniture, producing new furnishings out of plywood, bricks and crates, making curtains and bedspreads and many other items. The author emphasizes making use of articles that may at first seem old or of no value.

Responsive Customer Service, by Joe Dawson. *Management Quarterly,* v. 11. winter 1970–71: 20–24.

The Public Affairs Director of the Office of Consumer Affairs discusses consumer complaints against the utility industry and makes positive suggestions for improving the industry's customer relationships.

Room Air Conditioners, 1968. 14 p. Free. Council of Better Business Bureaus, 1101 17th St., N.W., Washington, D.C. 20036.

"How to choose the model best suited to four needs." Quantity prices available.

7 Ways to Reduce Fuel Consumption in Household Heating, n.d. 9 p. Free. Office of Consumer Affairs, New Executive Office Building, Washington, DC. 20506.

Seven practical steps to reduce the consumer's heating bill: weather stripping, storm windows, insulation, heating plants, draperies, attic air leakage, are among the areas considered.

Small Appliances, 1968. 39 p. 40¢. Good Housekeeping Bulletin Service, 959 Eighth Ave., New York, N.Y. 10019.

One of a series of appliance booklets from *Good Housekeeping.* Others include floor care appliances, dishwashers, ranges, washers, and refrigerators. These are brief booklets describing the items listed, telling the important things to consider in making your purchase, and providing a price range for each kind of appliance.

Warranties—What Are They Worth to You? by Herbert

Shuldiner. *Popular Science,* v. 197, Nov. 1970: 55–57.

Surveys the warranties of major producers of consumer products. Article indicates there is some improvement over the recent past, but states that additional improvement is needed.

Washing Machines: Selection and Use, 1964. 22 p. 15¢ (cat. no. A1.77:32/4) Supt. of Documents, GPO, Washington, D.C. 20402.

Your Rights and Responsibilities as a Public Utility User, 1968. 8 p. Free. Community Legal Assistance Office, 235 Broadway, Cambridge, Mass. 02139.

Although this pamphlet is written for the Massachusetts citizen, anyone working with low-income groups may find the material useful. Other titles: *Your Rights and Responsibilities as a Tenant,* 1968. 18 p. Free. *Your Rights and Responsibilities Under the AFDC Program,* 1968. 16 p. Free.

LEISURE

Bike-Ways (101 Things to Do with a Bike), Lillian and Godfrey Frankel, rev. ed., 1968. 128 p. $3.39. Sterling, New York.

Short, concise and easy-to-read information on how to: buy a bike and its parts and accessories, care for and repair it, earn money with your bike, and organize a bike club. Also included are bike games, trips and tours in this country and overseas, what is a good diet for touring and camping, and how to store food while camping. Well illustrated. Of special interest to teenagers.

Bonanza, U.S.A., 1966. 248 p. $1.00 (paper) Bantam Books, Inc. 666 Fifth Ave., New York N.Y. 10019.

A listing of a variety of items one may get free including travel brochures, maps, recipes, pictures, films, etc.

Camping in the National Park System, rev. 1970. 48 p. 25¢ (cat. no. I29.71:970). Supt. of Documents, GPO, Washington, D.C. 20402.

Containing informational and descriptive material of interest to campers, this booklet lists camping accommodations in each area, and gives definitions of categories of these accommodations.

The Complete Book of Bicycling, by Eugene A. Sloane, 1970. 342 p. $9.95. Trident. Orders to Simon & Schuster, New York.

A comprehensive guide to all aspects of bicycles and bicycling. It includes forty-six pages on buying a bicycle—where to buy, what to look for, the rating of bicycles in various price ranges—a chapter on accessories, plain and fancy, with prices, a complete maintenance guide with detailed instruction for caring for and repairing your machine, and an entertaining chapter on its history. Appendix of cycling organizations, bicycle supply sources, bicycling magazines and bibliography (pp. 315–323). Of special interest to teenagers.

Creative Crafts for Today, by John Portchmouth, 1970. 190 p $6.95. Viking Press, New York.

Hundreds of ideas for the teen-ager interested in making things that are useful and decorative—paintings, sculpture, collages, carvings—from inexpensive materials many of which can be found around the house such as buttons, wood, eggs, bottles, shells, nutshells, sand, and boxes. The author believes that everyone is basically creative and that one can experience joy and satisfaction from creating. Complete, concise instructions for each project, listing everything that is needed plus helpful drawings and photographs.

Enduro, by Thomas Firth Jones, 1970. 155 p. $5.50. Chilton, New York.

Although the title *Enduro* refers to

the motorcycle endurance run, this book includes twenty pages on buying a motorcycle—what to look for in an enduro machine and the advantages and the drawbacks of various machines on the market—and a chapter each on modifying your machine and on maintaining it. Readable, interesting and well illustrated. Of special interest to teenagers.

Guides to Outdoor Recreation Areas and Facilities, 1968. 116 p. 55¢ (cat. no. I66.15:G94/968) Supt. of Documents, GPO, Washington, D.C. 20402.

Lists sources of various publications of interest to those seeking information on outdoor recreation areas and facilities. Divided into national, regional and state guides, with cross-references for camping, canoeing, fishing, hiking, and hunting. Of special interest to teenagers.

Handbook for Recreation, rev. 1959, reprinted 1967. 148 p. 75¢ (cat. no. FS17.210:231) Supt. of Documents, GPO, Washington, D.C. 20402.

Plans for parties and picnics, for hundreds of games indoors and outdoors, and detailed suggestions for such activities as dances, dramas, story-telling and singing. Useful to parents, teachers, church and club leaders, and professional leaders.

National Forest Vacations, rev. 1968. 60 p. 45¢ (cat. no. A-13.2:V13/4/968) Supt. of Documents, GPO, Washington, D.C. 20402.

Inexpensive and memorable vacations for the family are detailed in this publication.

Official U.S. Coast Guard Recreational Boating Guide, 1966. 93 p. 60¢ (cat. no. T47.8/3:B63/966) Supt. of Documents, GPO, Washington, D.C. 20402.

For all boatmen—the novice and experienced alike. Information on boat numbering, minimum equipment re-

quirements, other equipment you should have, operating responsibilities, aids to navigation, hints on safety, etc. Includes text of Motorboat Act of 1940, and Federal Boating Act of 1958.

Outdoors, U.S.A., 1967. 448 p. $2.75 (cat. no. I27.2:R24/10/969) Supt. of Documents, GPO, Washington, D.C. 20402.

The *Yearbook of Agriculture, 1967.* "A handbook of resource conservation, a guide to the American outdoors with its great recreational potential and a primer of natural beauty. Designed for all Americans, conservationists, hunters, fishers, campers, children, farmers and rural developers."

See America Free, by Sallie Ann Robbins, 1968. 272 p. $4.95. Hearthside Press, New York.

A fifty state guide listing of free resources for the vacationer: such as museums, plant tours, and art galleries.

EDUCATION

Barron's Handbook of Junior and Community College Financial Aid, by Nicholas C. Proia and Vincent M. DiGaspari, 1970. 697 p. $6.95. Barron's Educational Series, Woodbury, N.Y.

Up-to-date information on the types and conditions of grants and loans available at over 800 two-year junior and community colleges in the United States and Puerto Rico, on how to determine college costs and where and when to apply for aid. Should prove invaluable to high school seniors, parents and guidance counselors.

Borrowing for College, 1965. 11 p. 20¢ (cat. no. FS5.255:55039) Supt. of Documents, GPO, Washington, D.C. 20402.

A "guide for students and parents." Discusses loans available through Federal, State, and college programs and commercial lending institutions.

College Education Financing, 1969. 48 p. 35¢. AFL-CIO, 815 16th St., N.W., Washington, D.C. 20006.

Details the many plans which are available to assist young people in financing a college education.

The College Handbook, by College Entrance Examination Board, 1969. 1327 p. $4.74. College Entrance Examination Board, Publications Order Office, Box 592, Princeton, N.J. 08540.

Comprehensive information on 832 accredited colleges which are members of the College Entrance Examination Board, giving terms of admission, size of student body, college life, yearly expenses, financial aid, etc. Also included for most are tables showing the scores earned on college admission tests by recent applicants and a recent freshman class. Two-year junior colleges are also included.

Comparative Guide to American Colleges, 1970–1971, by James Cass and Max Birnbaum, 1969, 837 p. $10.00. Harper and Row, New York.

Analyzes accredited four year colleges in the United States, giving information on such matters as admission requirements, makeup of student body, the intellectual, social and cultural environment, curriculum, faculty qualification, annual costs, religious orientation, scholarship aid available and percentage of students receiving aid. Also by the same authors: *Comparative Guide to Two-Year Colleges and Four-Year Specialized Schools and Programs* (Harper and Row, 1969, $7.95) Which covers community colleges, junior colleges, technical institutes and specialized schools and programs in art, dance, music, theater, radio-TV-film.

Directory of Private Home Study Schools, 1971. n.p. Free. Accrediting Commission of the National Home Study Council, 1601 18th St., N.W., Washington, D.C. 20009.

A directory of private correspondence schools offering a wide variety of practical and academic subjects. The 1971 directory lists 152 schools.

Facts You Should Know about Home Study Schools, 1959. 15 p. 15¢. Council of Better Business Bureaus, 1101 17th St., N.W., Washington, D.C. 20036.

How to choose a school, what to look for in your contract, advertising and selling practices—these are three of the general areas covered.

Financial Aids for Students Entering College, by Oreon Kesslar, 4th ed., 1969. 487 p. $8.75. Wm. C. Brown Co., Publishers, Dubuque, Iowa 52001.

Lists 1600 sources of financial assistance. For each source, there is information on the donor, restrictions, field of specialization, amount of aid, eligibility, basis of the award, and application procedures. Also included are an annotated list of books and pamphlets that will help select a college and guides for financial aids. Of value to students, parents, and guidance counselors.

Guide to Correspondence Study. Irreg. National University Extension Association, 900 Silver Spring Ave., Silver Spring, Md. 20910.

Lists courses available from regionally accredited colleges and universities which are members of the association. Copies are available on request from member institutions.

A Guide to Student Assistance, 1970. 129 p. 60¢ (cat. no. 91–2: H. doc. 221) Supt. of Documents, GPO, Washington, D.C. 20402.

This document of the House Committee on Education and Labor lists and describes major federal programs for financial assistance to students. Also discusses other selected graduate and undergraduate programs, scholarships and loans.

How the Office of Education Assists College Students and Colleges, rev. 1970. 67 p. 70¢ (cat. no. HE5.255:55051–70) Supt. of Documents, GPO, Washington, D.C. 20402.

How to Go to High School or College by Mail, by Kevin Martin, 1969. 254 p. $5.95. Frederick Fell, New York.

Fifty-nine accredited colleges and universities give correspondence courses (fifty-seven of them for credit) in college subjects and some of them in high school, junior high and elementary school subjects. This book gives detailed information on each institution—the courses, special programs for the employed, high school students, undergrads, post grads, drop outs, and G.I. Bill students. Bibliography of books and pamphlets on the subject and on financial aid (pp. 233–254).

Let Us Now Appraise Famous Writers, by Jessica Mitford. *Atlantic,* v. 226, July, 1970: 45–54.

Critical look at the correspondence course on writing offered by the Famous Writers School. The author questions the ethics of the school.

Lovejoy's Career and Vocational School Guide, by Clarence E.

Lovejoy, 1967. 176 p. $6.50; $3.95 (paper) Simon and Schuster, New York.

Information on 3,533 schools and opportunities for training in more than 200 careers, skills, and trades, including courses offered, length of time required for study, tuition costs, entrance requirements and certificates or diplomas conferred on completing the course. Included are schools for such diverse areas as bartending, flying, beauty culture, ballet, practical nursing, business electronics, hotel management, photography, modelling, drafting, acting, and welding.

Paying for a College Education, by Sidney Margolius, 1967. 28 p. 25¢ (Public Affairs Pamphlet no. 404) Public Affairs Committee, 381 Park Ave. South, New York, N.Y. 10016.

For parents and students. Discusses the realities of college costs and how to find the money for higher education.

Planning for College, by Sidney Margolius, 1965. 304 p. 75¢ (paper) Avon Books, 959 Eighth Ave. New York, N.Y. 10019.

Covers four broad areas: "College costs today and how to meet them," "Admission crisis," "How to choose a college," and "Scholarship aid." Of particular help is the "Directory of colleges" which lists costs, scholarship availability, earning opportunities and admissions data. Thirty additional sources and listed.

Consumer Education

CURRICULUM DEVELOPMENT

Begin with a Single Step, by Katherine Conafay. *National Association of Secondary School Principals. Bulletin,* v. 51, Oct. 1967: 55–63.

Contains concrete examples of innovative teaching in consumer education.

Bibliography of Research on Consumer and Homemaking Education, by Anna M. Gorman and Joel H. Magisos, 1970. #EDO36336. $3.29; 65¢ (micro-

fiche). ERIC Document Reproduction Service, P.O. Drawer O, Bethesda, Md. 20014.

A subject bibliography of materials available in such areas as teacher education, research methodology, homemaking education, vocational education programs, and the disadvantaged.

Buyer Beware, 1971. $12.00. Neighborhood Consumer Information Center, 3005 Georgia Ave., N.W., Washington, D.C. 20010.

Manual on how to set up a neighborhood consumers information and complaint handling facility in the inner-city. Describes the Neighborhood Consumer Information Center operated by Howard University law students.

The Changing Times Teachers Journal. 9 per year. Apply for price. Changing Times Education Service, 1729 H St., N.W., Washington, D.C. 20006.

A guide to the use of *Changing Times* as a classroom aid in teaching consumer education. Contains sample discussion questions, suggested activities, and brief consumer notes. Particularly suited to secondary and adult classes.

Consumer Education, 1969. 2 parts $1.50 each. Bureau of Curriculum Development, Board of Education, City of New York, 110 Livingston St., Brooklyn, N.Y. 11201.

Curriculum development aids with suggested lesson plans, audio-visuals, and resource materials. One part for elementary, intermediate and junior high schools; a second booklet for high schools.

Consumer Education, 1971. 2 parts (looseleaf) $6.50 each. Home Economics Instructional Materials Center, Texas Tech University, P.O. Box 4067, Lubbock, Texas 79409.

Curriculum manual designed for use with a one-semester course for both boys and girls at the 11th and 12th grade levels. Part one: "Behavioral Objectives," "Suggested Learning Experiences," "Key Points" and "References" for students and teacher. Part two: contains related teaching-learning materials for students and teachers.

Consumer Education: Curriculum Guide for Ohio, Grades K–12, 1970. 164 p. $2.75. Instructional Materials Laboratory, Trade and Industrial Education, Ohio State University, 1885 Neil Ave., Columbus, Ohio 43210.

Contains units developed for grade K–6 and 7–12; includes special material for mentally retarded and disadvantaged children. Selected bibliographies included. Descriptive brochure available free on request.

Consumer Education for Families with Limited Incomes, 1971. 360 p. (looseleaf) $10.50. Home Economics Instructional Materials Center, Texas Tech University, P.O. Box 4067, Lubbock, Texas 79409.

A resource manual specifically designed to develop those concepts of consumer education which will aid the teacher of adults in economically depressed areas. Many concepts and teaching aids could be applicable for high school programs.

Consumer Education for Mexican Americans, by Irene Gromatzky, 1968. EDO 16563 19 p. $1.05; 25¢ (microfiche) ERIC Document Reproduction Service, P. O. Drawer O, Bethesda, Md. 20014.

Study originates from New Mexico State University, University Park, N. Mex.

Consumer Education in an Age of Adaptation, by Sally R. Campbell, 1971. $1.00. Sears, Roebuck and Co., Consumer Information Services, Dept. 703-Public Relations, 303 E. Ohio St., Chicago, Ill. 60611.

An educator resource for consumer education curriculum development. Contains behavioral objectives stated as consumer competencies; evaluation materials for both teacher and student; and guidelines for adapting curriculum content to meet the needs of various age, ability and income groups. Free evaluation copy furnished to consumer education instructors.

Consumer Education—Materials for an Elective Course, 1967. 230 p. $1.25 (single copies only). University of the State of New York, The State Education Department, Bureau of Secondary Curriculum Development, Albany, N.Y. 12224.

Designed for an elective course at the 12th grade level, this guide provides curriculum guidelines and materials bibliography.

Consumer Education Package for Low Income Families, 1971. n.p. Apply for price. National Foundation for Consumer Credit, Inc., Federal Bar Building West, 1819 H St., N.W., Washington, D.C. 20006.

Unit outlines and teaching materials for an adult consumer education program for low-income groups.

Consumer Education: the Management of Personal and Family Financial Resources. 1970. 231 p. $2.25. Curriculum Division of the State Department of Vocational and Technical Education, 1515 West 6th Ave. Stillwater, Okla. 74074.

A basic curriculum manual for teachers of boys and girls in home economics and vocational education classes.

A Department Store in the Classroom, by Sally R. Campbell, 1971 $1.00. Sears, Roebuck and Co., Consumer Information Services, Dept. 703-Public Relations, 303 E. Ohio St., Chicago, Ill. 60611.

Instructor's guide to assist in bringing the marketplace into the classroom through the use of mail order catalogs. Free evaluation copy furnished to consumer education instructors.

Economic Education for Washington Schools, 3 parts. Superintendent of Public Instruction, Olympia, Wash. Order from Joint Council on Economic Education, 1212 Avenue of the Americas, New York, N.Y. 10036.

Teacher's manual with economic concepts and teaching suggestions; *Kindergarten through grade six,* 1966, 194 p. $3.00; *Grades seven, eight and nine,* 1967, 59 p. $1.75; and *Grades ten, eleven and twelve,* 1968, 129 p. $3.00.

Economic Literacy in the Elementary School, by David J. Simpson, 1963. 48 p. 75¢. Haverford House, Haverford, Pa. 19041.

"A curriculum guide on economics with particular emphasis on the free flow of money." Published under the auspices of Invest-in-America.

Educational Methods Used in Presenting Consumer Information to Homemakers Living in Low Income Urban Areas, by Virginia Norris, 1967. 214 p. Microfilm, $3.00 Xerography, 9.70. University Microfilms, 300 Zeeb Rd., Ann Arbor, Michigan 48106. Order no. 67–16, 321.

Unpublished doctoral dissertation, Ohio State University, Columbus, Ohio.

110

Educational Program in Consumer Education-Money Management, 1971 rev. 62 p. $2.00. Department of Education and Research, Credit Counseling Centers, Inc., 17000 W. Eight Mile Road, Suit 280, Southfield, Michigan 48075.

Identifies growing community problems as they relate to financial management and pleas for relevancy in consumer education.

Family Economics, 1967. 351 p. Apply for price. State Dept. of Education, Tallahassee, Florida.

"A curriculum guide for home economics education," based on a concept of family-focused economic knowledge.

Family Finance and Consumer Education for Secondary Schools and Adult Education. 1966. 196 p. $5.00. State Board for Vocational Education, 518 Front Street, Boise, Idaho 83702.

Teacher's guide with consumer education objectives, concepts and learning experiences for adult and young adult programs.

Family Financial Education for Adults, by Lawrence W. Erickson, 1969. 102 p. $4.00. Council for Family Financial Education, Twin Tower, Silver Spring, Md. 20910.

Suggested procedures and materials for a course in money management for adults.

Feminine Finance, 1965. 75¢. American Home Economics Association, 2010 Massachusetts Ave., N.W., Washington, D.C. 20036.

A portfolio of ideas for teaching consumer education at all academic levels.

Guidelines for Consumer Education, 1968. 89 p. Free. Office of Superintendent of Public Instruction, Springfield, Ill. 62706.

Developed to meet the requirement in the Illinois School Code which makes the teaching of consumer education mandatory. Included are 29 pages listing resource materials.

Helping Low-Income Homemakers, by Margaret Harding, 1969. 142 p. Apply for price. College of Human Ecology, Cornell University, Ithaca, N.Y. 14850.

"A selected, annotated bibliography" with abstracts containing many references not otherwise available. A basic resource for professionals and social science libraries.

Home Economics Learning Packages (HELP), 1971. $2.00 per packet. American Home Economics Association, 2010 Massachusetts Ave., N.W., Washington, D.C. 20036.

Twenty self-instructional "learning packages" for youth and adult consumer education programs. Areas such as "Advertising Appeal," "Changing Roles for Teachers and Learners" and "Dollars for Housing" are included.

Hunger, Hustlin' and Homemaking, by Camille Jeffers. *Journal of Home Economics,* v. 61, Dec. 1969: 755–761.

The author was director of the Model Cities District Office of the Child Service and Family Center in Atlanta, Georgia. This address was delivered in the opening session of the Conference on Innovation in Consumer Education for the Home Economics Curriculum. It makes observations about the factors that influence poor families' consumer choices.

Identifying Consumer Problems for Low-Income and Adequate-Income Students, by Sally Campbell. *Forecast for Home Economics,* v. 15, Jan. 1970: F22–23.

States the needs of students from both income levels. Outlines course planning for both groups, and surveys the similarities in consumer problems facing each.

Illinois Requires Instruction in Consumer Education, by Dan Bonne. *Business Education Forum,* v. 23, Feb. 1969: 21–22.

Brief summary of the contents of *Guidelines for consumer education* prepared by the Illinois Superintendent of Public Instruction in 1968.

Instruction in Consumer Health, by Carl E. Willgoose. *Instructor,* v. 80, Oct. 1970: 73–74.

Discusses the various consumer health topics appropriate for the upper elementary school grades.

Poverty Studies in the Sixties, 1970. 126 p. 60¢ (cat. no. HE3.-38:P86) Supt. of Documents, GPO, Washington, D.C. 20402.

This broad view of poverty and related problems covers the literature between 1960 and 1969—a selected and annotated bibliography.

Social Studies in Action, 1970. 2 parts $1.75 each. Division of Social Studies, Cleveland Public Schools, 1380 E. 6th St., Cleveland, Ohio 44114.

Teaching units for kindergarten through grade three, and for grades four through six. Contain objectives, identify economic understandings, skills, and attitudes, state questions for discussions, and suggest student activities.

State Education Department Lends a Hand, by Hillis K. Idleman. *National Association of Secondary School Principals. Bulletin,* v. 51, Oct. 1967: 76–78.

Describes the development and contents of a course guide in consumer education. The guide was prepared by the New York State Education Department.

Suggested Guidelines for Consumer Education, Grades K–12, 1970. 58 p. 65¢ (The Office of Consumer Affairs, cat. no. Pr36.8:C76/Ed8) Supt. of Documents, GPO, Washington, D.C. 20402.

A basic resource. Designed to serve as a springboard for use by teachers, faculties, curriculum teams and supervisory or administrative personnel in planning individual programs of Consumer Education. Of particular bibliographic interest: Section V. p. 43–58. "Instructional Resources for Consumer Education."

Survey and Evaluation of Consumer Education Programs in the United States, by Joseph Uhl and others, 1970. 2 vols. 666 p. $33.40; $2.50 (microfiche) ERIC Document Reproduction Service, National Cash Register Co., 4936 Fairmont Ave., Bethesda, Md. 20014.

Produced under a research grant of the United States Department of Health, Education, and Welfare, this study identifies and describes American consumer education. Volume I is a survey and evaluation of institutional and secondary school consumer education programs. Volume II is a sourcebook of consumer education programs.

A Survey of Consumer Education in Canada, 1970. 95 p. Free. Canadian Consumer Council, Box 94, Ottawa 2, Ontario, Canada.

Surveys consumer education activities by educational institutions and organization, labor unions, cooperatives and credit unions, and voluntary agencies.

Teaching about Drugs, 1970. 203 p. $4.00. American School Health Association, ASHA Bldg., Kent, Ohio 44240.

"A curriculum guide, K–12". Co-published with the Pharmaceutical Manufacturers' Association. Presents suggested curriculum and reference materials.

Teaching Adult Women from Puerto Rican Families in N.Y.C. How to Use Their Financial Resources More Effectively, by Irene Oppenheim. *Journal of Home Economics,* v. 57, Dec. 1965: 803.

Reports on a program dealing with the selection of food and clothing, choice of stores, and methods of payment. The program tested varying forms of audio-visual instruction.

Teaching Aids in Consumer Economics: 1970–71. 153 p. $1.00. New York State Council on Economic Education, State University of New York, 135 Western Ave., Albany, N.Y. 12203.

A twelfth grade guide consisting of twelve subject units. Each unit covers economic concepts, suggested vocabulary, economic attitudes and abilities, activities, and selected bibliography.

Teaching Consumer Education and Family Financial Planning. 170 p. $6.00. Council for Family Financial Education, 1110 Fidler Lane, Suite 1616, Silver Spring, Maryland 20910.

Classroom manual built around six major themes of planning, buying, borrowing, protecting, investing, and sharing. Classroom activities feature use of such teaching techniques as role playing visuals, student self-evaluation, and use of community resources.

Teaching a Course in Personal Economics. 1971. 69 p. $2.50 for 1–9 copies, $2.00 for over 10 copies. Joint Council on Economic Education, 1212 Avenue of the Americas, New York, N.Y. 10036.

Lesson plans emphasize individual's decision-making process and participation in economic roles as worker, consumer and citizen.

Teacher's Guide to Financial Education, 1967. 51 p. $1.00. National Education Association, 1201 16th St., N.W., Washington, D.C. 20036.

Provides practical information on loans, interest, budgets and mortgages. It includes patterns for making transparencies, and addresses from which resource materials may be obtained.

Teaching Personal Economics in the Business Curriculum, 1971. 92 p. $2.50. Joint Council on Economic Education, 1212 Avenue of the Americas, New York, N.Y. 10036.

"How to provide students with an understanding of the economic proccess by illustrating the impact of their behavior when they function in their roles as workers, consumers and citizens."—Preface. A curriculum guide for secondary school teachers edited by Roman Warmke.

Teaching Personal Economics in the Home Economics Curriculum, 1971. 99 p. $2.50. Joint Council on Economic Education, 1212 Avenue of the Americas, New York, N.Y. 10036.

"A new approach to the teaching of economic concepts and generalizations to secondary school students . . . emphasizes the crucial role of the consumer."—Preface. A curriculum guide for secondary school teachers edited by Richard Berge and Gerald Draayer.

Teaching Personal Economics in the Social Studies Curriculum, 1971. 80 p. $2.50. Joint Council on Economic Education, 1212 Avenue of the Americas, New York, N.Y. 10036.

"The first step in relating personal economics to the social studies is to examine its structure by identifying its basic content and its unique analytical modes of inquiry."—Part I. A curriculum guide for secondary school teachers edited by George Fersh, Roman F. Warmke, and David Zitlow.

Teachers' Attitudes Toward Consumer Issues and Their Appraisal of the Educational Relevance of These Issues, by John Robert Burton, 1970. 218 p. Available by interlibrary loan; photo-duplication $10.00; microfilm $4.00. Pub. #71–15965. Univ. of Michigan, Ann Arbor, Mich. 48106.

Doctoral dissertation examining attitudes of teachers of home economics and social studies.

Teacher's Guide to Financial Education, 1967. 50 p. $1.00. Stockno. 261–08398. American Home Economics Association, 2010 Massachusetts Ave., N.W., Washington, D.C. 20036.

Four booklets providing practical information on financial subjects. Offer suggestions to business education and home economics teachers for the cooperative development of units on finance.

Test of Understanding in Personal Economics. 1971. 27 p. $1.50 for 1–9 copies, $1.20 for 10 or more. Joint Council on Economic Education, 1212 Avenue of the Americas, New York, N.Y. 10036.

Interpretive manual and discussion guide to be used in conjunction with the Council's economic education series.

Training Home Economics Program Assistants to Work with Low Income Families, 1965. 110 p. $1.00 (cat. no. A1.68:681) Supt. of Documents, GPO, Washington, D.C. 20402.

The purpose of this publication is to assist in developing programs for training nonprofessional workers to help low-income families. Section 4 of this publication has been printed separately to use as a basis for the program assistants training: *Handbook for home economics program assistants,* 1965. 31 p. 25¢ (cat. no. A1.68: 680).

Which? In Secondary Schools: Math and Science—a Consumer Publication for Schools, 1967. 256 p. $3.60. Dept. of Arts, Science and Education, Goldsmith's College, London, Consumer's Association, 14 Buckingham St., London WC2.

Shows how consumer education may be applied in the teaching of math, physics, biology and chemistry.

Why Not Collect Labels? *Consumer Bulletin,* v. 53, Sept. 1970: 15–16.

The "consumer education value of collecting food and textile labels."

Working with Low-Income Families, 1965. 239 p. $2.00 (paper) American Home Economics Association, 2010 Massachusetts Ave., N.W., Washington, D.C. 20036.

Proceedings of a workshop constituting a basic published resource in the field. Contains a variety of articles of interest to consumer specialists. Resource list: p. 223–231.

Your Guide for Teaching Money Management, 1968. 30 p. 25¢. Household Finance Corporation, Money Management Institute, Prudential Plaza, Chicago, Ill. 60601.

To assist teachers and group leaders in developing effective programs in personal and family economics. Valuable for the beginning teacher and for those who wish to brush-up and re-evaluate teaching procedure.

TEXTBOOKS

Behind Every Face, by Arthur and Xenia Fane, 1970. 3 booklets (paper) Grade 9-up. $1.32 each. Ginn, Boston.

Contains a booklet entitled: *A challenge of success,* which includes such consumer topics as acquiring a home, personal finances, cash or credit buying, and life styles in family living. Treatment and illustrations are adult.

Buying Behavior and Marketing Decisions, by Chester A. Wasson and others, 1969. 547 p. $7.95 text ed. Appleton-Century-Crofts, New York.

A marketing text, approximately a third of which is devoted to "The consumer and his behavior."

Consumer Economic Problems, by W. Haimon Wilson and Elvin S. Eyster, 7th ed., 1966. 650 p. $5.96. South-Western Publishing Co., Cincinnati, Ohio.

The principles of both economics and consumer economics are included in this high school text. A workbook, achievement test, and a teacher's manual are also available.

Consumer Economics, by Fred T. Wilhelms, Ramon P. Heinerl, and Herbert M. Jelley, 3rd ed., 1966. 495 p. $6.56. Gregg Division, McGraw-Hill, New York.

Emphasizes the principles of economics for consumer education classes in high school. Supporting materials include a *Student activity guide* and a *Teacher's guide and key.*

Consumer Economics, by M. Rosenblum, July, 1970. 87 p. $3.95. Lerner, Minneapolis, Minn.

Describes the role of consumers in a free enterprise system, the effects of advertising on consumers, the problems of credit buying and the agencies and individuals who work for the consumers' interests. For grades 5 through 11.

Consumer Education Series. 1967. 5 booklets (paper) Grade 7—up. Books 1–5, $5.32. Instructor's guide $1.08. Ginn, Boston.

Five booklets of programmed texts entitled: *Dress Well for Little Money; Exchanges and Refunds; Buying Appliances; What's Good Furniture; Be Sharp! Don't be cheated.* Group leaders guide contains outlines of proposed role-playing situations and group discussion suggestions.

The Consumer and His Dollars, by David Schoenfeld & Arthur A. Natella, 1970. 365 p. $6.00. Oceana, Dobbs Ferry, New York.

Text designed to be used in high school and adult consumer education classes. Cover such topics as the family budget, buying a car, how and where to borrow, and taxes and investments.

The Consumer in American Society, by Arch W. Troelstrup, 4th ed., 1970. 668 p. $10.95. McGraw-Hill, New York.

A substantially revised consumer text which deals with personal and family finance. This 4th edition updates the changing consumer scene since 1965.

The Consumer in the Marketplace, by Leon Levy, Robert Feldman and Simpson Sasserath, 1970. 470 p. $7.33. Pitman, New York.

An illustrated high school text on consumer economics. It is divided into fifty teaching units which include questions, projects and consumer arithmetic problems.

The Consumer in Our Economy, by David Boyce Hamilton, 1962. 473 p. $8.75. Houghton Mifflin, Boston.

Interesting for its historical background of consumer protection; this book also contains a lengthy section on current consumer protection on the federal, state, and local level. Annotated bibliography.

Consumer Information: an Annotated Catalog, 1970. 116 p. $2.50. Consumers' Association of Canada, 100 Gloucester St., Ottawa 4, Canada.

An overview of literature of interest to consumers. Arranged by Dewey Decimal class numbers, with an author-title-subject index. All entries in English. Edited by Valerie Zacharias.

Economics, by Bernt P. and Marcia L. Stigum, 1968. 625 p. $8.95. Addison-Wesley, Reading, Mass.

A beginning text on the principles of economics, devoting eighty-one pages to the consumer and his consumption, savings and investment decisions.

Economics for Consumers, by Leland J. Gordon and Stewart M. Lee, 5th ed., 1967. 641 p. $8.95. Van Nostrand-Reinhold Books, New York.

An examination of consumer behavior, marketing and pricing processes, consumer control of purchasing decisions and private and governmental aids to consumers.

Economics of the Consumer, by Marc Rosenblum, 1970. 87 p. $3.95. Lerner, Minneapolis, Minn.

For the junior high student level, this well-illustrated text provides brief discussions of consumer issues. This is volume two of an eleven volume series, *Real world of economics.*

Essentials of Life Insurance, by J. D. Hammond and Arthur L. Williams, 1968. 168 p. $1.95. Scott, Foresman, Glenview, Ill.

Preface states "an introductory text for courses in insurance as well as a primer for company personnel both in the home office and agency operations." A presentation of life insurance from the seller's point of view.

The Family as Consumers, by Irene Oppenheim, 1965. 318 p. $7.25. Macmillan, New York.

Text on consumer economics and family finance, focusing on the important role of women in planning and managing family consumption.

General Business for Everyday Living, by Raymond G. Price and others, 3rd ed., 1966. 500 p. $6.96. McGraw-Hill, New York.

Relates business practices which will be of use to consumers of goods and services, including how to use money, banks, credit and insurance. A source book, activity guide and tests are also available.

Get Your Money's Worth, by Aurelia Toyer, 1965. 202 p. $1.68 (paper) Holt, Rinehart & Winston, New York.

An adult basic education book written for people with a third or fourth grade reading level and a modest income. Outlines a family's move from a company town to the city, and the problems arising in buying on credit, choosing a place to live, and saving and spending money.

Health, by Arthur L. Harnett, 1969. 438 p. $7.75. Ronald, New York.

An excellent and thoughtful textbook on personal and community health aimed at the young adult. Includes chapters on sexual behavior, physical fitness, mental and emotional health, family planning, diseases, drugs, alcohol, smoking, community health resources, costs of medical care and insurance, environmental health hazards, nutrition and consumer frauds in the field of health. The appendices include an excellent first aid and emergency care guide, recommended daily dietary allowances, weight charts, calorie charts, food composition table and the cholesterol content of food (pp. 395-418). Of special interest to teenagers.

How Money and Credit Help Us, by Elmer R. Kane, 1966. 97 p. $3.20. Benefic Press, Westchester, Ill.

A classroom textbook for early elementary grades. Questions and answers follow each chapter. Illustrated with photographs and charts. A color film-strip, $6.00—44 frames, is available to supplement the text.

How People Earn and Use Money, by Muriel Stanek, 1968. 48 p. $2.40. Benefic Press, Westchester, Ill.

Elementary text on money for use in grades 3–5. Well-illustrated with line drawings and photographs.

How the American Economic System Functions, by Sherwin S. Glassner, 1968. 96 p. $2.40. Benefic Press, Westchester, Ill.

Basic economics textbook for use in grades 5–9.

Life on Paradise Island, W. Harmon Wilson and Roman F. Warmke, 1970. 144 p. $2.10. Scott, Foresman and Co., Glenview, Ill. 60025.

Basic principles of economics for elementary school students.

Management for Better Living, by Mary Catharine Starr, 3d ed., 1968. 452 p. $6.68. Heath, Lexington, Mass.

A textbook for secondary school classes in homemaking, home management, personal development, and social problems.

Mathematics for the Consumer, by Francis G. Lankford, Jr. and William E. Goe, 1971. 480 p. $7.20. Harcourt Brace Jovanovich, New York.

Practical exercises illustrate basic mathematical principles for the consumer.

Mortgage Lending, by Willis R. Bryant, 2d ed., 1962. 423 p. $10.50. McGraw-Hill, New York.

A basic college text. Covers fundamentals of mortgage banking, sources of funds, procedures for loans, role of mortgage banker in developing new business, the FHA program, veterans' loans, and the credit analysis of the borrower.

Personal Finance, by E. Bryant Phillips and Sylvia Lane, 2d ed., 1969. 536 p. $9.95. John Wiley, New York.

Credit, savings, investments, personal expenditures, and lifetime financial security are some of the areas included in this college text.

Personal Finance, by Elvin F. Donaldson and John K. Pfahl, 4th ed., 1966. 803 p. $9.75. Ronald, New York.

Covers the standard topics of personal finance, with a final chapter on owning your own business.

Personal Finance, by Maurice A. Unger and Harold A. Wolf, 2d ed., 1969. 579 p. $9.95. Allyn & Bacon, Rockleigh, N.J.

College text covering the budgeting of income and purchases, insurance and annuities, investments, taxes, and assets.

Personal Finance, by Virginia Britton, 1968. 406 p. $4.95. Van Nostrand-Reinhold, New York.

A textbook designed for home economics classes in junior college and high school. The three major topics covered are: your family finances; your expenditures; your investments and long-run protection.

Real Estate Finance, by Henry Elmer Hoagland and L. D. Stone, 4th ed., 1969. 638 p. $13.25. Richard D. Irwin, Homewood, Ill.

A textbook for students and professionals which will be of considerable value to the inquiring layman. The section on mortgages is of particular interest.

Where Does the Money Go? by Hazel Taylor Spitze and Patricia

H. Rotz, 1969. 94 p. $1.08. Steck-Vaughn Co., P.O. Box 2028, Austin, Tex. 78767.

Designed for adult basic education courses, this simply written book focuses on wise consumer buying and money management while providing reading practice. Teacher's manual and key included with class orders. Apply for quantity price.

You and the Law, by Arthur P. Crabtree, 1964. 250 p. $2.48. Holt, Rinehart, & Winston, New York.

A title in the "Holt Adult Education Series." Especially important for the consumer are the chapters which cover contracts, negotiable instruments, debtors and creditors, property, mortgages, and landlord and tenant.

Your Family and Its Money, by Helen M. Thal and Melinda Holcombe, 1968. 280 p. $5.20. Houghton Mifflin, Boston.

High school text on family finance. Includes twenty pages of resource materials, including books and audio-visual aids.

AUDIOVISUAL MATERIALS

Films

Educators Guide to Free Films. Educators Progress Service, Randolph, Wis. 53956. $9.00.

Annual annotated listing of films and filmstrips including consumer education.

Guide to Government-Loan Film, 1969. 130 p. Serina Press, 70 Kennedy St., Alexandria, Va. 22305. $4.95.

A general list of about 2000 films which includes some subjects related to consumer education.

Library of Congress Catalog— Motion Pictures and Filmstrips. Library of Congress, Card Division, Building #159, Navy Yard Annex, Washington, D.C. 20541. $25.00 per year.

The largest single listing of films and filmstrips, but by no means comprehensive. Provides a subject breakdown including many areas or consumer topics. Published in book form quarterly, cumulated annually and every five years.

What's New on Smoking In: Films, 1969. 6 p. 10¢ (cat. no. FS2.2:Sm7/10/969) Supt. of Documents, GPO, Washington, D.C. 20402.

List of films for young people and adults on the relationship of smoking and health.

After the Applause. 1970. Social Security Administration. Available from nearest Social Security office. Free loan.

Film, 16mm., 28 min., color. Adult.

Explains retirement and disability benefits by following a circus performer's experience with the program. Set in an entertaining circus background.

At Home—2001. 1967. Union Carbide—CBS 21st Century. Modern Talking Pictures Service, Inc., 1212 Avenue of the Americas, New York, N.Y. 10036. Free loan, borrower pays postage.

Film, 16mm., 30min., color. Young adult, adult.

Presents the possibilities in housing for the 21st Century. A film to stimulate interest in home management.

The BBB Story. 1960. Council of Better Business Bureaus, Inc., 1101 17th St., N.W., Washington, D.C. 20036. Free, one week loan.

Film, 16mm., 27 1/2 min., color. Adult, high school.

What a Better Business Bureau is and how it aids consumers.

Banks and the Poor. 1970. National Educational Television, Indiana University, Audio Visual Center, Bloomington, Ind. 47401. Apply for price.

Film, 16mm., 60 min., b&w. Adult, young adult.

Analyzes ways that banks have fallen short of their stated aims in supporting poverty projects such as housing projects in the inner city. Reveals instances where loan companies have charged exorbitant interest rates. Indicates how the consumer can guard against these practices.

Beginning Responsibility: Using Money Wisely. 1967. Coronet Films, 65 E. South Water St., Chicago, Ill. 60601. $65.00 in b&w, $130.00 in color.

Film, 16mm., 11 min., color or b&w. Juvenile (grades 1–3).

Attempts to aid children in understanding how money is obtained and spent.

The Big Con. 1967. California Dept. of Justice. Ken Nelson Productions, 3718 Sunset Blvd., Los Angeles, Calif. 90026. Apply for price.

Film, 16mm., 10 min., color. Young adult, adult.

Points out the fradulent sales practices which are used most frequently with lower- and middle-income families.

A Bone for Spotty. n.d. American Bankers Association, Banking Education Committee, 90 Park Ave., New York, N.Y. 10016. Free loan.

Film, 16mm., 10 min., b&w. Juvenile.

Seeks to create a desire to save money and explains savings banks.

Budgeting. 1968. Bailey-Film Associates, 2211 Michigan Ave., Los Angeles, Calif. 90404. $155.00.

Film, 16mm., 12 min., color. Young adult, adult.

Discusses budgeting of personal finances.

Cities and Commerce: Where We Get Our Food. 1967. McGraw-Hill Films, 330 W. 42nd St., New York, N.Y. 10036. $100.00.

Film, 16mm., 8 min. color. Juvenile.

We follow the steps milk takes from dairy to store and we learn how wholesalers supply the stores that sell to us at retail prices. For second and third grades.

Cities and Commerce: Where We Get Our Goods and Services. 1967. McGraw-Hill Films, 330 W. 42nd St., New York, N.Y. 10036. $100.00.

Film, 16mm, 8 min., color. Juvenile.

At the supermarket we see how the store operates to make a profit, and we see how Suzie's family gets gas and electricity at home. For second and third grade level.

Cities and Geography: Where People Live. 1967. McGraw-Hill Films, 330 W. 42nd St., New York, N.Y. 10036. Apply for price.

Film, 16 mm., 10 min., color. Juvenile.

Visiting different families in different homes, we learn why families live in different places. For second and third grades.

College Profile Film Series. 1971. Visual Education Corporation, 364 Nassau St., Princeton, N.J 08540. Apply for price.

Film (16mm. and super 8mm. cartridges), set of 12 each 15–20 min., color. Young adult, adult.

A series of twelve documentary films which capture the quality of student life at twelve generically different types of institutions, such as a giant midwestern state university, a liberal arts college for men, a predominantly black college. Based on interviews and talk sessions with students. An aid to the prospective college student in gaining insight into the atmosphere and spirit of different campuses.

Consumer Education Film Series. 1968. Bailey-Film Associates, 2211 Michigan Ave., Los Angeles, Calif. 90404. $99.00 each.

Film, 16mm., 11–13 min., color. Young adult.

Consists of three films: *Budgeting, Installment Buying, Retail Credit Buying.* Clear and accurate presentation of the necessary information for junior and senior high school students and college students. The actors are white, middle-to upper-middle-income groups which limits the use of these films in inner-city situations. *Installment Buying* is probably the most helpful.

Consumers Want to Know. n.d. Consumers Union Film Department, Consumers Union of U.S., Inc., 256 Washington St., Mount Vernon, N.Y. 10550. Free loan.

Film, 16mm., 30 min., b&w. Grades 10–12.

This film is largely about the Consumers Union and what it does, but it also provides information to aid the student in competent personal economic decision-making.

Credit—Man's Confidence in Man. n.d. Modern Talking Picture Services, Inc., 1212 Avenue of the Americas, New York, N.Y. 10036. Free loan.

Film, 16mm., 30 min. Adults, young adult.

Story of individual and company credit in our economy. Historical sequences show the development of credit and credit reporting in the United States and how the expansion of our country was aided by credit recording of credit information for benefit of sellers.

Economics and the Individual. 1971. Dun & Bradstreet, Inc., 1290 Avenue of the Americas, New York, N.Y. 10019. Each individual film, $150.00. Complete set, $695.00.

Films, 16mm., set of 5, color. Young adult.

Series consists of five films: *Big Day Tomorrow* sets the contemporary scene against a backdrop of fundamental economic facts of life; *Crossroads*, focuses on earning an income, deciding upon a career, establishing a life style; *Which Comes First?* emphasizes savings and investment in terms of individual needs; *Of Dollars and Sense* covers sound spending, budgeting, and borrowing; *Something for a Rainy Day* deals with protection and security for the future.

Every Seventh Family. n.d. Modern Talking Pictures Services, Inc., 1212 Avenue of the Americas, New York, N.Y. 10036. Free loan.

Film, 16mm., 26 min. Adult.

The story of consumer credit for personal need; operations of a typical finance company; the influence of credit on the economic and social life of the consumer.

Families and Jobs: Risa Earns Her Dime. 1965. McGraw-Hill Films, 330 W. 42nd St., New York, N.Y. 10036. $110.00.

Film, 16mm., 9 min., color. Juvenile.

Explains how Risa earns money doing odd jobs around the house to buy things she wants, and how her father earns money to buy food and clothing for the family. For third and fourth grades.

Family Finances. 1965. National Consumer Finance Association, 1000 16th St., N.W., Washington, D.C. 20036. Apply for price.

Film, 16mm. Juvenile.

A three-film teaching unit from the "Living American Economy Series" developed for the elementary grades.

Food Buying. 1970. Consumers Union Film Department, 267 West 25th St., New York, N.Y. 10001. Free loan.

Film, 16mm., 28 min., b&w. Adult.

Walker Sandbach, Executive Director of Consumers Union, and Lois Simonds, Cooperative Extension Specialist, Ohio State University, discuss food buying activities such as grade labeling, unit pricing, and code stamping.

Fred Meets a Bank. 2nd ed., n.d. Ellis F. Hartford. Coronet Films, 65 E. South Water St., Chicago, Ill. 60601. b&w $75.00, color $150.00.

Film, 16mm., 13 1/2 min., color or b&w. Juvenile.

When Fred makes his first business trip to the bank, he learns about opening savings accounts, handling checking accounts, securing loans, and some of the other services which banks perform. This second edition takes us on a tour through a modern bank, where we see all the departments, from safety deposit box rental to bookkeeping department with its modern electronic computers.

The Great American Funeral. 1964. CBS News. McGraw-Hill Films, 330 W. 42nd St., New York, N.Y. 10036. Apply for price.

Film, 16mm., 54 min., b&w. Adult.

A documentary study of funeral practices and costs. Traces changes that have taken place in burial customs in the United States. Includes interviews with Jessica Mitford, morticians, ministers, and others. Compares practices in America, Denmark, England.

Hard Times in the Country. 1970. National Educational Television, Indiana University, Audio-Visual Center, Bloomington, Indiana 47401. $550.00.

Film, 16mm., 58 min., color. Adult.

An exceptionally thoughtful analysis of food pricing, especially in the package food industry, for consumers. Also indicates the plight of the farmer in the takeover of farms by large corporations.

Harvey's Dilemma. 1965. Modern Talking Pictures Services, Inc., 1212 Avenue of the Americas, New York, N.Y. 10036. Apply for price.

Film, 16mm., 20 min. Adult.

Explains the value of saving money and shows how loans made to home buyers by a savings and loan association benefit depositors and the entire community.

The Health Fraud Racket. 1967. U.S. Food and Drug Administration, Public Health Service, Audio Visual Facility, Atlanta, Ga. 30333. Free loan.

Film, 16mm., 28 min., color. Adult.

Exposes the cunning traps and trappings of the fraud, the quack, and the charlatan. Distinguishes between legitimate and fraudulent products; spots quackery, and explains how to combat it.

A House is a Living Thing. 1964. Council of Better Business Bureaus. 1150 17th St., N.W Washington, D.C. 20036. Free loan.

Film, 16mm., 14 min., color.

How to buy a home.

How to Use Your Bank. 1965. American Bankers Association, 90 Park Ave., New York, N 10016. Apply for price.

Film, 16mm., 10 min., b&w. Young adult, adult.

Describes three basic services of the bank: the checking account to care for day-to-day expenses, the savings account for future plans, and loan facilities for emergencies, investments, or purchases when ready cash is needed.

121

In Common Cause. John Hancock Life Insurance Co. Modern Talking Pictures Service, Inc., 1212 Avenue of Americas, New York, N.Y. 10036. Free loan, borrower pays postage.

Film, 16mm., 20 min., color. Grades 10–12.

Presents an historical development of insurance in the United States. Could be used as background material.

Installment Buying. 1968. Bailey-Film Associates, 2211 Michigan Ave., Los Angeles, Calif 90404. $155.00.

Film, 16mm., 13 min., color. Young adult, adult.

Discusses the principles of the installment plan. Points out the pitfalls to avoid.

It's Your Money! 1970. Henry Biesdorf. Videotape available from ETV Center, N.Y. State College of Human Ecology, Martha Van Rensselaer Hall, Cornell University, Ithaca, N.Y. 14850. Sale $125.00 per tape, rental free in N.Y. State, outside the state $25.00 per tape. Film available from Film Library, Roberts Hall, Cornell University, Ithaca, N.Y. 14850. Sale $55.00; rental $40.00 for 6 films or $10.00 per film.

Film or videotape, series of six 28½ min. programs. Adult.

How to manage personal finances.

Just Sign Here. 1969. Better Business Bureau of Harlem. Association Instructional Materials, 600 Madison Ave., New York, N.Y. 10022. Sale $150.00; rental $10.00.

Film, 16mm., 12 1/2 min. Adult, young adult.

A presentation which covers the experience of couples buying four different types of credit misrepresentations. Points out unethical and immoral practices which cannot be brought to court.

Lady and the Stock Exchange. n.d. New York Stock Exchange. Modern Talking Pictures Service, Inc., 1212 Avenue of the Americas, New York, N.Y. 10036. Free loan, borrower pays postage.

Film, 16mm., 30 min., color. Grades 10–12.

Shows the operation of the Exchange and the family conflicts which may arise over the investment of money. It stresses the importance of obtaining the services of a reliable broker.

Life Insurance—What It Means. n.d. Institute of Life Insurance. Modern Talking Picture Service, Inc., 1212 Avenue of the Americas, New York, N.Y. 10036. Free loan.

Film, 16mm., 16 min., color. Grades 10–12 and adults.

Presents the factors involved in determining premium rates and defines the net annual premium.

Manage Your Money Kit. 1969. American Bankers Association, 90 Park Ave., New York, N.Y. Sale: $125.00. Available for free loan in some states from bankers' associations.

Audio visual kit. Young adult.

Contains a 16mm color film, a 71 frame color filmstrip (using the same pictures as the film) accompanied by a record, a teacher's guide, and fifty student leaflets. It deals with spending, saving and borrowing. Geared for use with junior high and senior high school students.

Measurement in the Food Store. n.d. Herbert F. Spitzer, Coronet Films, 65 E. South Water St.,

Chicago, Ill. 60601. b&w $60, color $120.

Film, 16mm., 11 min. Juvenile.

As the Martin family does their shopping, they encounter some practical problems involving the standard units of measurement. Ounces and pounds, fluid ounces and pints, dry pints and quarts are some of the units illustrated as the family makes comparisons of quantities in answering the mathematical question of "How much"?

The Owl Who Gave a Hoot. 1968. Modern Talking Picture Services, Inc. 1212 Avenue of the Americas, New York, N.Y. 10036. Free loan.

Film, 16mm., 15 min., color. Adult.

Describes in an entertaining manner the problems of consumers in low-income areas. Especially concerned with door-to-door selling. Cartoon style. Produced by the Office of Economic Opportunity. Also available in Spanish.

A Penny Saved. n.d. Modern Talking Picture Service, Inc., 1212 Avenue of the Americas, New York, N.Y. 10036. Free loan.

Film, 16mm., 15 min. Young adult.

Story of three young couples and their ideas about thrift and money management. Explains the credit union system and how it contributes to a sensible family financial plan.

People Who Work at Night. n.d. Bailey-Film Associates, 2211 Michigan Ave., Los Angeles, Calif. 90404. Rental $3.00.

Film, 16mm., b&w. 14 min. Juvenile.

Describes the activities of people who work at night. Shows a taxi driver, a gas station attendant, a druggist, a bus driver, a hotel clerk, and news-paperman, dairy, baker, and factory workers. Explains that people who work at night make living in the city better and easier for all.

Personal Financial Planning. n.d. National Consumer Finance Association, 1000 16th St., N.W., Washington, D.C. 20036. Sale: $75.00; free loan.

Film, 16mm., 11 min., color. Grades 8–12.

Designed to orient high school students into economic problems of daily living. It defines terms of basic consumer economics and emphasizes personal financial planning as part of successful money management. Teacher's Guide is available.

The Poor Pay More. 1967. National Educational Television, Indiana University, Audio-Visual Center, Bloomington, Ind. 47401. Rental $9.15.

Film, 16mm., 60 min., b&w.

An excellent coverage of the subject, this film names names, and presents many of the problems confronting the poor and less educated in the marketplace. Has appeared on NET.

Quacks and Nostrums. 1959. McGraw-Hill Films, 330 W. 42nd St., New York, N.Y. 10036. Sale $120.00. Rental $8.50.

Film, 16mm., 19 min., b&w. Adult, young adult.

Shows the ways in which medical quacks dupe the consumer, and the steps taken by local and federal agencies to protect the public. Follows the story of a woman who takes an herb tea cure-all for her attacks.

Retail Credit Buying. 1968. Bailey-Film Associates, 2211 Michigan Ave., Los Angeles, Calif. 90404. $155.00.

Film, 16mm., 11 min., color. Young adult, adult.

Warns consumers of the pitfalls of buying on credit.

Revolution in our Time. n.d. U.S. Savings and Loan League. Modern Talking Pictures Service, Inc., 1212 Avenue of the Americas, New York, N.Y.

10036. Free loan, borrower expected to pay return postage.

Film, 16mm., 30 min., b&w. Grades 10–12.

The role of home buying in the American economy with emphasis on saving and loan associations as financers.

Security Regained. 1963. First National City Bank of New York, 399 Park Ave., New York, N.Y. 10017. Apply for price.

Film, 16mm., color. Adult.

Explains what happens when a man and his wife bring their estate problems to a trust officer at a bank. Shows how the bank helps put their financial affairs in order giving the customer more spendable dollars now and assurance that the bulk of their estate will be passed on to their heirs.

The Story of the Wholesale Market. n.d. Churchill Films, 662 N. Robertson Blvd., Los Angeles, Calif. 90069. b&w $60, color $120.

Film, 16mm., 11 min. Juvenile.

Follows the activities of a work day at the wholesale produce market. Introduces elementary concepts of economics and public health.

Strawberries with Cream. 1966. Co-Operative League of the U.S.A. Modern Talking Picture Services, Inc. 1212 Avenue of the Americas, New York, N.Y. 10036. Free loan.

Film, 16mm., 16 min., color. Adult, young adult.

A primitive boy discovers a new food source and later the need for cooperatives in producing food. Briefly discusses modern co-ops.

This is a Cooperative. 1967. Gilbert Altschal Productions. Journal Films, 909 W. Diversey Parkway, Chicago, Ill. 60614. Apply for price.

Film, 16mm., 28 min., color. Adult.

Lorne Greene discusses the role of consumer cooperatives in urban and rural society, showing the activities of a health cooperative, a credit union, and a farm family. Produced for the Co-operative League of the U.S.A.

Til Debt Do Us Part. Journal Films, 909 W. Diversey Parkway, Chicago, Ill. 60614. $55.

Film, 16mm sound b&w, 14½ min. Adult.

The credit union helps a couple find the answer to their marriage problems, and puts their marriage back on a sound basis. Good picture of the credit union as a family institution.

Too Good to Be True. 1962. Council of Better Business Bureaus, 1150 17th St., N.W., Washington, D.C. 20036. Free loan.

Film, 16mm., 25 min., color. Adult.

Demonstrates bait and switch techniques with a refrigerator in a store and a sewing machine sold by door-to-door salesman.

Using Your Money. 1970. Educational Dept., Credit Union National Association, Inc. Journal Films, 909 W. Diversey Parkway, Chicago, Ill. 60614. Film: $350.00. Filmstrips: $22.00 each or $120.00 for set of 6. Complete film and filmstrip set: $350.00.

Film, 16mm., 18 min., color. Young adult, adult.

Filmstrips (set of 6), 35 mm., 11–15 min., color. Young adult, adult. Guidelines for handling money effectively. Includes a teacher's guide, games, transparency masters and a record.

What Do Fathers Do? n.d. Churchill Films, 662 N. Robertson Blvd., Los Angeles, Calif. 90069. $120.00.

Film, 16mm., 11 min., Juvenile.

Toby learns about kinds of work fathers do. Watching his father on construction job, he meets the architect and workmen. Toby begins to see how father's earnings buy the things his whole family wants and needs.

What Makes Us Tick. 1958. New York Stock Exchange. Modern Talking Picture Services, Inc., 1212 Avenue of the Americas, New York, N.Y. 10036. Free loan; borrower expected to pay return postage.

Film, 16mm., 14 min., color. Young adult.

Presents an animated version of the "average American family," some answers to their financial needs and the several basic steps in investing.

What You Should Know Before You Buy a Home. 1962. United States Savings and Loan League. Modern Talking Pictures Services, Inc. 1212 Avenue of the Americas, New York 10036.

Film, 16mm., 28 min., color. Adult.

The Wise Use of Credit. 1961. National Consumer Finance Association. Association Films, Inc., 1000 16th St., N.W. Washington, D.C. 20036. Free loan.

Film, 16mm., 11 min., color and b&w. Young adult.

Provides a basic understanding of consumer credit, introduces economic terms, types of credit, cost factor, and guidelines for wise use of credit. A teacher's guide is available.

Working Dollars. n.d. New York Stock Exchange. Modern Talking Pictures, Inc., 1212 Avenue of Americas, New York, N.Y. 10036. Free loan, borrower expected to pay postage.

Film, 16mm., 15 min., color. Grades 10–12 and adults.

Shows, in cartoon form, the use of money for investment dealings, mainly the Monthly Investment Plan and the importance of dealing with a reliable broker. A follow-up to "What makes us tick."

Filmstrips and slides

Color Filmstrips and Slide Sets of the U.S. Department of Agriculture, 1970. 13 p. Free. Office of Information, U.S. Dept. of Agriculture, Photography Division, Washington, D.C. 20250. Free.

Subjects include housing, food and nutrition, grading and inspection, and home economics.

Index to 35mm Educational Film Strips, 2nd ed., 1970. 872 p. $34.00. National Information Center for Educational Media. University of Southern California. R. R. Bowker Company, 1180 Avenue of the Americas, New York, N.Y. 10036.

An extensive listing of curriculum-oriented filmstrips.

All Kinds of Houses. 1964. McGraw-Hill Films, 330 W. 42nd St., New York, N.Y. 10036. $6.00.

Filmstrip, 35mm., 25 frames, color. Juvenile.

The "Children's World" series. From a snail's shell through Eskimo, Indian and pioneer dwellings to the houses of today, the material which is available controls the type of construction.

The 'Basic Four' Way to Good Meals. 1969. Slide set available from: Photography Division, Office of Information, U.S. Dept. of Agriculture, Washington, D.C. 20250. $8.00. Filmstrip available from: Photo Lab Inc., 3825 Georgia Ave., N.W., Washington, D.C. 20011. $5.50.

Slide set or filmstrip, 50 frames, color. Young adult, adult.

Number 1 in the "Food Makes a Difference" series of the U.S. Dept. of Agriculture Consumer and Marketing Service in cooperation with the Evaporated Milk Association. Basically a home economics nutrition guide.

Be a Better Shopper: Buying in Supermarkets. 1967. Heinz B. Biesdorf and Mary Ellen Burris. Cooperative Extension, College of Home Economics, Martha Van Rensselaer Hall, Cornell University, Ithaca, N.Y. 14850. $20.00.

Audio-visual teaching kit. Young adult, adult.

100 35mm color slides, leader's guide, set of Better Shopping Record Sheets, Cost-Weight Table, and a sample bulletin. Four-page leaflet with the kit is free. (Eight 30-min video tapes and 8 16mm sound films have also been produced by the same authors with basically the same content—apply for price) .

Be Credit Wise. 1970. Money Management Institute, Household Finance Corp., Prudential Plaza, Chicago, Ill. 60601. With record and teacher's guide, $2.50; silent with script, $1.75.

Filmstrip, 35mm., 87 frames, color. High school adult.

Dramatizes the credit experiences of three young consumers. It illustrates the various types and sources of consumer credit, as well as the advantages, disadvantages and responsibilities involved.

Buying Beef for Your Freezer. 1968. Visual Communications Section, Dept. of Communication Arts, 442 Roberts Hall, Cornell University, Ithaca, N.Y. 14850. $15.00.

Slide set with kit, 40, color. Young adult, adult.

Kit contains a script, copies of *Home Freezers, their Selection and Use*, and *Handbook for Freezing Foods*, a set of audience participation activities and the leaflets *How to Buy Beef Roasts* and *Selecting Beef of Quality*.

Charge It, Please. 1969. Visual Education Consultants, Madison, Wis. 53701. $3.50.

Filmstrip, 35mm., 18 frames, 7 min., color. Young adult, adult.

Explains the principles of charge accounts, their advantages and dangers.

Cigarettes and Health. 1966. National Interagency Council on Smoking and Health. Training Films, Inc., 150 W. 54th St., New York, N.Y. 10019. Sale $3.00, free loan.

Filmstrip, 35mm., 93 frames, 33 1/3 rpm record, 17 min., color. Young adult, adult.

Warning of the effects of cigarette smoking on health.

The Consumer Decides. 1968. $4.25. J. C. Penney Company, Inc., 1301 Avenue of the Americas, New York, N.Y. 10019.

Filmstrip, 35mm., color. Young adult.

With accompanying record relates consumer rights and responsibilities to consumer satisfaction with purchases.

Consumer Filmstrip Series: 1. Our Role as Consumers, 2. Consumers in the Marketplace, 3. Consumers in Action. 1968. Institute of Life Insurance, Educational Division, 277 Park Ave., New York, N.Y. 10017. $10.35.

Filmstrip, silent, color. Junior high.

The third filmstrip is more advanced than the first two, the dramatic situation being that of a married man. Basic economic information provided includes scarcity, goods and services, opportunity costs.

Consumer Finance Elementary Class Filmstrips. n.d. National Consumer Finance Association, 1000 16th St., N.W., Washington, D.C. 22036. $18.00; Free loan.

Filmstrips, 35mm., set of 3, color. Juvenile.

Provides a basic explanation of the functions of our consumer loan and credit industries. For use with elementary school children. Accompanied by a teacher's guide.

Consumer Tips on Fresh Citrus. 1969. Sunkist Growers, Consumer Services, P.O. Box 2706, Terminal Annex, Los Angeles, Calif. 90054. Free loan.

Filmstrip, 35mm. 42 frames, color. Adult, young adult.

Contains consumer tips on fresh citrus: how to buy, store, use and enjoy citrus all year around.

Credit Concepts. 1969. Visual Education Consultants, Madison, Wis. 53701. $6.95.

Filmstrip, 35mm., 45 frames, 14 min., color. Young adult, adult.

Discusses the basic principles of credit.

Credit Education Package. 1969. National Foundation for Consumer Credit, Inc., Suite 510, 1819 H St., N.W., Washington, D.C. 20006. $7.50.

Filmstrip, 35mm., 50 frames, Color. Junior-Senior high school.

Two filmstrips, "The Cost of Credit" and "Credit in the U.S. Economy" and an accompanying long-playing record present a basic approach to the elements of credit.

Credit Sources. 1960. Visual Education Consultants, Madison, Wis. 53701. $3.50.

Filmstrips, 35mm., 18 frames, 7 min., color. Young adult, adult.

Explains the principles of credit to young people.

Deceptive Packaging. n.d. Consumers' Research, Washington, N.J. 07882. Rental $5.00.

Slide set, 24 slides, 12 min., color. Young adult, adult.

Illustrates examples of deceptive packaging and labeling. Shows partially filled packages, misleading gimmicks, and other ways in which the consumer is beguiled and confused.

Dr. Quack's Lab. 1970. U.S. Food and Drug Administration. Photo Lab, Inc., 3825 Georgia Ave., N.W., Washington, D.C. 20011. $4.25.

Slide set, 40 slides, 13 min., color. Young adult, adult.

Deals with fraudulent medical devices which have been taken off the market.

Facts and Pesticides. n.d. Women's Activities, Manufacturing Chemists Association, 1825 Connecticut Ave., N.W. Washington, D.C. 20009. Apply for price.

Filmstrip, 35mm. Young Adult, adult.

Presents the advantages and dangers of pesticides.

Feeding Our Nation. n.d. Wayne State University, Detroit, Mich. 48233. $3.50.

Filmstrip, 35mm., 35 frames, silent, b&w. Juvenile.

Discusses the harvesting, processing, and marketing of food.

Food Additives. n.d. Consumers' Research, Washington, N.J. 07882. $5.00 rental.

Slide set, 28 slides, 13 min., color. Young adult, adult.

Describes what they are and how they are used.

Homes Are to Live In. n.d. Encyclopedia Britannica Educational Corp., 425 N. Michigan Ave., Chicago, Ill. 60611. $19.90.

Filmstrip, 35mm., 14 frames, silent. Juvenile.

One of the "Learning about people series." Discusses the importance of homes. Shows examples of various types of homes in the United States and other countries.

How to Handle $300,000—A Little at a Time. Journal Films, 909 W. Diversey Parkway, Chicago, Ill. 60614. $15.

Filmstrip, 355mm., with record, color, 15 min.

A money management filmstrip which graphically explains how an average family can best use its lifetime income through wise saving and borrowing. Gives couples of all ages helpful hints on money management.

How We Get Our Clothing. n.d. Society for Visual Education, Inc., 1345 Diversey Parkway, Chicago, Ill. 60604. Each captioned filmstrip $5.00. Set of 4 captioned filmstrips $16.25.

Filmstrip, 35mm. Juvenile.

Introduces children to the essential task of providing clothing. Includes *The Story of Cotton, The Story of Wool.*

How We Get Our Foods. n.d. Society for Visual Education, 1345 Diversey Parkway, Chicago, Ill. 60604. Each captioned filmstrip $5.00, set of 4 captioned filmstrips $1.25.

Filmstrip, 35mm. Juvenile.

Explains the necessity of providing food for the family. Includes *The story of Milk and The Story of Bread.*

How We Get Our Homes. n.d. Society for Visual Education, 1345 Diversey Parkway, Chicago, Ill. 60604. Each captioned filmstrip $5.00, set of 4 captioned filmstrips $16.25.

Filmstrip, 35mm. Juvenile.

Explains the concept of providing basic shelter. Includes *Planning the Home and Building the Foundation.*

The Installment Contract. n.d. Visual Education Consultants, Madison, Wis. 53701. $3.50.

Filmstrip, 35mm., 18 frames, 7 min., color. Young adult, adult.

Explains the advantages and dangers of buying on the installment plan.

Johnny Goes to the Store. n.d. McGraw-Hill Films, 330 W. 42nd St., New York, N.Y. 10036. $5.50.

Filmstrip, 35mm., 27 frames, silent, color. Juvenile.

"Growing Up Series." Tells of new experiences in childhood.

The Kilos are Coming! 1969. Extension Service, University of Vermont, Burlington, Vt. 05401. $7.50 to $13.75 depending on size of order.

Slide set, or transparency set, 44. Young adult, adult.

Contains material on the metric system including a script. "Metric units of measurement" and "Metric supplement to mathematics," a 20cm plastic ruler, and a list of sources for teaching materials.

Laws and Labels. 1968. Visual Instruction Service, 121 Pearson Hall, Iowa State University, Ames, Iowa 50010. $6.25.

Slide set, 25 slides. Young adult, adult.

Deals with the Truth in Packaging Law. Accompanied by a script.

Learning from Labels. 1968. Evaporated Milk Association, 228 N. LaSalle St., Chicago, Ill. 60601. Free loan.

Filmstrip, teacher's script and guide, 35mm., color. Adult, young adult.

Evaporated milk is used as the example for pointing out the information obtainable from present labeling.

Learning to Use Money Wisely. n.d. Society for Visual Education, Inc., 1345 Diversey Parkway, Chicago, Ill. 60604. $6.50.

Filmstrip, 35mm., 37 frames, 7 min., color. Juvenile.

Part of "Learning to Live Together Series." Teaches money concepts. Teacher's guide included.

Living and Working without Money, etc. (Filmstrip series no. 7220). n.d. Horace Taylor, Encyclopaedia Britannica Educational Corp., 425 N. Michigan Ave., Chicago, Ill. 60611. Each filmstrip $6.00, series of 8, boxed $48.00.

Filmstrip, 35mm. (set of 8), average 60 frames each. Juvenile.

Traces the development of an economic system on Enterprise Island, an imaginary community which gradually introduces money, taxation, banking, borrowing, and lending into its society. Adapted from Hans Christian Sonne's *Enterprise island.*

Managing Your Clothing Dollar. n.d. Money Management Institute, Household Finance Corp., Prudential Plaza, Chicago, Ill. 60601. $1.50 each or $6.00 for complete set of five.

Filmstrip, 35mm., 63 frames, 15–20 min., color. Young adult.

Discusses principles of selection for wise consumer spending. Humorous treatment of key points, study guide included.

Marriage and Money. 1963. Educational Division, Institute of Life Insurance. Association Films, Inc., 600 Madison Ave., New York, N.Y. 10017. Sale $3.00; free loan.

Filmstrip, 35mm., 67 frames, 15 min., color. Grades 10–12 and young married or newly married adults.

Discusses the importance of money and budget problems that young people must face.

Money and How We Use It. 1965. Savings Banks Association of New York State, 200 Park Ave., New York, N.Y. 10017. Apply for price.

Filmstrip, 35mm., 58 frames, color. Young adult, adult.

Discusses benefits and techniques of sound money management and explores thrift practices and outlets for savings and investments. Comes with a teacher's manual.

Money Management Filmstrip Library. Money Management Institute, Household Finance Corp., Prudential Plaza, Chicago, Ill. 60601. $7.00 set of five; $1.75 each.

Filmstrip, 35mm., color. Adult.

Dramatizes five areas of personal finance. Includes teacher's guide.

Money Management Series. 1968. Bailey-Film Associates, 2211 Michigan Ave., Los Angeles, Calif. 90404. Filmstrips $7.25 each, records $5.00 each, complete series $72.00.

Filmstrips (set of 6), 35mm., from 7–12 min., with 12" 33 1/3 rpm records. Young adult.

Titles included are: *Charge account applications, Charge cards and charge statements, The bank loan, The loan company, The credit union, The retail merchants association.* Based on the "Consumer Education Film Series." Designed for use with junior and senior high school students and college students.

Our Neighborhood Workers. n.d. Eye Gate House, Inc., 146–01 Archer Ave., Jamaica, N.Y. Prices vary from $5.00 for individual Teach-A-Tape to $67.50 for complete set of Teach-A-Tapes and teacher's manual.

Filmstrip, 35mm. Juvenile.

A filmstrip series designed to introduce a variety of workers and progessions to students eager to learn more about them, the Baker, the Dairyman. Taken from children's experiences, the subject matter is sufficiently familiar to be understood by all viewers.

Planning a Home. n.d. Long Filmslide Service, 7505 Fairmont Ave., El Cerrito, Calif. 94530. $5.00.

Filmstrip, 35mm, silent. Juvenile.

Family living in trailer decides to move to permanent home. Financing, location, planning shown. "Family Shelter Series."

Power Tool Safety, 1970. Power Tool Institute, Inc., 604 Davis Street, P.O. Box 1406. Evanston, Ill. 60204.

Slide Presentation, "Power tool safety," 19 slides (color) and script on safe use of power tools. $5.00. Flyer—"Safety rules for power tools," single copies free; $10.00 per 1,000 plus 25¢ to cover postage and handling. Film, "Give the man power," 5 minutes, $40.00 per print for purchase or free loan from Modern Talking Pictures, 1212 Avenue of the Americas, New York, N.Y. 10036.

Protecting the Consumer. 1968. The New York Times, 229 W. 43rd St., New York, N.Y. 10036. Apply for price.

Filmstrip, 35mm., 75 frames, b&w. Adult.

Examines the new concern with consumer problems: Ralph Nader and automobiles, meat inspection, new laws on finance charges, and the reaction of industry. Discusses the role of government in providing corrective legislation. Comes with a discussion manual.

The Role of Consumers, n.d. Joint Council on Economic Education, 1212 Avenue of the Americas, New York, N.Y. 10036. $7.00.

Filmstrip, 130 frames, 35mm. Young adult, adult.

Covers the importance and status of the consumer, and the role of an intelligent consumer citizen. An accompanying booklet gives teaching suggestions, discussion questions, student activities, and a bibliography. Extra copies 70¢, special rates for schools.

Safety in the Home, n.d. Consumers' Research, Inc., Washington, N.J. 07882. Rental $5.00.

Slide set, 34 slides, color. Young adult, adult.

Illustrates safety hazards the consumer encounters in his daily life. Special emphasis is given to electrical hazards, and the efforts of Consumers' Research to detect and minimize them.

Sears Audio Visual Series. n.d. Association Films, Agents for Sears Consumer Information Services, 512 Burlington Ave., La Grange, Ill. 60525. Apply for price.

Six filmstrips, 35mm., 1 transparency unit.

Includes a reading script and fifty *Sears hidden values* booklets. Topics covered include diving equipment, kitchen equipment, window treatments, home furnishings.

Spending Your Food Dollar. 1967. Money Management Institute, Household Finance, Corp., Prudential Plaza, Chicago, Ill. 60601. $1.75.

Filmstrip, 35mm., 77 frames, color. Young adult, adult.

How to save money, time and energy through proper skills of food buying, using comparative shopping, i.e. check labels, brands in season, frozen, prepackaged foods. Has a review at end of film. Accompanying study guide provided.

Teenage Allowances. n.d. Society for Visual Education, 1345 Diversey Parkway, Chicago, Ill. 60614. $6.50.

Filmstrip, 35mm., Young adult.

Stresses family finances, management, and wise spending. Accompanied by a record.

Testing at Consumers' Research, n.d. Consumers' Research, Inc., Washington, N.J. 07882. Rental $5.00.

Slide set, 34 slides, color. Young adult, adult.

Shows the methods used by Consumers' Research in testing products. Some of the examples shown are tests on electric mixers, toasters, electric blankets, and vacuum cleaners.

That's Life, Insurance, That Is.
1962. The Travelers Companies, Sterling Movies, U.S.A., Inc., 43 W. 61st St., New York, N.Y. 10023. Free.

Filmstrip, 35mm., 17 min., color. Adult, young adult.

Tells the story of a Martian spy who returns from Earth to report to his king on his discovery of life insurance. In humorous format, the basic types of life insurance are explained.

Truth in Lending. 1970. Public Services, Div. of Administration, Federal Reserve System, Washington, D.C. 20551. Sale; $10.00, free loan from the 12 Federal Reserve banks or their branches.

Filmstrip, 35mm., 93 frames, with record. Adult.

Explains the meaning of "finance charge" and "annual percentage rate" as used in Truth in Lending.

The United States Economy in Action. n.d. Joint Council on Economic Education, 1212 Avenue of the Americas, New York, N.Y. 10036. Free loan, borrower pays postage.

Filmstrips, 35mm., 38 frames, color. Grades 10–12.

Three filmstrips which define the term "consumer," consider the role of production on consumption, and discuss the difficulties of becoming an intelligent consumer. A reading script is provided.

The Value of Your Dollar, n.d. Current Affairs Films, 527 Madison Ave., New York, N.Y. 10022. $7.50.

Filmstrip, 35mm., 44 frames, silent, color. Young adult, adult.

Explains the underlying reasons for the diminishing purchasing power of the dollar. Points out ways in which the U.S. can strengthen its economy. Pictorial discussion guide included.

The Why and How of Packaging. 1968. Studio One Animation, 1220 Glenwood Ave., Minneapolis, Minn. 55405. $3.50.

Filmstrip, 35mm., 68 frames, 9 min., color. Young adult, adult.

A narration guide and twenty-five student booklets are provided with the filmstrip.

You, the Shopper. 1966. Becker & Goessl. Money Management Institute, Household Finance Corporation, Prudential Plaza, Chicago, Ill. 60601. Apply for price.

Filmstrip, 35mm., 63 frames, b&w. Young adult, adult.

Explains the role of the shopper as the family purchasing agent, the customer, and the citizen.

Your Money Matters and You Take the Credit. 1970. National Consumers Finance Association, 1000 16th St., N.W., Washington, D.C. 20036. $20.00 per set.

2 Filmstrips, 35mm., 80 frames, color, each with a record. Young adult.

Deals with financial decision making before and after marriage, and introduces concepts of credit.

Your Money's Worth in Shopping. n.d. Money Management Institute, Household Finance Corp., Prudential Plaza, Chicago, Ill. 60601. $1.75.

Filmstrip, 35mm., 63 frames, color. Young adult.

This demonstrates how intelligent shopping can help consumers get more for their money by establishing goals for spending and understanding the role of consumers. Study guide included.

Your Wardrobe and You. 1967. Money Management Institute, Household Finance Corp., Prudential Plaza, Chicago, Ill. 60601. $1.75.

Filmstrip, 35mm., 67 frames, 15–20 min., color. Young adult, adult.

Advice on stretching your clothing budget. Discusses quality and style.

Visuals

Posters and Charts, Price List 81. Free. Supt. of Documents, GPO, Washington, D.C. 20402.

A subject listing of general teaching aids available at low cost from the Government Printing Office. Each item is described as to both content and dimensions. Catalog numbers are given for each entry.

Visual Teaching Materials, 1971. 65 p. Free. Visual Products Division, 3M Company, Box 3344, St. Paul, Minn. 55101.

Annotated catalog and price list of overhead projection transparencies including units related to consumer education. Also lists booklets available for purchase to assist teachers plan management lessons based on visuals listed in catalog. For all grade levels, adult and special education programs.

Buyer Beware, 1971. 11″ by 7″ posters. 25 for $50, 50 for $90. Neighborhood Consumer Information Center, 3005 Georgia Ave., N.W., Washington, D.C. 20010.

Cartoon posters designed by Howard University law students depicting consumer problems such as over-extended credit and fraud & deception. Available in Spanish.

Consumer Protection Sources. 1968. $35.00. cat. no. 15–4784–3, Visual Products Division, 3M Company, Box 3344, St. Paul, Minn. 55101.

Transparency. Juvenile.

Citing examples of agencies, groups, laws and standards that protect the health of the consumer.

Cows Are To Be Milked, Not People, 1969. Free. Georgia Consumers Services Program, 15 Peachtree St., N.E., Room 834, Atlanta, Ga. 30303.

Posters designed to alert low-income consumers to pitfalls in the marketplace.

Household Weights and Measures, 1960. 11″ x 8.5″ [Wall card, printed on both sides.] 10¢ (cat. no. C13.10:234) Supt. of Documents, GPO, Washington, D.C. 20402.

The purpose of this card is to present in convenient form the weights and measures tables most useful for household purposes, together with associated weights and measures information of general household interest.

Know the Eggs You Buy, rev. 1967. 12 p. 10¢ (cat. no. A1.68: 70/3) Supt. of Documents, GPO, Washington, D.C. 20402.

Color chart, that illustrates the difference in size between the six U.S. weight classes, and provides photographs that compare the quality of the three U.S. grades as they are broken out of the shell, fried and poached. Measures 1′ x 1.5′ when opened. Same poster revised in 1968 is 45″ x 30″ and available from GPO for 30¢. Cat. no. A88.40/2:62.

The Modern Metric System, rev. 1969. Chart. 29″ x 45″. 50¢ (cat. no. C13.10:304) Supt. of Documents, GPO, Washington, D.C. 20402.

"The international system of units and its relationship to U.S. customary units."

101 Meat Cuts, 1970. 36p. 25¢. Dept. VT, National Livestock and

Meat Board, 36 South Wabash Ave. Chicago, Ill. 60603.

Close up photographs of most common meat cuts together will full descriptions and basic cookery methods.

Posters, 1956, reprinted 1968. 18 p. 15¢ (cat. no. A1.38:796) Supt. of Documents, GPO, Washington, D.C. 20402.

"Making posters, flashcards, and charts for extension teaching."

A Primer for Consumer Thinking. 1970. $15.00 Educational Services Division, Consumers Union of U.S., 256 Washington St., Mt. Vernon, N.Y. 10550.

Transparency. Young adult, adult.

Ten transparencies useful in introducing general consumer topics such as "Buying," "Information" and "Where to Live." Instructor's guide included.

Silhouettes of Fashion, 1968. 19 p. $1.00. Sears, Roebuck and Co., Public Relations, 7401 Skokie Blvd., Skokie, Ill. 60076.

Booklet.

Seven decades of American fashions traced by printed illustrations from Sears catalogues. Intended for use with opaque projection.

Smoking, 1969. 12″ x 9″ Poster 5¢ (cat. no. FS2.26:C48) Supt. of Documents, GPO, Washington, D.C. 20402.

Cautions cigarette smoking may be hazardous to your health, tar and nicotine content of cigarettes.

What is Consumer Credit, by Elsie Fetterman, 1969. 8 p. 17″ x 22″ $2.50. Agriculture Publications Dept., U–35, University of Connecticut, Storrs, Conn. 06268.

Flip charts designed for teaching consumer credit. Available in Spanish.

Audio

Buyer Beware. 1970. WILL Radio, University of Illinois, Urbana, Ill. 61801. $65.00 for the series, but $26.00 if purchaser provides the blank tape to WILL for dubbing.

Audio tapes, series of 13 thirty-minute programs. Adult.

Touches on thirteen subject areas including "What is a consumer," "Clothes on my back," "A roof over my head," "If I die," "The new consumer." Among the many specialists who speak are Ralph Nader, Walker Sandbach, and Jessica Mitford.

Consumer Credit in Family Financial Management. 1967. American Home Economics Association, 2010 Massachusetts Ave., Washington, D.C. 20036. $6.00 each tape, $55.00 set of 10 tapes.

Tapes, vary in length from 40–120 min. Adult.

A series of ten tape recordings. These are the tapes of the AHEA National Workshop on "Consumer Credit in Family Financial Management." For an order form with the complete listing of speakers, titles and lengths, write to the AHEA.

Consumer Protection—A Federal or Private Responsibility? 1968. Washington Tapes, Inc., 5540 Connecticut Ave., Washington, D.C. 20015. $10.00.

Audio tape, 20 min. Adult.

Senator Gaylord Nelson and Mr. Daniel Parker (representing the National Association of Manufacturers) present opposing views concerning federal consumer legislation.

Credit Card Blues, by Montie Montana, Jr. 1969. Montana Associates, Inc., Box 102, Calabasas, Calif. 91302. $1.00.

45 rpm record.

Song highlighting difficulties one can get into by overextending the use of a credit card. Song in country music style.

Health-Cleanliness-Safety. Soap and Detergent Association, 475 Park Ave., South, New York, N.Y. 10016. Free.

Phonograph record, preschool.

"Songlets for Project Head Start by Irving Caesar." Approximately ten minutes of recorded songs covering such topics as cleanliness, working, health and nutrition. Designed for class use.

Laundry Story; Bakery Story. n.d. Berliner Music Shop, 154 Fourth Ave., New York, N.Y. 10003. $2.70.

Recordings, Disc, 78 rpm. Juvenile.

A parent visits a laundry, then a bakery with her child. Songs such as "Checking our list" and "Cake decorating song" are presented. For use with preschool children.

Money Management Recordings. 1969. National Consumer Finance Association, 1000 16th St., N.W., Washington, D.C. 20036. $15.00.

Recordings, tape or disc, set of 5; teacher's manual.

Money management dramatizations designed as discussion starters for use at the junior high level. They feature such topics as budgeting, savings accounts, time-purchases, use of credit, and borrowing.

Report to Consumers. 1970. Consumers Union of U.S., 256 Washington St., Mt. Vernon, N.Y. 10550. Free.

Record, 12 in., 50 min. Adult.

This is a service of Consumers Union for radio stations.

TEACHING AIDS

All About Furniture, 1969. $15.00 for kit; $16.00 for kit with 33 1/3 LP record to accompany filmstrips. Southern Furniture Manufacturers Association, P.O. Box 951, High Point, N.C. 27261.

Course in home furnishings. Kit includes two filmstrips, 100 frames each, with printed scripts, and optional LP scenario record, one on furniture construction and materials, and one on furniture styles; fabric and wood samples; student text which includes guidelines to selecting and buying furniture; and teacher's guide.

Better Buymanship Series. Apply for price. Co-ed/Forecast Books, Junior-Senior High School Division of Scholastic Magazines, Inc., 904 Sylvan Ave., Englewood Cliffs, N.J. 07632.

A series of paperback books offering elementary advice to young consumers. Topics, include home furnishings, budgeting, foods, and clothing.

Clothes, Money and You, by Ruth Ann Nine, 1965. 28 p. Free. Reference Unit of Selected Readings and References for State Clothing Specialists, State 4-H Staffs, Pennsylvania State University, University Park, Pa. 16802.

Books that the teacher and student may use successfully in a consumer education class or club activity. Basic teaching unit for courses in consumer education on the high school level.

Consumer Buying Guides, 4 p. each. 5¢ each. J. C. Penney Co., Inc. 1301 Ave. of the Americas, New York, N.Y. 10019.

Twenty guides planned for classroom use, covering such subjects as buying slips, young men's slacks, and small appliances. You may also request, free of charge, J. C. Penney's Educational Materials, a four page catalog.

Consumers Cost Calculator. 50¢.
Food Advisory Services, Sir John Carling Building, Carling Ave., Ottawa, Canada.

A 5¾ inch by 4¼ inch plastic calculator for determining price per unit.

Consumer Education Series, 1967. 56 p. 6 pamphlets $1.00 each; $5.25 for series. Xerox Education Division, 352 Park Ave. South, New York, N.Y. 10010.

Five programmed instruction booklets on the buying of appliances, clothing, furniture; on not being cheated, on refunds and exchanges, and a Group Leader's Guide. Tailored for school dropouts, VISTA programs, head start mothers, and other low income persons with limited education. Descriptive brochure free on request.

Consumer Facts. n.d. CUNA, Inc., 1617 Sherman Ave., Box 431, Madison, Wis. 53701.

A series of leaflets on Consumer Education giving worthwhile facts and information on consumer subjects.

Consumer Game, by Gerald Zaltman, 1969. $30.00. Western Publishing Co., 850 Third Ave., New York, N.Y. 10022.

Simulates problems and economics of installment buying. For 11 to 34 players; time required 1½ to 2½ hours. Kit includes all necessary materials, profile folders, money, score sheets, contracts, display board, instructor's manual.

Consumer Information, Price List 86, 5th ed., 1971. Single copy free; $7.50 per 100 copies. Supt. of Documents, GPO, Washington, D.C. 20402.

A bibliography of consumer-type publications that provide helpful information on family finances, appliances, clothing and other related subjects which are available for sale by the Government Printing Office.

Consumer Mathematics Series, by David H. Knowles, 1965–66. $21.68 complete kit, apply for individual price. Behavioral Research Laboratories, Box 577, Palo Alto, Calif. 94302.

Course containing seven units, each with teacher's manual, text and test booklet. Titles are *Vocational Opportunities and Lifetime Earnings*, *The Pay Check*, *The Household Budget*, *The Wise Buyer*, *Income Tax*, *Insurance*, and *Investments*. Junior to Senior high school level.

Consumer Purchasing: Purchasing Food, Clothing, Furniture and Appliances, and Housing, 1968. Paging varies. 25¢ each. Center for Economic Education, State University of New York, 135 Western Ave., Albany, N.Y 12203.

Teaching aids, including economic concepts and attitudes, suggested vocabulary, activities and a bibliography. These aids are correlated with the New York State Education Department's 12th grade syllabus, *Consumer Education*.

Decision Making for Consumers. 1969. $10.00. Education and Consumer Relations, J. C. Penney Co., Inc., 1301 Avenue of the Americas, New York, N.Y. 10019.

Contains recorded playlets, paper hand puppets, a filmstrip with a record, a bulletin board puzzle, and a teacher's guide. Provides a tool for teaching the intellectual approach to decision making.

Decision Making in Consumer Affairs (Credit), 1970. Student Resource Book. 61 p. 41¢. Teacher's Guide. 65 p. 68¢. Office of School Publications, School District of Philadelphia,

219 N. Broad St., Philadelphia, Pa. 19103 (Single copies free to members of the American Council on Consumer Interests.)

The first in a series of curriculum materials for senior high school consumer education classes.

Economic Man, 1971. Booklets, game, teacher's resource booklet (parts sold separately). Apply for prices. Benefic Press, 10300 W. Roosevelt Road, Westchester, Ill. 60153.

A program in elementary economics for grades 6–9. "Developed and field tested over a period of three years by the Industrial Relations Center staff of the University of Chicago." Game may be used separately from the text and is suitable for adult education classes. Game title: *Market*.

Economic System, by T. Robert Harris and James S. Coleman. $25.00. Western Publishing Co., Wayne, N.J. 07470.

A game designed for 7–13 players of highschool age, 2–4 hours playing time. "Simulates [the] basic features common to a wide variety of economic systems."

Economics Cases for Discussion. 20 p. Single copy $1.00. Phi Chapter of Delta Pi Epsilon, 117 Burton Hall, University of Minnesota, Minneapolis, Minn. 55455.

Describes twenty situations which call for economic decisions. Possible decisions and various justifications are considered.

Educational Materials on Automobile Insurance-Homeowners Insurance. 1967. Free. Educational Division, Insurance Information Institute, 110 William St., New York, N.Y. 10038.

Designed for high school and college units on property and liability insurance.

Educator's Information Service. 1968. 27 p. Free to teachers. Bureau of Education and Research, American Advertising Federation, 655 Madison Ave., New York, N.Y. 10021.

A consolidated list of informational and educational materials currently available. A number of the materials listed deal with the relationship between the advertisers and the consumer.

FDA's [Food and Drug Administration] Life Protection Series. The pamphlets in this series are brief and simply written. They can serve as springboards to classroom discussion and as resource materials for school libraries. Sample items from this series are annotated elsewhere in this bibliography. A list of appropriate titles follows. All are available from: Supt. of Documents, GPO, Washington, D.C. 20402.

Additives In Our Food, 1968. 8 p. 15¢ cat. no. FS13.111:43/2

Citizenship and the Strawberry Jam, 1967. 4 p. 5¢ cat. no. FS13.111:49

How Safe Are Our Drugs? 1968. 11 p. 15¢ cat. no. FS13.111:44/2

How Safe Is Our Food? 1968. 11 p. 20¢ cat. no. FS13.111:41/2

Making a Safe Home Environment, 1968. 4 p. 5¢ cat. no. FS13.111:50/2

Protection of Human Life, 1968, 4 p. 5¢ cat. no. FS13.111:48/2

Use and Misuse of Drugs, 1968. 15 p. 15¢ cat. no. FS13.111:46/2

Young Scientists Look at Drugs, 1968. 14 p. 15¢ cat. no. FS13.111:45/2

Young Scientists Look at Food, 1968. 6 p. 10¢ cat. no. FS13.111:42/2

FDA's [Food and Drug Administration] Science Project Series. These projects, suitable for high school biology or chemistry classrooms, include experiments and procedures, subjects for classroom discussion, and sources of additional information. They could be utilized to introduce the technical study of consumer items into the curriculum. All are available from: Supt. of Documents, GPO, Washington, D.C. 20402.

Analysis for Spoilage Indicators in Butter, 1968. 8 p. 10¢ cat. no. FS13.111:55/2

Identity of Artificial Color on Oranges, 1968. 8 p. 10¢ cat. no. FS13.111:54/2

Identity of Synthetic Colors in Foods, 1968. 8p 10¢ cat. no. FS13.111:57/2

Rapid Identity of Margarine and Butter, 1968. 8 p. 10¢ cat. no. FS13.111:56/2

Qualitative Analysis of APC Tablets, 1968. 8 p. 10¢ cat. no. HE20.4015:53

Family Money Management.
$1.00. National Consumer Finance Association, 1000 16th St., N.W., Washington, D.C. 20036.

A counseling kit containing pamphlets, budget sheets, and a sliding guide to family expenditures.

Financing a New Partnership,
1968. $1.00 J. C. Penney Co., Inc., 1301 Avenue of the Americas, New York, N.Y. 10019.

A teaching kit designed to help young people understand the need for money management. Included are a number of leaflets and a group money management game.

The Good Foods Coloring Book,
1970. 32 p. 20¢ (cat. no. A1.68:912) Supt. of Documents, GPO, Washington, D.C. 20402.

A children's coloring book describing nutritive foods. Also available in a Spanish edition, cat. no. A1.68:912–S.

Handle Yourself With Care,
1969. The Administration on Aging and the National Safety Council. U.S. Department of Health, Education and Welfare, Social Rehabilitation Service, Washington, D.C. 20201.

An instructor's guide (No. 804) and separate illustrated booklet (No. 805) for an accident prevention course for older Americans with suggested lessons and references to audio-visual aids. AOA Publications No. 804, 46 p. and 805, 20 p. Free to instructors from the AOA (also available for 50¢ and 30¢ respectively from the Supt. of Documents, GPO, Washington, D.C. 20402).

Home Economics Program, 1970.
$39.50. Home Furnishings Council, National Home Furnishings Association, 1150 Merchandise Mart, Chicago, Ill. 60654.

Classroom home economics program of multi-media teaching aids comprised of three kits: "Home Furnishings Buymanship," "Basic Decorating" and "Budgeting and Care." Kits contain curriculum guides, audio-visuals, evaluations, and bibliographies.

Home Laundry Classroom Kit.
n.d. $15.00. Association of Home Appliance Manufacturers, 20 N. Wacker Dr., Chicago, Ill. 60606.

A selection of teacher and consumer aids and booklets related to laundry, washers, dryers, and detergents.

Home Safety Course. Apply for price. National Safety Council, 425 N. Michigan Ave. Chicago, Ill. 60611.

This is a multi-media teaching kit which includes four slide sets and accompanying pamphlets on falls, fires, electrical hazards and poisons. Designed for young adults and adults. Graduation certificates can also be ordered.

How to Furnish a First Home.
n.d. $2.00. J. C. Penney Co., Inc., Educational Relations, 1301 Avenue of the Americas, New York, N.Y. 10019.

Teaching kit includes cut-outs of three couples of different backgrounds. Explains goals and values that each must accomplish in purchasing of goods.

Instructional Material for Classroom Use, by the Council for Family Financial Education. 1971. Free. Savings Bond Division U.S. Department of the Treasury, Washington, D.C. 20226.

Teaching kit on savings designed primarily for junior and senior high school; contains research projects, two mini-dramas, a cartoon strip, two transparencies, and a bulletin board display.

Kaleidoscope. Semi-annual. Free. Consumer Information Services, Dept. 703, Public Relations, 303 E. Ohio St., Chicago, Ill. 60611.

Hints for consumers and teachers of consumer education.

Male Manners, by Kay Corinth and Mary Sargent, 1969. 336 p. $6.95. David McKay, New York.

Includes information for young people on how to handle money on dates and in other daily life situations, plan and buy clothes, choose a college and pay for it, make the most of one's looks with the help of the right food and aids for skin problems, spend leisure time and "everything you need to know about travel by car, plane, bus, ship and rail."

Medical Care, 1970. 36 p. 40¢ (cat. no. HE3.2:M46/8) Supt. of Documents, GPO, Washington, D.C. 20402.

"The size and shape of the medical care dollar, [a] chart book."

A Miss and Her Money, 1971. 24 p. Free. Institute of Life Insurance, 277 Park Ave., New York, N.Y. 10017.

How a young woman should wisely spend and save her money.

Modern Consumer Education. 1970. $274.00 with player; $249.00 without player. 39 lessons, 27 programmed texts, 12 audio cassettes, 2 filmstrips, 180 student record books, answer key cards, wall chart, and instructor's manual with a 33 1/3 rpm record. Grolier Educational Corporation, 845 Third Ave., New York, N.Y. 10022.

Six units covering Food, Clothing, and Shelter; Cars, Furniture, and Appliances; Protecting Family Health and Security; You and the Law; Ways to Handle Money; and Ways to Shop. Conductive to self-instruction. Created originally for the Job Corps under a U.S. Government contract.

Money and Credit Management Education. 1970. 16 p. Free. National Consumer Finance Association, 1000 16th St., N.W., Washington, D.C. 20036.

A descriptive catalog of educational materials for the classroom teacher or counselor.

Money Talk, 1968. $5.00. National Board, YWCA, 600 Lexington Ave., New York, N.Y. 10022.

Kit contains a 30 minute LP record discussing consumer loans, installment buying, and consumer gyps; a group of government consumer pamphlets, a bibliography and film list for consumer groups.

No Smoking Pamphlets, 1967. 65¢ per kit. Supt. of Documents, GPO, Washington, D.C. 20402.

A portfolio of five pamphlets "for parents, teenagers, grade school children on why and how to avoid smoking." Sample pamphlets from this kit are annotated elsewhere in this bibliography. Each is available for separate purchase.

The Nutrition Ladder, n.d. 12 p. Free. Florida Citrus Commission,

Institutional and School Marketing Dept., Lakeland, Fla. 33802.

One of several aids distributed by the Commission. Teaches the role of vitamin C and other nutrients in good dietary habits.

1968-1969 Catalog of Teaching Aids on Life and Health Insurance and Money Management, 1968. 14 p. Free. Educational Division, Institute of Life Insurance, 277 Park Ave., New York, N.Y. 10017.

Listings include pamphlets, leaflets, booklets, filmstrips, and motion pictures on money management and health and life insurance.

Personal Money Management, 1970. 63 p. Free. Marketing/ Savings Division, American Bankers Association, 90 Park Ave., New York, N.Y. 10016.

Simply writtten booklet on money management for high school and adult students.

The Poor Don't Have to Pay More, 1970. 4 p. Apply for Price. Bay Area Neighborhood Development, 4801 Central Ave., Richmond, Calif. 94804.

One of a series of pamplets for low-income consumers. Available in Spanish. Write for catalogue and current price list.

Resource Kit for Teaching Consumer Education. $22.50. Changing Times Educational Service, 1729 H St., N.W., Washington, D.C. 20006.

A teaching kit with five consumer topics: Earning, Spending, Borrowing, Saving, and Budgeting. A teaching guide is provided.

Savings—the Salvation of Mankind, 1968. 10 p. 10¢. Invest-in-America Council, 121 South Broad St., Philadelphia, Pa. 19102.

One of seven "Money in Motion" booklets distributed by the Council. Together they constitute a basic course in the principles and methods of capital formation.

Sears Hidden Values Series. 10 booklets. Free. Consumer Information Services, Sears Roebuck and Co., Dept. 703, Public Relations, Chicago, Ill. 60611.

Complimentary set available to educators. Covers such consumer topics as furniture, bathrooms, floor coverings, fashions. Each booklet has hints for purchasing and maintenance. Available in quantities at a minimal charge.

Self-Correcting Problems in Personal Finance, by Robert Dolphin, Jr., 1970. 129 p. $2.50 (text ed.) Allyn & Bacon, Rockleigh, N.J.

A programmed student workbook surveying eighteen areas of personal finance. Among the areas covered are budgeting, insurance, consumer purchasing power, and personal income tax.

Shoppers Almanac, by Donald Smith, 1969. 264 p. $1.69 +15¢ for handling. Consumer Publishing Co., 26 Park Place, Paramus, N.J. 07652.

"A quick method of price weight comparison." Provides information on coding and dating. Two hundred and thirty-one pages are price—weight comparison tables.

Smart Spending. 1971. $65.00. Recordings, filmstrips, documents, supplemental materials. Olcott Forward, Inc. 234 N. Central Ave., Hartsdale, New York, 10530.

A multimedia instructional unit for secondary school classes, stressing personal values, self-identity, and concepts leading to decision-making skills based on real life experiences. Developed in cooperation with the Better Business Bureau of Metropolitan New York.

Socio-Economic Aspects of Money Management, 1971. 6 p. Free. Women's Division, Institute of Life Insurance, 277 Park Ave., New York, N.Y. 10017.

A short bibliography of materials of interest to finance and consumer specialists.

The Story of Checks, 4th ed., 1970. 21 p. Free. Public Information Dept., Federal Reserve Bank of New York, 33 Liberty St., New York, N.Y. 10045.

A comic book description of checks and the Federal Reserve System. Available in classroom supply quantity. Suitable for grades 6–10.

Supplementary Consumer Bibliography, edited by Stewart Lee, 1970. 16 p. $1.00. Stewart Lee, Geneva College, Beaver Falls, Pa. 15010.

One of the leading authorities of the literature of consumer information edits a bibliography of more than one hundred valuable resource items. Mr. Lee is editor of the American Council on Consumer Interests' *Newsletter*.

Teaching Aids from Procter and Gamble. Free. Procter and Gamble Co., Public Relations Dept., P.O. Box 599, Cincinnati, Ohio 45201.

Five units on laundering, home care, personal grooming, and foods. Each unit consists of teacher materials, visuals, and leaflets for high school students.

A Teacher's Guide on Cooperative Enterprise in the American Economy, 1967. 53 p. $1.00. Cooperative League of the USA, 59 E. Van Buren St., Chicago, Ill. 60605.

For use in the upper high school grades and in colleges.

Teachers Guide, Teaching Taxes Program, 31 p. Free. (Publication 19) Internal Revenue Service, Department of the Treasury, Washington, D.C. 20224 or local Internal Revenue Office.

Contains background information, sample lesson plans in a teaching taxes unit for young adults and adults. Also available, free, are student texts, *Understanding Taxes*, Publication 21 covering general tax information and Publication 22 containing additional material devoted to farm tax problems.

Teacher's Kit: a One Week Advanced Teaching Unit on Consumer Credit. $1.00. National Consumer Finance Association, Educational Services Division, 1000 16th St., N.W., Washington, D.C. 20036.

A selection of classroom aids for teaching a one week course on consumer finance at the high school level. Includes a teacher's manual and sample tests.

Teaching Social Living Skills, 1968. $18. National Association for Public Continuing & Adult Education and the National Education Association, 1201 16th St., N.W., Washington, D.C. 20036.

Kit designed to help the wage earner spend his money more wisely and to alert him to the high cost of credit. Includes teacher's manual, lesson plans and worksheets, *Shopping for Money* transparency masters and text, filmstrip and manual for *Getting Credit* with tape-recorded narration, and 25 33 1/3 rpm, 7″ discs (plastic) on *Getting Credit* and *Banking Services*.

Today's Economics: Case Studies for Student Understanding, 1965. 64 p. 35¢. American Education Publications, Education Center, Columbus, Ohio 43216.

An American Education Publications Unit Book. Examples and illustrations designed to serve as classroom aids in describing basic economic decision-making.

Understanding Economics. 10 booklets, discussion group kit, Eco-tape set (parts sold separately). Apply for price. Chamber of Commerce of the United States of America, 1615 H St., N.W., Washington, D.C. 20006.

Materials designed for use with a discussion group covering the broad areas of economics, finance, production, government and the economy, and science and the economy. Booklets provide a basis for the discussion and list a short bibliography in each field. Booklets are approximately thirty-five pages in length.

Using Bank Services, 1969. 40 p. Free. American Bankers Association, 1120 Connecticut Ave., N.W., Washington, D.C. 20036.

Bank services for individuals, families, businesses and government.

Using Our Credit Intelligently, by William J. Cheyney, rev. 1970. 54 p. Apply for price. National Foundation for Consumer Credit, Inc. 1819 H Street, N.W., Washington, D.C. 20006.

Booklet designed for high school and young adults.

Volunteer Income Tax Assistance Program (VITA), Internal Revenue Service U.S. Department of the Treasury. VITA materials available free at District Offices of Internal Revenue Service.

A self-instructional course for volunteers who can help low-income, the elderly and other citizens prepare tax returns. Annual revisions.

Your Credit Health. 1971. 5 p. 9¢. Department of Education and Research, Credit Counseling Centers, Inc., 17000 West Eight Mile Road, Suite 280, Southfield, Michigan 48075.

One of a series of pamphlets on money management. Others in the series available at the same price are: *Living Better for Less, Teaching Children to Manage Their Money, Eating Better for Less, Your Gift Planning Guide,* and *Savings Makes Dollars and Sense.*

SPANISH TEACHING AIDS

Gastos y entradas (Money Management)

¡**Cuidado! Es su Dinero,** s.a. [12] p. Gratis. Federal Trade Commission, 26 Federal Plaza, New York, N.Y. 10007.

"Debe comparar precios y mercancías y asegurarse de que consigue más por su dinero, especialmente cuando compra a crédito."

"You should compare prices, merchandise, and make sure you're getting more for your money, especially when buying on credit."

El Ahorro, por Carmen P. Busquets, 1969. 5 p. Gratis. Servicio de Extensión Agricola, Universidad de Puerto Rico, Box AR, Río Piedras, Puerto Rico.

Razones por las cuales se debe ahorrar, principios que deben tenerse en cuenta y características de las distintas instituciones en que puede colocarse el dinero.

Reasons for saving. The different institutions where you can save your money.

Lista de Publicaciones para Agricultores, Amas de Casa, Juventudes de Puerto Rico, 1969. 13 p. Gratis. Servicio de

Extension Agrícola, Universidad de Puerto Rico, Apartado AR, Río Piedras, Puerto Pico 00928.

Bibliografía de las publicaciones del Servicio de Extensión Agrícola de la Universidad de Puerto Rico.

Bibliography of publications of the extension service of Dept. of Agriculture of the University of Puerto Rico.

Plan de Gastos y Entradas del Hogar, por Carmen P. Busquets, s.a. 16 p. Gratis. Servicio de Extensión Agrícola, Universidad de Puerto Rico, Box AR, Río Piedras, Puerto Rico.

Cómo trazar el presupuesto familiar por un año e instrucciones para la distribución de los gastos. Muy detallado y completo.

How to make a family budget for one year and instructions for the distribution of expenses. Very detailed and complete.

Utilice Bien su Dinero, por Carmen T. P. Busquets, 1970. 8 p. Gratis. Servicio de Extensión Agrícola, Universidad de Puerto Rico, Box AR, Río Piedras, Puerto Rico.

Cómo utilizar sabiamente el dinero con un plan de gastos y entradas para poder llevar una vida mejor.

How to utilize your money wisely with a plan for expenses and income to be able to lead a better life.

Ventajas y Limitaciones del Plan de Gastos y Entradas en el Hogar, por Carmen P. Busquets, 1969. 4 p. Gratis. Servicio de Extensión Agrícola, Universidad de Puerto Rico, Box AR, Río Piedras, Puerto Rico.

Utilidad de un presupuesto familiar de acuerdo con las entradas.

Annoted advantages and limitations of the Expense and Income Plan of the Home.

Credito (Credit)

Acta de la Union de Credito Federal y Estatutos Afines, Segun Reformada Hasta el 1 de Agosto, 1968, 1970. 24 p. 55¢ (cat. no. HE3.305:F31/968 Spanish) Supt. of Documents, GPO, Washington, D.C. 20402.

Contiene las disposiciones del Acta de la Unión de Crédito Federal (acta del 26 de junio, 1934), a segun fue reformada hasta el 1 de agosto, 1968, y ostros estatutos pertinentes.

Act of the Federal Credit Union

Como Determinar el Costo del Credito, 1969. 4 p. Gratis. Servicio de Extensión Agrícola, Universidad de Puerto Rico, Box AR, Río Piedras, Puerto Rico.

Fórmula para determinar el costo real de un artículo comprado a crédito.

How to determine the cost of credit.

¿Compra usted Ahora y Paga Despues?, s.a. [1] p. Gratis. Sales Finance Division, State Banking Department, 100 Church Street, New York, N.Y. 10007.

Breve información sobre las leyes que protegen al consumidor que compra a plazos.

Brief information on laws that protect the customer that buys on credit.

Credito al Consumidor, por Carmen P. Busquets, 1970. 8 p. Gratis. Servicio de Extensión Agrícola, Universidad de Puerto Rico, Box AR, Río Piedras, Puerto Rico.

Cuándo se justifica comprar a crédito y explicación detallada de cómo hacer uso del mismo y de sus variaciones.

When should you buy on credit and a detailed explanation on how to use it.

¿Debe Usted Usar su Credito?, 1969. 4 p. Gratis. Servico de Extensión Agrícola, Universidad de Puerto Rico, Box AR. Río Piedras, Puerto Rico.

Razones para usar el crédito y razones para no usarlo. Preguntas que debe un comprador hacerse antes de utilizar su crédito o pedir dinero prestado.

Reasons for using credit. Questions that a buyer should ask before using his credit or asking for a loan.

Guia Rapida Para Credito Al Consumidor, 1965. 5¢. Superintendent of Documents, Washington, D.C. 20402.

Folleto aconsejando al consumidor sobre el crédito.

Pamphlet advising the consumer on credit.

Las Compras al Contado, por Carmen P. Busquets, 1969. 4 p. Gratis. Servicio de Extensión Agrícola, Universidad de Puerto Rico, Box AR, Río Piedras, Puerto Rico.

Recomendaciones respecto a las ventas y desventajas de comprar al contado.

Recommendations on the advantages and disadvantages on buying by cash.

¿Piensa Usted Comprar a **Plazos?,** rev. 1967. 23 p. Gratis. New York State Banking Department, 100 Church Street, New York, N.Y. 10007.

Información bastante complete acerca de las distintas clases de ventas a crédito, haciendo énfasis en los derechos y obligaciones del comprador y en la importancia de un cuidadoso estudio del contrato. Contiene un cuadro de reembolsos.

Information on the different kinds of credit.

¿Que es Credito?, 1969. 4 p. Gratis. Servicio de Extensión Agrícola, Universidad de Puerto Rico, Box AR, Río Piedras, Puerto Rico.

Explicación de lo que es el crédito y de las obligaciones de quienes lo utilizan.

Explanation of credit.

Reglamento Union de Credito Federal, Agosto de 1968, 1968. 23 p. 30¢ (cat. no. FS3.302: B99/970) Supt. of Documents, GPO, Washington, D.C. 20402.

Alcance de las actividades de la unión de crédito y sus poderes así como las obligaciones y responsabilidades de sus funcionarios.

Regulations of federal credit unions.

Sea precavido, Consulte la Guia de Credito Rapido al Consumidor, 1964. [2] p. 5¢ (Cat no. A1.11/3:C86) Supt. of Documents, Washington, D.C. 20402. (100 ejemplares $2.50).

Detalles para ayudar a comprender mejor el sistema de ventas a crédito y a plazos, así como los procedimientos para obtener crédito.

Details to help understand the system of credit sales and the procedures on how to obtain credit.

Una Vida Mejor por Medio de las Cooperativas Federales de Credito, 1962. [1] p. 5¢. Supt. of Documents, GPO, Washington 25, D.C. (100 ejemplares por $3.00).

Funcionamiento, ventajas y organización de las Cooperativas Federales de Crédito.

Functions, advantages and organizations of the Federal Cooperative Credit.

Union de Credito Federal, Reglamentos y Regulaciones, Agosto 1969, 1969. 30 p. 40¢ (Cat. no. HE3.306:F31/2/969) Supt. of Documents, Washington, D.C. 20402.

Edición revisada a fin de que con-
tenga las últimas modificaciones.

Federal credit union rules and regulations.

Compras (Shopping)

Actua de Acuerdo con la Realidad, c. 1969. 14 p. 25¢. Good Reading Communications, Inc., 505 Eight Ave. New York, N.Y. 10019.

Necesidad de hacer un cuidadoso examen antes de realizar una compra a plazos y consejos para comprar artículos de calidad a su justo precio.

Analyze purchasing decisions.

Almidones, por Carmen T. P. de Busquets, 1969. 4 p. Gratis. Servicio de Extensión Agrícola, Universidad de Puerto Rico, Box AR, Río Piedras, Puerto Rico.

Diferentes usos del almidón y distintos tipos existentes en el mercado.

Different uses of starch and the different types in the market.

Blanqueadores, por Carmen T. P. de Busquets, 1969. 3 p. Gratis. Servicio de Extensión Agrícola, Universidad de Puerto Rico, Box AR, Río Piedras, Puerto Rico.

Características de las distintas clases de blanqueadores y recomendaciones para su uso.

Different kinds of whiteners and recommendations for their use.

Combata el Fraude, s.a. [1] p. Gratis. Harlem Consumer Education Council, 2325 Seventh Avenue (planta baja), New York, N.Y. 10132.

Ocho reglas para comprar inteligentemente tanta en la puertoa de la casa como en la calle.

Rules for protection from fraudulent sales practices, including dishonest door to door sales.

¡Comprador Sea Precavido!, por Sidney Margolius, 1970. 12 p. 25¢ (Asuntos Públicos, Panfleto no. 382) Public Affairs Committee, 381 Park Avenue South, New York, N.Y. 10016. (Tarifas reducidas para más de nueve ejemplares).

Cómo comprar artículos de calidad sin pagar más de lo que valen y de acuerdo a un presupuesto familiar.

How to buy articles of quality without paying more than what they are worth.

Corte y Confeccion, c. 1966. 491 p. $1.90. Meredith Publishing Co., 1946 E., 6th, S., Salt Lake City, Utah 84102.

Este libro proporciona información muy útil acerca de qué clase de telas y patrones comprar, cómo comprobar su calidad y cómo adaptarlos a las necesidades de cada cual. También ofrece muchas ideas para comprar ropa barata, ya confeccionada, y darle una apariencia mejor.

Book on clothing. Includes information on buying patterns, comparison shopping for fabrics, and hints on purchasing ready-made clothes.

Cosmeticos, (1) p. Gratis. Departamento de Alimentos y Drogas (FDA), U.S. Dept. of Health, Education, & Welfare, Washington, D.C. 20204.

Información sobre el uso de cosmeticos.

Information on the use of cosmetics.

Cuidado y Limpieza del Hogar, por Annie Fabre, c.1964. 155 p. $3.50. Editorial Juventud, Calle Proenza 101, Barcelona 15, España.

Cuando se consulta este libro se aprenden las más variadas formas de cuidar, limpiar y renovar los artículos del hogar de modo económico y eficaz, sin necesidad de recurrir a la compra de productos muy costosos.

Different ways of caring for the home.

144

El Libro del Auto, por Alexandre Spoerl, c.1965. 271 p. $2.50. Ediciones Daimon, Manuel Tamayo, Provenza 284, Barcelona.

Contiene advertencias y consejos sobre las acechanzas que aguardan a los compradores de automóviles desde que lo adquieren hasta que lo revenden, incluyendo como evitar caer en las manos de un mal técnico a la hora de repararlo.

Contains advice for the buyers of automobiles.

El Mundo Loco de las Ollas y Cacerolas, por Amelita V. Reyna, 1970. 6 p. Gratis. Servicio de Extensión Agrícola, Universidad de Puerto Rico, Box AR, Río Piedras, Puerto Rico.

Distintas clases de enseres de cocina que un ama de casa puede adquirir en el mercado. Descripción de los materiales de que están hechos, sus características y guía para cuidarlos.

Different kinds of cooking utensils for the homemakers. Description of the construction materials.

El Senor y la Senora Perez Resuelven el Misterio del Precio, c. 1966. [4] p. Bay Area Neighborhood Development, 4801 Central Ave., Richmond, Calif. 94804.

Historieta ilustrada sobre cómo averiguar el precio correcto que debe pagarse por un artículo. Escriba pidiendo el catálogo y la lists de precios.

An illustrated booklet on how to get the best price for an article.

Juego para Analizar al Consumidor, s.a. [6] Gratis. Departamento de Comercio del Estado de Nueva York, Programa Femenino.

Doce preguntas para comprobar la habilidad de una compradora.

Game with 12 questions to analyze the consumer.

Obtenga Valor Completo por su Dolar, s.a. [1] p. Gratis. Department of Consumer Affairs, 80 Lafayette Street, New York, N.Y. 10013.

Veinte puntos para economizar dinero al hacer las compras.

20 points to economize while shopping.

Pinte y Barnice Usted Mismo, por Louis Morréel, 2a., ed., 1965. 64 p. $1.25. (Colección "Hágalo usted mismo") Espasa-Calpe, Río Rosas 26, Madrid.

Distintos tipos de pinturas y brochas que deben adquirirse según la superficie sobre la que se vayan a utilizar. Limpieza y conservación de brochas y accesorios.

Different types of paints and brushes to buy and instructions on how to keep them.

¡Pregunte! Cuando Compre un Automovil, 1971. 4 p. 10¢ Office of Consumer Affairs, order from Supt. of Documents, GPO, Washington, D.C. 20402.

Folleto con sugestiónes en como comprar un autómovil y con énfasis en como comprar a crédito y también el precio del automóvil.

Information on buying an automobile.

Progreso en la Proteccion del Consumidor: Su Guia Para una Compra Cuidadosa. [1] p. Gratis. Estado de Nueva York, Departamento de Leyes, 80 Centre Street, New York, N.Y. 10013.

Diez consejos para evitar ser engañado al efectuar una compra e información acerca de cómo la Oficina de Protección al Consumidor Contra Fraudes protege al ciudadano.

Ten rules to avoid being cheated when buying.

¿Quien Toca a su Puerta?, c. 1966. [4] p. Bay Area Neighborhood Development. 4801 Central Ave., Richmond, Calif. 94804.

Historieta ilustrada que explica lo que debe hacerse cuando un vendedor toca a la puerta. Escriba pidiendo el catálogo y la lesta de precios.

Hints on shopping with door to door salesmen.

Sea un buen Comprador, por Judith Fías Ramírez, 1969. 7 p. Gratis. Servicio de Extensión Agrícola, Universidad de Puerto Rico, Box AR, Río Piedras, Puerto Rico.

Magnífico folleto para ayudar a hacer una buena compra, con recomendaciones para comprobar precios y calidad, para saber leer las garantías y las etiquetas y para aprovechar las ventas especiales.

Booklet to help when shopping, with recommendations to verify prices and quality. Information on how to read quarantees and labels and to profit by sale specials.

Seleccion, Uso y Cuidado del Aspirador de Polvo, por Andreita V. Reina, 1969. 6 p. Gratis. Servicio de Extensión Agrícola, Universidad de Puerto Rico, Box AR, Rio Piedras, Puerto Rico.

Diversas clases de aspiradores de polvo, su funcionamiento y características que deben tenerse en cuenta al comprarlos.

A selection, use and care of vacuum cleaners.

Tu Hogar, por G. Oheim, 4a. ed. 1967. p. 51–69. $6.00. Ediciones Daimon, Manuel Tamayo, Provenza 284, Madrid.

En el capítulo titulado El arte de comprar bien, se ofrecen normas básicas para aprender a comprar alimentos y artículos para el hogar, así como consejos para distribuirlos y conservarlos de modo que rindan lo más posible.

Book on ways to buy food and articles for the home.

Uso y Cuidado de la Plancha Electrica, por César Maldonado

Sierra, 1969. 8 p. Gratis. Servicio de Extensión Agrícola, Universidad de Puerto Rico, Box AR, Río Piedras, Puerto Rico.

Orientaciones sobre las distintas clases de planchas eléctricas, su funcionamiento y datos sobre su uso y cuidado.

Information on the different kinds of electric irons, their funcitons and data on their use and care.

Alimentos (Food)

¡Ahorre! Compre en Temporada, s.a. Gratis. Department of Consumer Affairs, 80 Lafayette Street, New York, N.Y. 10013.

Como escoger frutas y vegetales de acuerdo a la temporada del año.

How to select fruits and vegetables in accordance with the time of year.

Cocina Hispanoamericana. c. 1967. 399 p. $4.50. Ediciones Garriga, Paris 143, Barcelona.

Libro bilingüe muy valioso para el ama de casa hispana residente en EE.UU. pues indica la forma de adaptar los productos norteamericanos a los platos hispanos. Muy útil a la hora de comprar los alimentos.

Bilingual book for the Spanish-American housewife who lives in the U.S. It shows the housewife how to use North-American products.

Consuma Diariamente los Cuatro Alimentos Basicos, s.a. Carteles (18'X36') y (12'X6'). Gratis. Del Monte Corporation, P.O. Box 3575, San Francisco, California 94119.

Los cuatro grupos de alimentos básicos que no deben faltar en la comida diaria presentados en forma muy atractiva y con gran colorido. En el reverso del cartel más pequeño hay una información muy exacta y concisa de los productos incluidos en cada grupo.

The Four Basic Food Groups.

Defienda su Dinero al Comprar Alimentos, 1969. Hoja suelta. Gratis. Servicio de Extensión Agrícola, Universidad de Puerto Rico, Box AR, Río Piedras, Puerto Rico.

Información sobre cómo comprar los productos alimenticios de forma que rindan más y cuesten menos.

Information on how to buy food products for less.

El Mercadeo de Nuestros Alimentos, 1970. 3 p. Gratis. Servicio de Extensión Agrícola, Universidad de Puerto Rico, Box AR, Río Piedras, Puerto Rico.

Explicación del proceso y manipulación de un alimento hasta que llega a su mesa.

Explanation of the process and distribution of food before it gets to our table.

Los Patos A Distancia, 23 p. 30¢. Superintendent of Documents, U.S. Government Printing Office, Washington, D.C.   20402.

Guía para la identificación de aves acuáticas.

Guide for the identification of acuatic birds.

¿Invierte Usted Bien su Dinero al Comprar Alimentos?, por Nilda O. Muriente, 1969. 4 p. Gratis. Servicio de Extensión Agrícola, Universidad de Puerto Rico, Box AR, Río Piedras, Puerto Rico.

Consejos para antes de comprar alimentos, para el momento de comprarlos y para conservarlos el mayor tiempo posible en buen estado.

Hints for buying and caring for food.

Las Etiquetas le Ayudan a Comprar, 1969. 4 p. Gratis. Servicio de Extensión Agrícola, Universidad de Puerto Rico, Box AR, Río Piedras, Puerto Rico.

Información acerca de los productos enlatados y de los requisitos que la ley obliga a cumplir a los empacadores para proteger la salud de los consumidores.

Information on canned product labels.

Lo que debe dar de Comer a su Familia, c. 1968. 5 p. Gratis. National Dairy Council, Chicago, Ill. 60606.

Comidas sanas y nutritivas que el organismo necesita diariamente. Ilustrado. Adaptado a las posibilidades de una familia de escasos recursos.

Leaflet on nutritious foods that the body needs daily.

El Niño De Uno A Seis Años, 1961. 192 p. Comité Interdepartamental de Cooperación Cientifica y cultural por el Servicio de Lenguas Extranjeras de la Secretaría de Estado de los Estados Unidos, Washington, D.C.

Éste libro, cubre las cosas importantes que los padres necesitan considerar según su hijo va pasando de la infancia a la niñez.

This book covers the important things that parents need to know as their child passes from infancy to childhood.

Saneamiento en el Departamento de Carnes, 1968. 6 p. Gratis. Supermarket Institute, Inc., 200 East, Ontario Street, Chicago, Illinois 60611.

Instrucciones para un saneamiento eficiente del departamento de carnes y ventajas que ello representa.

Instructions for sanitary efficiency in the meat department.

Una Guia Para Comer Bien, 3era. ed. 1968. Carteles (8½' X 11') y (18' X 28'). Gratis. National Dairy Council, Chicago, Ill. 60606.

Alimentos que deben comerse diariamente para mantenerse en buena salud. En la parte del frente tienen fotos en colores de los principales productos, y en el reverso del cartel más pequeño hay una información muy detallada sobre las características y propiedades de cada grupo alimenticio.

Foods that should be eaten daily to maintain good health.

El Primer Año De Vida De Su Bebe, 1969. 28 p. 20¢. Superintendent of Documents, U.S. Government Printing Office, Washington, D.C. 20402.

Éste corto folleto, ilustrado, sobre el cuidado de un bebé durante su primer año de vida, está diseñado para leerse con facilidad y cubre los puntos más importantes del buen cuidado del bebé.

Pamphlet on baby's care during his first year.

Salud (Health)

Aborto, s.a. [15] p. Gratis. Inter-Agency Council on Family Planning, New York (Distributed by Planned Parenthood of New York City, Inc., 300 Park Ave. South, New York, N.Y. 10010.

Datos claros y precisos, en forma de cuestionarío, acerca de cuándo, dónde, y cuánto cuesta hacerse un aborto en el Estado de Nueva York.

Data in question form on costs, how, and where to get an abortion in the State of New York.

Datos Sobre el Habito de Fumar y la Salud, rev. 1970. 12 p. (cat. no. HE 20.2602:Sm 7/4 Spanish) Supt. of Documents, GPO, Washington, D.C. 20402).

Sumario sobre lo que hasta el momento se conoce en relación con el hábito de fumar y la salud. Ultimas investigaciones científicas, índice de mortalidad y relaciones entre diversas enfermedades y el tabaco.

Summary on what is known about cigarette smoking and health.

El Problema Del Retraso Mental, 1970. 19 p. 20¢. Superintendent of Documents, U.S. Government Printing Office, Washington, D.C. 20402.

Folleto para intreducir el problema del retraso mental. Está ideado para ahondar en la comprención de los problemas que afectan a los retrasados mentales y para fortalecer nuestro empeño en encontrar soluciones para ellos.

Pamphlet to introduce the problem of mental retardation.

Mientras Su Bebé Está En Camino, 1969. 29 p. 20¢. Superintendent of Documents, U.S. Government Printing Office, Washington, D.C. 20402.

Este librito, relacinado con el cuidado de la madre encinta, es para leerse detenidamente y cubre los puntos mas importantes de su cuidado.

This booklet is in relation to the care of the mother to be. It covers the most important points of prenatal care.

Su Hijo De Uno A Tres Años, 1968. 21 p. 20¢. Superintendent of Documents, U.S. Government Printing Office, Washington, D.C. 20402.

Éste corto folleto, cubre la mayor parte de las cosas importantes que los padres necesitan considerar según su hijo va pasando de la infancia a la niñez.

Leaflet on child's care from 1 to 3 years.

Envases De Alimentos, (1) p. Gratis. Departamento de Alimentos y Drogas (FDA) U.S. Dept. of Health, Education, & Welfare, Washington, D.C. 20204.

Explicación de alimentos en envases de lata.

Leaflet on the explanation of canned food.

Usted y Estampillas Para Alimentos, (4) p. Gratis. U.S. Department of Agriculture, Food & Nutrition Service. FNS-5.

Éste folleto explica como podra recibir estampillas para alimentos.

This pamphlet explains how you can receive food stamps.

Derechos (Rights & Remedies)

¡A Sequrese bien . . . antes de Firmar Contratos!, 1971. 4 p. 10¢ Office of Consumer Affairs, order from Supt. of Documents, GPO, Washington, D.C. 20402.

"Lea también la letra pequeña."

"Read every word—even the small print"

Como Entablar un Debate ante la Corte de Pequenas Reclamaciones de la Ciudad de Nueva York, por Sue R. Prenner, 1970. 29 p. Gratis. Department of Consumer Affairs, 80 Lafayette Street, New York, N.Y. 10013.

Información detallada, sencilla y clara sobre el procedimiento que debe seguirse para entablar una demanda por una cantidad no mayor de $300 sin necesidad de abogado. El Apéndice A incluye mapas que señalan las rutas hacia las cortes y el Apéndice B contiene las direciones de los oficiales de la Corte.

Information on using the Small Claims Court in New York City.

Conociendo los Nuevos Textiles. n.p. Gratis. J. C. Penney y Compania, Relaciones Educativas, 1301 Avenue of the Americas, New York, N.Y. 10019.

Fibras naturales, fibras sinteticas, fibras artificiales.

Information on natural fibres, synthetic fibres, and artificial fibres.

Conozca sus Derechos, lo que una Esposa que Trabaja debe Saber Sobre sus Derechos, 1967. 14 p. 15¢ (cat. no. L13.11:39–A) Supt. of Documents, GPO, Washington, D.C. 20402.

Guía general en forma de preguntas y repuestas sobre los derechos de una mujer casada en relación con la propiedad, el matrimonio, el divorcio y las relaciones entre padres e hijos de acuerdo con las leyes en vigor.

General guide in question and answer form on the rights of a working wife in relation to property, marriage, and divorce.

Direcciones para Tareas Domesticas—Una Quia Facil. s.a. 62 p. Gratis. Soap and Detergent Association, 475 Park Ave., South, New York, N.Y. 10016.

"Es más fácil mantener la casa lempia cuando se hace un plan para cada tarea de limpieza."

Annoted directions for domestic tasks— an easy guide.

Doce Secretos para la Buena Compra de los Viveres, 1966. 4 p. Gratis. Bay Area Neighborhood Development. 4801 Central Ave., Richmond, Calif. 94804.

Doce consejos illustrados sobre como comprar víveres de buena calidad a bajo precio.

Twelve hints for the thrifty shopper.

¿Espere! Que Esta Firmando? 1966. 4 p. Gratis. Bay Area Neighborhood Development, 4801 Central Ave., Richmond, Calif. 94804.

Qué debe hacerse para saber a qué se compromete un comprador cuando firma un contrato.

Things to know when you sign a contract.

¿Quien Toca?, 1971. 4 p. 10¢. Office of Consumer Affairs, Order from Supt. of Documents, GPO, Washington, D.C. 20402.

"Cuando un extraño toca a su puerta, probablemente es un vendedor" recuerde "¡Nunca tema decir no!"

Hints on buying from door to door salesmen.

FREE AND INEXPENSIVE MATERIALS

Bibliographies

Bibliography of Publications, 1971. 19 p. Free. National Canners Association, 1133 20th St., N.W., Washington, D.C. 20036.

An annotated guide to the publications of the Association. Teachers will especially want to examine p. 8–13. Materials will interest all grade levels from elementary through college.

Bibliography on Marketing to Low-Income Consumers, 1969. 49 p. 55¢ (Dept. of Commerce, Business and Defense Services Administration, cat. no. C-41.12: M34/4) Supt. of Documents, GPO, Washington, D.C. 20402.

Surveys two hundred and thirty-six items treating of many aspects of marketing to lower income groups. Includes many periodical references.

Catalog of Teaching Aids on Life and Health Insurance and Money Management, 1968–1969. 14 p. Free. Educational Division, Institute of Life Insurance, Health Insurance Institute, 277 Park Ave., New York, N.Y. 10017.

Annotated lists of material available to instructors.

Consumer Information, Price List 86, 5th Ed. 1971. Supt. of Documents, GPO, Washington, D.C. 20402.

Selected list of Federal publications concerning consumer problems and interests.

Consumer Information Series. Single copies free. $4.00 per 100; $30.00 per 1,000. Council of Better Business Bureaus, 1101 17th St., N.W. Washington, D.C. 20036.

A series of fold-out six page booklets devoted to such general topics as *Homework Schemes; Unordered Merchandise; Truth in Lending.* Sample titles are annotated elsewhere in this bibliography.

Consumer Product Information, 1971. 15 p. Free. Consumer Product Information Distribution Center, Washington, D.C. 20407.

An index of selected Federal publications on consumer products.

Educators Guide(s)

The guides listed below give sources of materials for classroom use. They are arranged by broad curricular areas with subject and title indexes and an index to sources, which gives addresses, terms and conditions, and probable availability of loan. Pagination and price vary; recent editions range from 170 to 798 pages and cost $5.75–$9. The guides are available from Educators Progress Service, Randolph, Wis. 53956.

Educators Grade Guide to Free Teaching Aids. 1st+ ed.; 1955+ loose-leaf. annual.

Educators Guide to Free Films. 1st+ ed.; 1941+ annual.

Educators Guide to Free Filmstrips. 1st+ ed.; 1949+ annual.

Educators Guide to Free Guidance Materials. 1st+ ed.; 1962+ annual.

Educators Guide to Free Health, Physical Education and Recreation Materials. 1st+ ed.; 1968+ annual.

Educators Guide to Free Science Materials. 1st+ ed.; 1960+ annual.

Educators Guide to Free Social Studies Materials. 1st+ ed.; 1961+ annual.

Educators Guide to Free Tapes, Scripts and Transcriptions. 1st+ ed.; 1955+ annual.

Educators Index of Free Materials.
(Mar.) 1937+ issued in card form.

*Elementary Teachers' Guide to Free
Curriculum Materials.* 1st+ ed.; 1944+
annual.

Free and Inexpensive Educational Aids, by Thomas J. Pepe.

3d rev. ed., 1966. 175 p. $1.75.
Dover Publications, New York.

An annotated list of materials grouped
by such topics as agriculture, arts,
business, energy and fuels, and transportation. Grade level is indicated. Index of audiovisual aids and general
index are included.

Free and Inexpensive Learning Materials, 13th ed., 1966. 267 p.

$2.00. George Peabody College
for Teachers, Division of Surveys and Field Services, Nashville, Tenn.

Free and Inexpensive Material, 1969. 91 p. $1.00. Council for

Family Financial Education,
Twin Towers, Silver Spring, Md.
20910.

An annotated bibliography for teaching consumer education and financial
planning.

Free for Housewives, by Mark

Milton, 1970. 190 p. 60¢ (paper).
Ace Publishing Corp., 1120 Avenue of the Americas, New York,
N.Y. 10036.

Free for Teens, by Mark Milton,

1969. n.p. 60¢ (paper) Ace Publishing Corp., 1120 Avenue of
the Americas, New York, N.Y.
10036.

Free Learning Material for

Classroom Use, by Guy W.
Wagner and Darlon Mork, 1967.
75 p. $1.50. Extension Service,
State College of Iowa, Cedar
Falls, Iowa 50613.

Free Material for Earth Science Teachers, by W. Matthews and

R. Bartholomew, 1964. n.p.
$1.32. Prentice-Hall, Englewood
Cliffs, N.J.

Guide to Student and Consumer Aids, by Theodore J. Halatin,

1968. 88 p. Apply for price. Theodore J. Halatin, Abbey Lane,
Clifton, N.J. 07013.

Guide to 200 Free Periodicals in the Social Sciences, by Steven

E. Goodman, 1970. 32 p. $4.00.
Education and Training Associates, Box 304, Dunellen, N.J.
08812.

Helpful Tax Literature, 1970. 1

p. Free (Publication 610), Internal Revenue Service, Department
of the Treasury, Washington,
D.C. 20224 or local Internal Revenue Office.

List of free publications on specific
tax problems.

1001 Valuable Things You Can Get Free, by Mort Weisinger,

6th ed., 1968. 163 p. 75¢ (paper)
Bantam Books, 271 Madison
Ave., New York, N.Y. 10016.

An annotated list grouped by such
topics as career guidance, benefits for
veterans, scholarships, pets, paintings,
and travel.

Over 2000 Free Publications, by

Frederic J. O'Hara, 1968. 352 p.
95¢ (paper) New American Library, 1301 Avenue of the Americas, New York, N.Y. 10019.

A list of free or inexpensive government publications on a wide variety
of subjects. Includes detailed descriptions of the activities and functions
of the units of government and how
they can benefit the public.

The Poor, a Selected Bibliography, 1969. 56 p. 60¢ (cat. no. A1.38:1145). Supt. of Documents, GPO, Washington, D.C. 20402.

Spanning fifteen years, this listing includes citations from the fields of anthropology, demography, economics, physical and mental health, psychology, sociology, and social psychology. An index to authors is included.

Price Lists. Supt. of Documents, GPO, Washington, D.C. 20402.

Frequently revised series of lists of U.S. Government publications by subject (e.g., PL11—home economics, PL-86—Consumer Information PL 50—American history, PL79—aviation). Publications included are topical and currently available; some are inexpensive. The price lists, which include order blanks, are issued free by the Superintendent of Documents, U.S. Government Printing Office, Washington, D.C. 20402.

The biweekly leaflet, *Selected United States Government Publications*, listing current publications on varying topics, is also issued by the Superintendent of Documents.

Selected and Annotated Bibliography of Reference Materials in Consumer Finance, 1968–1969. 32 p. 50¢. Educational Services Division, National Consumer Finance Association, 1000 16th St., N.W., Washington, D.C. 20036.

Includes texts, study guides, pamphlets, films and filmstrips. Primarily for the serious student, the research worker, and professional worker in the field.

Selected Free Materials for Classroom Teachers, edited by Ruth H. Aubrey, 3d ed., 1969. 124 p. $2.00. Fearon Publishers, 2165 Park Blvd., Palo Alto, Calif. 94306.

An annotated list of materials grouped by such topics as agriculture, art, business, health education, music, and social science. Includes grade level, film services, and index. Selected by curriculum specialists in the Division of Education at San Jose State College.

Selected United States Government Publications. Biweekly. 2 p. Free. Supt. of Documents, GPO, Washington, D.C. 20402.

Virtually every issue lists some government publications of interest to consumers.

Sources of Free and Inexpensive Educational Materials, by Esther Dever, 3d ed., 1965. 652 p. $5.25. The author, P.O. Box 186, Grafton, W. Va. 26354.

An annotated list of materials grouped by such topics as astronomy, aviation, chemistry, Indians, languages, photography, steel, and welding. Includes sections on audiovisual aids, fundraising projects, and curriculum aids.

Sources of Free and Inexpensive Pictures for the Classroom, by Robert Bruce Miller, rev. ed., 1965. 31 p. 50¢. The author, Box 369, Riverside, Calif. 92502.

Includes references to illustrations in periodicals.

Sources of Free Pictures, by Merton B. Osborn and Robert Bruce Miller, 1963. 31 p. Apply for price. The authors, Box 369, Riverside, Calif. 92502.

Includes references to illustrations in periodicals.

Vertical File Index. Monthly, except Aug. $8.00. H. W. Wilson, 950 University Ave., Bronx, N.Y. 10452.

A subject and title index to selected pamphlet material, some of which is free or inexpensive.

What Business Teachers Can Get Free! by Theodore J. Sielaff,

1965. 200 p. $3.80. Lansford Press, 2516 Lansford Ave., San Jose, Calif. 95125.

Where to Get and How to Use Free and Inexpensive Teaching Aids, by Robert Schain and Mur-ray Polner, 1963. 63 p. $1.95. Teachers Practical Press. Orders to Atherton Press, New York.

An annotated list of materials grouped by such topics as art, foreign languages, home economics, science, and social studies. Includes a section especially for the elementary school with sample lesson plans. Grade level is indicated.

Land grant universities

Listed below are the land grant universities with Extension offices in each State which provide free and inexpensive Consumer Education materials. Other state offices, such as the Department of Agriculture, Attorney General's Office, consumer protection agencies, Department of Commerce, and Office of Weights and Measures, may also supply free and inexpensive materials to State residents.

Alabama Agricultural and Mechanical College
Normal, Ala. 35762
Richard D. Morrison, President

Auburn University
Auburn, Ala. 36830
Harry M. Philpott, President

University of Alaska
College, Alaska 99701
William R. Wood, President

University of Arizona
Tucson, Ariz. 85721
Richard Harvill, President

Agricultural, Mechanical and Normal College
Pine Bluff, Ark. 71601
Lawrence Davis, President

University of Arkansas
Fayetteville, Ark. 72701
David Mullins, President

University of California
Berkeley, Calif. 94720
Charles J. Hitch, President

Colorado State University
Fort Collins, Colo. 80521
Adrian R. Chamberlain, President

University of Connecticut
Storrs, Conn. 06268
Homer D. Babbidge, President

Delaware State College
Dover, Del. 19901
Luna Issac Mishoe, President

University of Delaware
Newark, Del. 19711
E. Arthur Trabant, President

Federal City College
Washington, D.C. 20001
Harland L. Randolph, President

Florida Agricultural and Mechanical University
Tallahassee, Fla. 32307
Benjamin L. Perry, President

University of Florida
Gainesville, Fla. 32601
Stephen C. O'Connell, President

Fort Valley State College
Fort Valley, Ga. 31030
Waldo W. E. Blanchet, President

University of Georgia
Athens, Ga. 30601
Fred C. Davidson, President

University of Hawaii
Honolulu, Hawaii 96822
Harlan Cleveland, President

University of Idaho
Moscow, Idaho 83843
Earnest W. Hartung, President

University of Illinois
Urbana, Ill. 61801
David D. Henry, President

Purdue University
Lafayette, Ind. 47907
Frederick L. Hovde, President

Iowa State University
Ames, Iowa 50010
W. Robert Parks, President

Kansas State University
Manhattan, Kan. 66502
James A. McCain, President

Kentucky State College
Frankfort, Ky. 40601
Carl M. Hill, President

University of Kentucky
Lexington, Ky. 40506
Otis A. Singlethary, President

Louisiana State University
Baton Rouge, La. 70803
John A. Hunter, President

Southern University
Baton Rouge, La. 70813
G. Leon Netterville, Jr., President

University of Maine
Portland, Maine 04102
Donald R. McNeil, Chancellor

University of Maryland
College Park, Md. 20742
Wilson H. Elkins, President

University of Maryland State College
Princess Anne, Md. 21853
John T. Williams, President

Massachusetts Institute of Technology
Cambridge, Mass. 02139
Howard W. Johnson, President

University of Massachusetts
Amherst, Mass. 01002
Robert C. Wood, President

Michigan State University
East Lansing, Mich. 48823
Clifton R. Whaton, Jr., President

University of Minnesota
Minneapolis, Minn. 55455
Malcom C. Moos, President

Alcorn Agricultural and Mechanical College
Lorman, Miss. 39096
Walter Washington, President

Mississippi State University
State College, Miss. 39762
William L. Giles, President

Lincoln University
Jefferson City, Mo. 65101
Walter C. Daniel, President

University of Missouri
Columbia, Mo. 65201
C. Brice Ratchford, Interim
President (1970)

Montana State University
Bozeman, Mont. 59715
Carl W. McIntosh, President

University of Nebraska
Lincoln, Nebr. 68508
Durward B. Varner, Chancellor

University of Nevada
Reno, Nev. 89501
Neil D. Humphrey, Chancellor

University of New Hampshire
Durham, N.H. 03824
John W. McConnell, President

Rutgers University
New Brunswick, N.J. 08903
Mason W. Gross, President

New Mexico State University
Las Cruces, N. Mex. 88001
Gerald W. Thomas, President

Cornell University
Ithaca, N.Y. 14850
Dale R. Corson, President

North Carolina Agricultural and
   Technical College
Greensboro, N.C. 27411
Lewis C. Dowdy, President

North Carolina State University
Raleigh, N.C. 27607
John T. Caldwell, Chancellor

North Dakota State University
Fargo, N.D. 58102
Laurel D. Loftsgard, President

Ohio State University
Columbus, Ohio 43210
Novice G. Fawcett, President

Langston University
Langston, Okla. 73050
William E. Sims, President

Oklahoma State University
Stillwater, Okla. 74074
Robert B. Kamm, President

Oregon State University
Corvallis, Ore. 97331
Robert W. MacVicar, President

Pennsylvania State University
University Park, Pa. 16802
John W. Oswald, President

University of Puerto Rico
Rio Piedras, P.R. 00931
Jaime Benitez, President

University of Rhode Island
Kingston, R.I. 02881
Werner A. Baum, President

Clemson University
Clemson, S.C. 29631
Robert C. Edwards, President

South Carolina State College
Orangeburg, S.C. 29115
M. Maceo Nance, Jr., President

South Dakota State University
Brookings, S.D. 57006
Hilton M. Briggs, President

Tennessee State University
Nashville, Tenn. 37203
Andrew P. Torrence, President

University of Tennessee
Knoxville, Tenn. 37916
Edward J. Boling, President

Prairie View A & M College
Prairie View, Tex. 77445
Alvin I. Thomas, President

Texas A & M University
College Station, Tex. 77843
Alvin R. Luedecke, Acting President

Utah State University
Logan, Utah 84321
Glen L. Taggart, President

University of Vermont
Burlington, Vt. 05401
Edward C. Andres, President

Virginia Polytechnic Institute
Blacksburg, Va. 24061
T. Marshall Hahn, Jr., President

Virginia State College
Petersburg, Va. 23803
Wendel Russel, President

Washington State University
Pullman, Wash. 99163
Glen Terrell, President

West Virginia University
Morgantown, W. Va. 26506
James G. Harlow, President

University of Wisconsin
Madison, Wis. 53706
John C. Weaver, President

University of Wyoming
Laramie, Wyo. 82070
William D. Carlson, President

Trade, Professional and Business Associations

Alcoa Wrap
1501 Alcoa Building
Pittsburgh, Pa. 15219

American Bankers Association
Banking Education Committee
1120 Connecticut Avenue, N.W.
Washington, D.C. 20036

American Council on Consumer Interests
Edward J. Metzen, Executive Secretary
238 Stanley Hall
University of Missouri
Columbia, Mo. 65201

American Cyanamid Company
Fibers Division
Berdan Ave.
Wayne, N.J. 07470

The American Dairy Association
20 N. Wacker Drive
Chicago, Ill. 60606

American Dental Association
211 East Chicago Ave.
Chicago, Ill. 60611

American Federation of Labor and Congress of Industrial Organizations
815 16th St., N.W.
Washington, D.C. 20206

The American Gas Association
1515 Wilson Boulevard
Arlington, Virginia 22209

American Home Economics Association
2010 Massachusetts Avenue
Washington, D.C. 20036

American Meat Institute
59 East Van Buren St.
Chicago, Ill. 60605

American Medical Association
535 N. Dearborn St.
Chicago, Ill. 60610

American Standard
40 W. 40th St.
New York, N.Y. 10018

Associated Press News Features
50 Rockefeller Plaza
New York, N.Y. 10020

Association Films
600 Madison Ave.
New York, N.Y. 10022

Association of Home Appliance
  Manufacturers
20 N. Wacker Drive
Chicago, Ill. 60606

Baltimore Urban League
2404 Pennsylvania Ave.
Baltimore, Md. 21217

Bay Area Neighborhood Development
4801 Central Avenue
Richmond, Calif. 94804

Benjamin Moore and Company
511 Canal St.
New York, N.Y. 10013

Better Business Bureau of Metropolitan New York
220 Church St.
New York, N.Y. 10013

Channing L. Bete Co., Inc.
45 Federal St.
Greenfield, Mass. 01301

Better Homes and Gardens
Reader Service—Department A
1716 Locust St.
Des Moines, Iowa 50303

Bigelow-Sanford, Inc.
140 Madison Ave.
New York, N.Y. 10016

Black & Decker Manufacturing
  Co.
701 E. Joppa Road
Towson, Maryland 21204

The Borden Company
Consumer Services—Room 1701
350 Madison Ave.
New York, N.Y. 10017

Bulova Watch Company, Inc.
630 Fifth Ave.
New York, N.Y. 10020

Canada Dry Corporation
100 Park Ave.
New York, N.Y. 10017

Cannon Homemaking Service
Cannon Mills, Inc.
P.O. Drawer 7
Kannapolis, N.C. 28081

Celanese Fibers Marketing Company
522 Fifth Avenue
New York, New York 10036

Chamber of Commerce of the
  United States
1615 H St., N.W.
Washington, D.C. 20006

Conso Products Company
27 West 23rd St.
New York, N.Y. 10010

Consolidated Edison
4 Irving Place
New York, N.Y. 10003

Consumer Federation of America
1012 14th St., N.W.
Washington, D.C. 20005

Consumer Information Clearing
  House

University of Vermont
Terrill Hall
Burlington, Vt. 15401

Council of Better Business Bureaus, Inc.
1150 17th St., N.W.
Washington, D.C. 20036

Council for Family Financial Education
Twin Towers
Silver Spring, Md. 20910

CUNA International, Inc.
1617 Sherman Ave.
Madison, Wisconsin 53701

Del Monte Corporation
Del Monte Kitchens
215 Freemont St.
San Francisco, Calif. 94119

Dow Chemical Company
Specialty Products Division
Midland, Michigan 48640

Dow Jones & Company
Educational Service Bureau
P.O. Box 300
Princeton, New Jersey 08540

Dun & Bradstreet, Inc.
Business Education Division
99 Church St.
New York, N.Y. 10007

E. I. du Pont de Nemours and Company
DuPont Building
Wilmington, Delaware 19898

Eastman Chemical Products, Inc.
1133 Avenue of the Americas
New York, N.Y. 10036

Eastman Kodak Company
343 State St.
Rochester, N.Y. 14650

EKCO Housewares Department NY
4834 W. Cicero Ave.
Chicago, Ill. 60639

Evaporated Milk Association
910 17th St. N.W.
Washington, D.C. 20006

Family Circle Magazine
488 Madison Ave.
New York, N.Y. 10022

Frigidaire Division
General Motors Corporation
3500 Taylor St.
Dayton, Ohio 45401

General Aniline and Film Corporation
Floor Products Division
1139 Lehigh Ave.
Fullerton, Pa. 18052

General Electric Company
570 Lexington Ave.
New York, N.Y. 10022

General Electric Company
Kitchen Laundry Guide Office
P.O. Box 8369
Chicago, Ill. 60607

General Foods
250 N. St.
White Plains, N.Y. 10602

Good Housekeeping Magazine
959 Eighth Ave.
New York, N.Y. 10019

Good Reading Rack
Good Reading Communications, Inc.
505 Eighth Avenue
New York, New York 10018

The B. F. Goodrich Company
500 S. Main Street
Akron, Ohio 44318

Goodyear Tire & Rubber Company
Public Relations Department
1144 E. Market St.
Akron, Ohio 44316

Grocery Manufacturers of America
1133 Avenue of Americas
New York, N.Y. 10036

Gulistan Carpet
1185 Avenue of Americas
9th Floor
New York, N.Y. 10036

Humble Oil and Refining Company
800 Bell Avenue
Houston, Texas 77002

Health Insurance Institute
277 Park Avenue
New York, N.Y. 10017

Home Furnishings Council
P.O. Box 262
Flossmoor, Ill. 60422

Institute of Life Insurance
Education Division
277 Park Ave.
New York, N.Y. 10017

Institute of Life Insurance
Women's Division
277 Park Ave.
New York, N.Y. 10017

Insurance Information Institute
110 William St.
New York, N.Y. 10038

International Ladies' Garment Workers' Union
1710 Broadway
New York, N.Y. 10019

Invest-in-America Council
121 South Broad St.
Philadelphia, Pa. 19107

Johnson and Johnson
501 George St.
New Brunswick, N.J. 08903

Johnson Wax
Consumer Education Department
1525 Howe Street
Racine, Wisconsin 53403

Joint Council on Economic Education
1212 Avenue of the Americas
New York, N.Y. 10036

Kellogg Company
Home Economics Services
235 Porter St.
Battle Creek, Mich. 49016

Kittinger Company
1893 Elmwood Avenue
Buffalo, N.Y. 14207

Kraftco Corp.
500 N. Peshtigo Court
Chicago, Ill. 60690

Ladies Home Journal
641 Lexington Ave.
New York, N.Y. 10022

Lees Carpet
Advertising Department

1000 Adams Ave.
Valley Forge Industrial Park
Norristown, Pa. 19401

Lever Brothers
Consumer Education Department
390 Park Avenue
New York, N.Y. 10022

Man-Made Fiber Producers Association, Inc.
350 Fifth Ave.
New York, N.Y. 10001

Manufacturers Hanover Trust Company
Public Relations Department
350 Park Avenue
New York, N.Y. 10022

Manufacturing Chemists' Association
1825 Connecticut Ave., N.W.
Washington, D.C. 20009

Marine Midland Banks
Public Relations Department
241 Main St.
Buffalo, New York 14203

The Maytag Company
403 W. 4th St., N.
Newton, Iowa 50208

McCall Corporation
230 Park Ave.
New York, N.Y. 10017

Metropolitan Life Insurance Company
1 Madison Ave.
New York, N.Y. 10010

Modern Talking Picture Service
1212 Avenue of Americas
New York, N.Y. 10036

Money Management Institute
Household Finance Corporation
Prudential Plaza
Chicago, Ill. 60601

Monsanto Company
Textiles Division Department RJW
800 N. Lindbergh Blvd.
St. Louis, Mo. 63166

Montgomery Ward and Co., Inc.
619 W. Chicago Avenue
Chicago, Ill. 60607

Morgan-Jones, Inc.
104 W. 40th St.
New York, N.Y. 10018

Motorola Company
9401 W. Grand Avenue
Franklin Park, Ill. 60131

Mutual of New York
1740 Broadway
New York, N.Y. 10019

National Association of Manufacturers
277 Park Avenue
New York, N.Y. 10017

National Automatic Laundry & Cleaning Council
7 South Dearborn St.
Chicago, Ill. 60603

National Automobile Dealers Association
2000 K Street, N.W.
Washington, D.C. 20006

National Canners Association
Consumer Service Division
1133 20th St., N.W.
Washington, D.C. 20036

National Consumer Finance Association
1000 Sixteenth Street, N.W.
Washington, D.C. 20036

National Consumer's League, Inc.
1029 Vermont Ave., N.W.
Washington, D.C. 20005

National Dairy Council
111 N. Canal St.
Chicago, Ill. 60606

National Foundation for Consumer Credit
1819 H Street, N.W.
Washington, D.C. 20006

National Gypsum Company
Distribution Department
325 Delaware Ave.
Buffalo, N.Y. 14202

National Home Furnishings Association
1150 Merchandise Mart
Chicago, Illinois 60654

National Institute of Dry Cleaning
909 Burlington Ave.
Silver Spring, Md. 20910

National Institute of Rug Cleaning, Inc.
1815 N. Fort Myer Drive
Arlington, Va. 22209

National Paint, Varnish & Lacquer Association, Inc.
1500 Rhode Island Ave., N.W.
Washington, D.C. 20005

National Safety Council
425 N. Michigan Avenue
Chicago, Illinois 60611

The Nestle Company
100 Bloomingdale Road
White Plains, N.Y. 10605

New York State Banking Department
100 Church St.
New York, N.Y. 10007

New York State Bar Association
1 Elk St.
Albany, N.Y. 12207

New York Stock Exchange
11 Wall St.
New York, N.Y. 10005
ATT: Publications Division

Olivetti Underwood Corporation
1 Park Ave.
New York, N.Y. 10016

Pellon Corporation
1120 Avenue of the Americas
New York, N.Y. 10036

J. C. Penney Company, Inc.
Educational Relations Department
1301 Avenue of the Americas
New York, N.Y. 10019

Pet Incorporated
Home Economics Department
400 S. 4th
St. Louis, Mo. 63166

Power Tool Institute, Inc.
604 Davis Street
P.O. Box 1406
Evanston, Illinois 60204

Procter and Gamble
301 E. 6th St.
Cincinnati, Ohio 45202

Public Affairs Committee, Inc.
381 Park Ave., S.
New York, N.Y. 10016

Quaker Oats Company
Merchandise Mart Plaza
Chicago, Ill. 60654

Revlon, Inc.
767 Fifth Ave.
New York, N.Y. 10022

Sears, Roebuck and Company
Department 703—Public Relations
Consumer Information Services
925 S. Homan Ave.
Chicago, Ill. 60607

Simplicity Pattern Company
200 Madison Ave.
New York, N.Y. 10016

The Soap & Detergent Association
485 Madison Avenue
New York, N.Y. 10022

Southern Furniture Manufacturers Association
P.O. Box 951
High Point, North Carolina 27261

The Sperry and Hutchinson Company
Consumer Relations Department
330 Madison Ave.
New York, N.Y. 10017

Sterling Movies U.S.A.
Booking Office
43 West 61st St.
New York, N.Y. 10023

Sunbeam Corporation
5400 Roosevelt Road
Chicago, Illinois 60650

Sunkist Growers
P.O. Box 2706
Terminal Annex
Los Angeles, Calif. 90054

Sylvania Electric Products, Inc.
730 Third Avenue
New York, N.Y. 10017

Syracuse China Corporation
Dinnerware Advertising
1858 W. Fayette St.
Syracuse, N.Y. 13204

The Taylor Wine Company, Inc.
425 Park Ave.
New York, N.Y. 10022

Tire Industry Safety Council
National Press Building
Washington, D.C. 20004

Union Dime Savings Bank
1065 Avenue of the Americas at 40th
New York, N.Y. 10018

United Medical Service, Inc.
Labor and Community Relations
2 Park Ave.
New York, N.Y. 10016

Vinyl Fabrics Institute
60 E. 42nd St.
New York, N.Y. 10017

Wallcovering Information Bureau
969 3rd Ave.
New York, N.Y. 10022

Winthrop Laboratories
Division of Sterling Drug, Inc.
90 Park Ave.
New York, N.Y. 10016

Woman's Day
1 Astor Plaza
New York, N.Y. 10036

Westinghouse Electric Corporation
Lamp Division
3 Gateway Center
Pittsburgh, Pa. 15230

Wurlitzer Company
DeKalb Division
105 W. Adams St.
Chicago, Ill. 60603

PROFESSIONAL READING

ACCI Newsletter. 9 per year. Controlled circulation to members. American Council on Consumer Interests, 238 Stanley Hall, University of Missouri, Columbia, Mo. 65201.

Current news of consumer interests. Invaluable for its listing of current consumer resource materials. A basic collection building resource for all libraries concerned with consumer affairs.

A Brief History of ACCI, by Henry Harap, 1969. 8 p. Free (with eight-cent stamped, self-addressed envelope) Dr. Henry Harap, 753 3rd St., S.W., Washington, D.C. 20024.

Brief but inclusive history of ACCI (American Council on Consumer Interests) by its first and third president.

The Capable Consumer Teacher, by Gladys Bahr. *National Association of Secondary School Principals. Bulletin,* v. 51, Oct. 1967: 97–102.

A plea for recency and flexibility in materials and methods used in consumer courses.

Changing Times. Monthly. $6.00. The Kiplinger Washington Editors, Inc., 1729 H St., N.W., Washington, D.C. 20006.

An informal and practical approach to daily living problems is the running theme of this magazine. It provides new, easy-to-apply ideas that will help the consumer to get more for his money. No advertising. Not sold on newstands.

Concepts and Generalizations. 1967. 63 p. $2.00. American Home Economics Association, 2010 Massachusetts Ave., N.W., Washington, D.C. 20036.

"Their place in high school home economics curriculum development."

Consumer Concerns 1970: Conference Proceedings, 1970. 132 p. $2.00. Colorado State University, Office of Conferences and Institutes, Ft. Collins, Colo. 80521.

Conference proceeding of eighteen speakers including Betty Furness on general consumer concerns, Doris Sasser on consumer education. Kenneth Monfort on the beef industry and Richand L. D. Morse on consumer credit.

Consumer Education, 1969. 115 p. $2.00. National Education Association of the United States, 1201 16th St., N.W., Washington, D.C. 20036.

Twenty educators from a variety of disciplines consider the burgeoning field of consumer education and consumer economics. Articles are drawn from the October, 1967 *National Association of Secondary School Principals. Bulletin;* many are separately cited in this bibliography.

Consumer Education, by Joseph G. Bonnice. *Business Education World,* v. 50, no. 1, Oct. 1969: 10. Free to business educators.

Discusses the need for cooperation among business educators, home economics and social studies teachers for better consumer education.

Consumer Education—a Major Responsibility of Business Teachers. *Business Education Forum,* v. 25, Mar. 1971: 8–10.

A plea for the addition of consumer education to the school curriculum.

Consumer Education and the Madison Avenue Morality, by David K. Gast. *Phi Delta Kappan,* v. 48, June 1967: 485–487.

A plea for the development of vital programs of consumer education in the public schools.

Consumer Education: Dynamics of Teaching, by Helen M. Thal and Lois Guthrie. *Journal of Home Economics,* v. 61, Dec. 1969: 762–767.

Reviews the objectives of consumer education and emphasizes that for many consumers "buying becomes more a means of self-expression than a process of acquisition".

Consumer Education Forum. 3 per year. Controlled circulation to members. American Council on Consumer Interests, 238 Stanley Hall, University of Missouri, Columbia, Mo. 65201.

A newsletter published to encourage an interchange of ideas among consumer specialists.

Consumer Education in the Business Program, by Virginia H. Knauer. *Business Education Forum,* v. 25, Mar. 1971: 8–10.

The Special Assistant to the President for Consumer Affairs discusses the present state of consumer education programs in our schools. She notes the reasons such programs have developed and comments on their future growth.

Consumer Education: Its New Look. *National Association of Secondary School Principals. Bulletin,* v. 51, Oct. 1967: 1–116. $2.00. 1201 16th St., N.W., Washington, D.C. 20036.

"Background Papers," "Practice Illustrated," "Supporting Programs," and "Teacher and Tools" are the area headings devoted to Consumer Education. Included is a 13-page section, "Reference Shelf," which is an annotated listing of Consumer Education materials.

Consumer Education Rides Again, by Edward Damon. *Clearing House,* v. 40, Mar. 1966: 391–396.

A capsulated survey of the history of the consumer education movement.

Consumer Education vs. Consumer Information, by Virginia H. Knauer. *Penneys Forum,* spring/summer, 1971: 3.

A discussion of the lasting values of consumer education as compared to the immediate values of consumer information.

Consumer Legislative Monthly Report. Monthly. Free. Office of Consumer Affairs, New Executive Office Building, Washington, D.C. 20506.

A subject classified listing of legislation introduced in the Congress on consumer oriented subjects. Provides bill numbers, sponsors, a numerical index to bills, and lists of legislation of consumer interests passed by either house and by both houses. An indispensable resource for large public and academic libraries.

Consumer Messages. Free as available. House Document Room, Room H226, The Capitol, Washington, D.C. 20510.

Transmitted by the President to the Congress. Each message comments on presidential consumer concerns. All consumer messages appear in the *Congressional Record.*

Consumer News. Monthly 4 p. $1.00. (Office of Consumer Affairs, cat. no. PREX16.9:) Supt. of Documents, GPO, Washington, D.C. 20402.

Newsletter describing regulations, legal actions and continuing programs of Federal agencies in the field of consumer affairs.

Contribution of Consumer Education to General Education, by Kenneth A. Scott. *Business Education Forum,* v. 24, Jan. 1970: 16–18.

A plea for an increase in the number of education programs offered in public and private schools. Includes a section on consumer instruction for "poor, culturally different consumers."

Contributions of Business Education, by Anne Scott Daughtrey. *National Association of Secondary School Principals. Bulletin,* v. 51, Oct. 1967: 46–54.

Discusses the role of business education as "a natural vehicle for consumer education." A well written, brief and lucid exposition.

Do Your Students Realize How Important the Youth Market Is? by Dickson S. Mullin. *Business Education World,* v. 46, May 1966: 24–26.

Describes the size and direction of the present youth market and appeals for modern methods and materials in the education of today's teenage consumers.

Economic Literacy and Consumer Education, by Herbert M. Jelley. *National Association of Secondary School Principals Bulletin,* v. 51, Oct. 1967: 21–26. Same condensed: *Education Digest,* v. 33, Dec. 1967: 46–48.

"Is it possible to tie consumer education and economic education together?" The author contends that the answer is an emphatic "yes".

Everybody's Money. Quarterly. Subscription to credit unions in quantities of fifty or more at 25¢ per member. CUNA, Inc., *Everybody's Money,* 1617 Sherman Ave. Madison, Wis. 53701.

A magazine for credit union members. Sample issue covers everything from employment agencies to how to buy a spool of thread. A magazine designed for credit union members. Each issue covers a variety of pertinent topics.

The Family: Focus on Management, 1970. 76 p. $3.00. American Home Economics Association, 2010 Massachusetts Ave., N.W., Washington, D.C. 20036.

Seven selected conference papers considering such varied family related topics as social decision making, home management research, and an ecological approach to the study of family managerial behavior.

Financial Facts Newsletter. Monthly. Free (single subscription). National Consumer Finance Association, 1000 16th St., N.W., Washington, D.C. 20036.

Regular report on indexes of consumer financial behavior, personal income, personal savings, indicators of business activity, consumer price indexes, and other areas of interest to those in the industry. Published since 1958. Designed for teachers. Available in bulk for class use, cost: 25¢ per year.

For the Consumer: What Breakthroughs? by Helen G. Conoyer. *Journal of Home Economics,* v. 58, Sept. 1966: 523–527.

A review of the growth of interest in consumer education in the mid-sixties. Briefly evaluates some programs and activities of the period.

Forecast for Home Economics. 9 per year. $6 per school year. *Forecast*, 902 Sylvan Ave., Englewood Cliffs, N.J. 07632.

Teacher's edition of *Co-ed*. Includes a copy of the student edition of *Co-ed*. Contains a variety of articles of interest to consumer specialists on such topics as food and nutrition, clothing and textiles, and family relations. A special section of professional reading for teacher precedes the students' edition.

Formal Consumer Education. 1968. 42 p. International Organization of Consumers Unions (IOCU) Information Center, 9 Emmastraat, The Hague, Holland.

Series of presentations on consumer education articles from ten nations.

A Forum on Low-Income Consumer Programs. *Journal of Consumer Affairs*, v. 2, summer 1968: 107–123.

Contents includes: "educating the low-income consumer," "some viewpoints from an action program," "consumer education and low income families."

General Business or Personal Economics? by Richard D. Brown. *Business Education World*, v. 49, Oct. 1968: 17+.

Contends that the general business course should try to reflect the ways in which consumer decisions control the economy.

Government and Consumer Education. *National Association of Secondary School Principals Bulletin*, v. 51, Oct. 1967: 69–75.

"What the government has available to help educate students for their role as consumers of goods and services."

Home Economics and Consumer Advice, by Rosemary McRobert. *Times Educational Supplement*, no. 2687, Nov. 18, 1966: 1227.

Describes the role of the home economist in consumer education.

Home Economics Learning Packages, by Twyla Shear and Elizabeth Ray. *Journal of Home Economics*, v. 61, Dec. 1969: 768–770.

A theoretical explanation of the use of learning packages as a means of individualizing instruction in the area of consumer education.

Home Economics Research Abstracts. Annual. Various prices. American Home Economics Association, 2010 Massachusetts Ave., N.W., Washington, D.C. 20036.

A continuing series which compiles abstracts of masters' theses and doctoral dissertations completed in colleges and universities offering graduate programs in home economics. For a list of available abstract annuals contact the Association.

Home Furnishings Industry Seeks to Educate Consumers, by Nancy Mills. *Forecast for Home Economics*, v. 13, Nov. 1967: 34–35.

"The industry that ranks second in retail sales in the United States" is now participating in consumer education. Includes a nationwide list of firms wanting to cooperate with home economics teachers.

Journal of Consumer Affairs. Semi-annual. $6.00. American Council on Consumer Interests, 238 Stanley Hall, University of Missouri, Columbia, Mo. 65201.

A journal designed for use by professionals in consumer education and consumer affairs. Provides scholarly research, book reviews, and information on current consumer topics. Indexed in several standard periodical indexes.

Journal of Home Economics. Monthly. $12.00. American

Home Economics Association, 2010 Massachusetts Ave., N.W., Washington, D.C. 20036.

A broad survey of all aspects of home economics and consumer topics. Often contains articles on family relations, child development, food and nutrition, textiles and clothing, housing and household equipment, and family economics. Basic reading for professionals.

Key to Many Doors, by Fred T. Wilhelms. *National Association of Secondary School Principals Bulletin,* v. 51, Oct. 1967: 3–13.

The associate director of the Consumer Education Study, 1942–1948, considers consumer education as an instrument for liberalizing traditional education.

The Most for Their Money: a Report on the Panel on Consumer Education For Persons With Limited Income, 1965. 57 p. 40¢ (cat. no. Pr36.8:C76/M74). Supt. of Documents, GPO, Washington, D.C. 20402.

Surveys the problem of the poor as consumers, the consumer education work being carried on, and makes recommendations for community and nationwide programs. Of special help to community, government and business leaders, as well as educators.

The New Approach to Consumer Education, 1968. 58 p. 25¢. Publications Distribution Unit, New York State Education Dept., Albany, N.Y. 12224. (Free to educational institutions in New York State.)

The proceedings of the first regional conference on consumer education held at Lincoln High School, Yonkers, N.Y. on March 15, 1968. Series of speeches geared to spark more consumer education in the schools of New York State.

New Developments in Teaching Consumer Education, by Herbert M. Jelley. *Business Education Forum,* v. 22, Mar. 1968: 7–9.

Suggests various consumer principles and projects appropriate to classroom study.

Of Consuming Interest. 2 per month. $24.00. Federal-State Reports, P.O. Box 654, Court House Station, Arlington, Va. 22216.

Reviews federal and state legislation related to consumer issues; covers a wide variety of other consumer related news items.

Payoff for Intelligent Consumer Decision-Making, by E. Scott Maynes. *Journal of Home Economics,* v. 61, Feb. 1969: 97–103.

"Discusses in detail some of the avenues open to consumers that aid in the decision-making process and concludes with recommendation for consumers."

Penneys Forum. 2 per year. Free to educators. J. C. Penney Co., Inc., Educational Relations, 1301 Avenue of the Americas, New York, N.Y. 10019.

A periodical of particular interest to consumer educators.

Pennywise Teenagers, by Esther Peterson. *American Education,* v. 2, Apr. 1966: 24–28.

Discusses the phenomenon of an immense adolescent market, and describes consumer education measures necessary to its wise direction.

Plight of the Consumer. *PTA Magazine,* v. 62, Mar. 1968: 28–29.

Lists those consumer problems and issues which ninety-one members of the PTA's National Board of Managers considered most important in 1968. A provocative variety are mentioned.

Principal's Case for Consumer Education, by Arthur A. Natella. *National Association of Secondary School Principals Bulletin,* v. 51, Oct. 1967: 41–45.

A brief description of the consumer education program offered by Lincoln High School in Yonkers, New York. The author is the principal of Lincoln.

Teaching Consumer Education, by Sally Campbell. *Forecast for Home Economics,* v. 14, Jan. 1969: F26–7.

A review of the ways in which a teacher can vivify consumer education for teenagers.

Things Go Better with Consumer Education, by Esther Peson. *PTA Magazine,* v. 60, May 1966: 7–9.

A statement of the non-materialistic and non-commercial values of consumer education courses.

Tips and Topics. Quarterly. $3.00. College of Home Economics, P.O. Box 4170, Texas Tech University, Lubbock, Texas 79409.

A newsletter surveying the various fields of home economics. Special rates available to students majoring in home economics education.

Under-Elevens Learn To Handle the High-Pressure Salesman, by Alma Williams. *Times Educational Supplement,* no. 2788, Oct. 25, 1968: 885.

Discusses ways in which children can be prepared for their role as consumers in modern society.

Values and American Youth, by Walter L. Thomas. *Journal of Home Economics,* v. 61, Dec. 1969: 748–754.

The author is the Director of the Project on Student Values in Grand Rapids, Michigan. This is a condensed version of his address to the Conference on Innovations in Consumer Education in the Home Economics Curriculum, 1969.

What Should Be Taught in General Business about the Role of the Consumer in Our Economy, by R. Pierce Lumpkin. *Business Education Forum,* v. 20, Mar. 1966: 5–7.

A tightly written overview of the consumer oriented subject matter appropriate to business classes.

What's New in Home Economics. 8 per year. $8.00 per year. Controlled circulation, available only to professional home economists. Magazine Publishing Division, Reuben H. Donnelley Corp., 466 Lexington Ave., New York, N.Y. 10017.

Magazine designed for the professional home economist and consumer specialist. Each issue has a coupon-resource section for teaching aids.

Who Carries the Ball in Consumer Education? by Eleanor Adams. *Forecast for Home Economics,* v. 13, Apr. 1968: F8–9+.

The author concludes that consumer education is primarily the responsibility of the home economics teacher. She urges them to assert their leadership.

Youth Needs and School Responsibilities, by James E. Mendenhall. *National Association of Secondary School Principals Bulletin,* v. 51, Oct. 1967: 14–20.

Details the need for consumer education programs at the high school level.

Children's Books

Children are already consumers although they may seldom consult consumers' guides and there are no children consumers' guides per se. However, it is important to prepare them for their role as consumers. With this in mind, information books on business and industries, jobs and careers, government and law, health and safety, machinery and ecology have been included. The special interests, hobbies and games of children are represented by books on pets, bicycles, crafts, model-making, sports, sewing, parties, and musical instruments. Good books which tell children how to do things such as train a dog, make a bird house, play a harmonica, learn a sport or redecorate a bedroom offer in the clearest possible manner, information on the selection, evaluation, use and maintenance of items children consume.

Aids to Choosing Books for Children, by Ingeborg Boudreau, n.d. 19 p. $1.95, paper. The Children's Book Council, 175 Fifth Ave., New York, N.Y., 10010.

A selected and annotated bibliography of book lists and review media arranged by subject and including special information for parents. This is an expanded edition, published in 1969, of an on-going list.

Best Books for Children, compiled by Doris Solomon, 1970. 272 p. $3.50, paper. R. R. Bowker Co. (a Xerox Company), 1180 Avenue of the Americas, New York, N.Y., 10036.

The 12th edition of a useful annual list of 4,000 approved books currently available, arranged by grade and subject with title and author indexes. Prepared and annotated in the offices of *School Library Journal.*

The Black Experience in Children's Books, Augusta Baker, compiler, 1971. 109 p. .50¢. paper. New York Public Library, Office of Children's Services, 8 East 40th Street, New York, 10016.

A comprehensive annotated bibliography listing more than 700 books with additional titles noted in many of the annotations. Compiler is Coordinator of Children's Services for The New York Public Library. All books on the list may be consulted in the Countee Cullen Regional Branch of the New York Public Library as they comprise the James Weldon Johnson Memorial Collection for children. Full author and title index.

The Dobler World Directory of Youth Periodicals, compiled and edited by Lavinia Dobler and Muriel Fuller, 1970. 108 p. $4.25 (available only in paperback). Citation Press (Scholastic Book Services), New York.

The 3rd enlarged edition of the guide to periodicals for children and young people. Lavinia Dobler is the librarian of the Scholastic library which has a large and current collection of children's magazines from the U.S.A. and abroad.

Films for Children, a Selected List, compiled by the New York Library Association—Children's and Young Adults Services Committee, 2d ed., 1969. 32 p. $1.00, paper. New York Library Association, P.O. Box 521, Woodside, N.Y., 11377.

An annotated list arranged by film title with an introduction on the accessibility of films for children, the criteria for selection and how to plan, publicize, project, stage and present film programs for children. A bibliography and subject index is appended.

Guide to Children's Magazines, Newspapers, Reference Books,
revised edition, 1968. 8 p. $0.10, paper. Association for Childhood Education International, 3615 Wisconsin Ave., Washington, D.C., 20016.

A selected annotated list of value to parents and teachers.

Let's Read Together, Books for Family Enjoyment, third ed.,
1969. 103 p. $1.50, paper. American Library Association, 50 East Huron Street, Chicago, Ill. 60611.

An annotated list of books for parents and teachers to read aloud to children. The compilers are members of a Special Committee of the National Congress of Parents and Teachers and the Children's Services Division American Library Association.

Libros en Espanol; an Annotated List of Children's Books in Spanish,
compiled by Mary K. Conwell and Pura Belpré, 1971. p. $0.50, paper. The New York Public Library Office of Children's Services, 8 E. 40th St., New York, N.Y. 10016.

A list of over 200 children's books in Spanish based on the collection in the New York Public Library. Books are arranged for the most part by age with annotations in both Spanish and English. The list was made possible by funds from the Library Services and Construction Act for the South Bronx Project which was set up to serve the Spanish speaking in the South Bronx area. An author title index is included.

CHILDREN AS CONSUMERS
Money and Money Management

Barter, Bills, and Banks, by Barry Tarshis, 1970. 80 p. $3.95. Messner (Simon and Schuster), New York.

The author traces the development and uses of money and how banking started. He discusses inflation, "tight money", credit cards, "wage-price spiral", giving a great deal of information for such an easy-to-read book. Grades 4–7.

The Bulls and the Bears, How the Stock Exchange Works, by Adrian A. Paradis, 1967. 94 p. $3.95. Hawthorn Books, New York.

The complicated workings of the New York Stock Exchange are explained for children in conversational style through the device of following an individual inventor through the various steps by which he ultimately attains a listing of his company on the exchange. A final chapter addressing the child on how to invest in stocks is practical and informative with a glossary of terms and explanatory tables. Grades 4–6.

Economics of the Consumer, by Marc Rosenblum, 1970. 87 p. $3.95. Lerner Publications Co., Minneapolis, Minn.

An elementary school textbook which discusses the consumer's role in the market, consumer behavior, government laws and agencies, consumer protection, consumer credit and how to be an intelligent consumer. This is one of the publisher's series on economics called "the real world series". Grades 4–7.

How Money and Credit Help Us, by Elmer R. Kane, 1966. 97 p. $3.20 Benefic Press, 10300 W. Roosevelt Road, Westchester, Ill. 60153.

A classroom textbook for early elementary grades. Questions and answers follow each chapter. Illustrated with photographs and charts. A color filmstrip, $6.00—44 frames, is available to supplement the test.

How People Earn and Use Money, by Muriel Stanek, 1968. 48 p. $2.00. Benefic Press, 10300 W. Roosevelt Road, Westchester, Ill. 60153.

A simple explanation of money and its uses which is better looking than the average primary grade supplementary text book. Grades 3–5.

Let's Go To a Bank, by Laura Sootin, 1957. 45 p. $2.29. Putnam, New York.

A social studies reader planned to supplement first, second and third grade class visits to a bank. Grades 2–4.

Money, by Dyno Lowenstein, 1963. 68 p. $2.95. Franklin Watts, New York.

An explanation of money and how it works, including credit and banking throughout the world but especially in the U.S.A. Useful still, despite the date of publication. Grades 4–6.

Money and Banking, by Kenneth H. Smith, 1970. 86 p. $3.95. Lerner Publications Co., Minneapolis, Minn.

A brief summary of the development of money from barter to the United States monetary policy of today. Explains the thinking behind large scale banking operations, how money is created, and how it can be managed successfully. Grades 4–7.

Money-go-round, by John J. Floherty, 1964. 192 p. $4.50. Lippincott, Philadelphia.

The second edition of a useful and interesting history of money, including information about the Treasury Department, credit and foreign exchange. Indexed. Grades 5–8.

Money Isn't Everything, by Kathlyn Gay, il. by Dan Nevins, 1967. 96 p. $3.25, Delacorte, New York.

A simple explanation of our economic system showing how personal economics fit into the national economy. Grades 3–6.

Spending Money, by Frederic Rossomando and others, 1967. 47 p. $2.95. Franklin Watts, New York.

Family and household economics in an easy to read text for elementary school children. A companion title is *Earning Money* by the same author. Grades 5–7.

The Stock Market, by Marc Rosenblum, 1970. 94 p. $3.95. Lerner Publications Co., 231 First Avenue N., Minneapolis, Minn. 55401.

A brief introduction to the history of securities trading in the United States. The trading process is described and the need for securities regulations in the public interest is explained. A glossary of terms such as "blue chip", "bull market", and "bear market" is included. Grades 4–7.

White Gloves and Party Manners, by Marjabelle Young and Ann Buchwald, 1965. 65 p. $3.95. Robert Luce, Inc., 2000 N. Street, N.W., Washington, D.C. 20036.

A simple and practical first book of etiquette and grooming for younger boys and girls. The authors who are themselves parents, direct a school for social graces in Washington, D.C. Grades 3–6.

Young Teens & Money, by Mary Beery, 1971. 159 p. $4.33 McGraw-Hill, New York.

Useful information on earning, saving, borrowing and spending money and on how to stretch one's allowance is presented as the answers to questions proposed by a board of girls and boys in their early teens. The formation of mature, responsible and honorable attitudes toward money and property are also discussed. Grades 7 and up.

Health, Drugs, and Safety

Danny Goes To the Hospital, by James Lincoln Collier, 1970. unp. $3.00. W. W. Norton (Grosset), New York.

Realistic photographs and a matter-of-fact text reassuringly explain a small boy's surgical operation to correct his defective eyesight. Grades K–3.

The Drug Epidemic, What It Means and How to Combat It, by Dr. Wesley C. Westman, 1970. 163 p. $4.95. The Dial Press, New York.

The drug problem is discussed within the social setting from which it has grown. Various therepeutic programs are explored with the warning of the need for further evaluation of the programs. Of interest to adults, young adults, and older boys and girls. The author is a clinical psychologist who has had wide experience in public health service to addicts. 7 and up.

Drugs, Facts on Their Use and Abuse, by Norman W. Houser in consultation with Julius B. Richmond, 1969. 48 p. $3.75. Lothrop, Lee & Shepard, New York.

An objective discussion of the use of both chemical and natural drugs with the primary focus on their deleterious effect. Easy-to-read with illustrations. Grades 5–8.

Emergency Room, by Anita Feagles, 1970. 91 p. $3.95. Cowles Book Co., 488 Madison Avenue, New York, 10022.

A brief text and photographs of emergency room procedures in a busy, integrated hospital reflect the experiences of a young volunteer worker. Good information on hospital services and vocational opportunities. Grades 3–6.

The Emergency Room, by Eleanor Kay, R.N., 1970. 65 p. $2.95. Franklin Watts, New York.

The operation of a large urban hospital emergency room is described and illustrated in relation to its services to a young boy who has had a serious accident at a construction site. Good photographs. A First Book. Grades 3–7.

Firefighting, A New Look at the Old Firehouse, by Paul C. Ditzel, 1969. 192 p. $4.95. Van Nostrand, New York.

Career information, rescue work and the new equipment used in firefighting is related to descriptions of famous fires in the 19th and 20th centuries. Much of the research done for the book was done in New York City. Grades 4–8.

The Good Drug and the Bad Drug, by John S. Marr, 1970. $3.95. M. Evans & Co., Inc., 216 E. 49 St., New York, N.Y. 10017.

A brief but straight-forward presentation that can be understood by young children aged about 8 to 10 years about what happens inside the body and mind when drugs are taken for personal experimenting and for kicks rather than for illness under medical direction. Grades 3–6.

Mind Drugs, edited by Margaret O. Hyde, 1968. 150 p. $4.50. McGraw-Hill, New York. Also available in paperback: 95¢, Pocket Books, Inc., 19 West 44th Street, New York.

A collection of nine articles on alcohol, marijuana, LSD, heroin, and other drugs, their effects and reasons for and against their use. Written by experts in medicine, psychiatry, social psychology or public health. Includes glossary, index, and "where to find help in New York". For older boys and girls. Grades 6 and up.

The Truth About Drugs, by Geoffrey Austrian, 1971. 131 p. $3.50. Doubleday, New York.

The author classifies and describes all kinds of "dangerous drugs" except alcohol in a clearly written book which addresses those who are unfamiliar with the drug culture among adults and children and those young adults who do not require this kind of material to be written in their own language. A glossary of drug terms is appended but the book's tone and point of view reflects that of law enforcement and treatment personnel with whom the author did his major research. Some addicts were interviewed and a number of case histories are included. Also available in paperback from the same publisher. $1.75. Grades 5 and up.

Safety, by Polly Bolian and Shirley Hinds, 1970. 64 p. $3.25. Franklin Watts, New York.

"A First Book". Simple pointers on all forms of outdoor safety—hiking, swimming, boating, camping, etc., with a brief reference chapter. Grades 4–7.

What You Should Know About Drugs, by Charles W. Gorodetzky and S. Christian, 1970. 121 p. $4.95. Harcourt, New York.

Straight talk about the nature and dangers of drug use, utilizing the experiences and actual conversations of young people who have experimented with drugs. The authors believe that the use, abuse or non-use of drugs rests with the individual. Color photographs add interest. Suitable for children of elementary and junior high school age. Grades 5–8.

You, Your Child and Drugs, 1971. 73 p. $1.50 paper + 35¢ postage. Child Study Association, 9 East 89th Street, New York, N.Y. 10028.

This practical book to help parents understand and cope with the drug problems of their children was prepared by the staff of the Child Study Association of America. Adult.

Young Scientist and the Dentist, by George Barr, 1970. 160 p. $4.50. McGraw-Hill, New York.

A detailed scientific account of modern dentistry for children which is useful as career information as well as hygiene. Grades 6 and up.

Young Scientist and the Doctor, by George Barr, 1969. 160 p. $4.50. McGraw-Hill, New York.

A visit to the doctor will take on happier dimensions after a reading of this book which is one of the publisher's series on the scientific approach to a variety of areas in nature and society. Grades 6 and up.

Your Health and You, by Charles Gramet, 1968. 192. p. $4.95. Lothrop, New York.

Informative book for pre-teens and teens on developing good habits conducive to physical and mental health. Some problem subjects discussed are venereal diseases, drinking, smoking and the use of drugs. Grades 7 and up.

Ecology

The Air We Live In, by James Marshall, 1968. 95 p. $3.64. Coward-McCann, New York.

Diagrams of proposed systems for the control of air pollution accompany a readable text on air pollution and what a citizen can do to overcome it. Addresses of agencies involved in the promotion of clean air appended. Grades 5–8.

How Do They Get Rid of It, by Suzanne Hilton, 1970. 117 p. $2.00. Westminster Press, Philadelphia, Pa.

Describes new methods of reusing and disposing of trash. Interesting and informative. Grades 5–8.

The Only Earth We Have, by Laurence Pringle, 1969. 86 p. $4.50. Macmillan, New York.

A plea that man recognize limitations in his freedom to abuse the planet and an alert to the many aspects of the problems of pollution together with suggestions for individual action. Grades 5–8.

Shadows Over the Land, by J. J. McCoy, 1970. 152 p. $4.95. Seabury Press, New York.

Combines many aspects of environmental deterioration in a readable style—depletion of soil and wildlife, urban blight, air, water and noise pollution with specific examples such as the pet trade, effect of furrier industry on the probably elimination of species, the Trans Alaska Pipeline System, and pros and cons on the activities of the Army Corps of Engineers. Grades 5–8.

This Vital Air, This Vital Water, by Thomas G. Aylesworth, 1968. 192 p. $4.95. Rand McNally, Chicago.

A useful and instructive book on air, water and noise pollution and ways of overcoming it. Grades 5–8.

Food

Around America, Cookbook for Young People, by Mildred O. Knopf, 1969. 209 p. $4.50. Knoph, New York.

Regional recipes preceded by notes about the history and the origin of the dishes to be prepared. A book which reflects the ethnic diversity of American cooking. Grades 5 and up.

Food Facts for Young People, by Pauline Arnold and Percival White, 1968. 95 p. $4.95. Holiday House, New York.

The authors have incorporated material from their adult book, *Food: America's biggest business* to describe food producing and food producing industries for children. Included also is material on wholesaling, retailing, packaging, advertising, and research. Grades 4–8.

Food From Farm To Home, by Walter Buehr, 1970. 94 p. $3.75. Morrow, New York.

The farm and farm life yesterday, today and tomorrow. How crops and products are raised, grown, gathered and processed. Grades 4 to 6.

Kids Cooking, by Aileen Paul and Arthur Hawkins, 1970. $3.95. Doubleday, New York.

Helpful hints for young cooks written by a woman who conducts cooking classes for boys and girls and a man who is the author of several cooking books for adults. The directions are clear and the material well-organized. Includes meal planning and parties with rules for safety. Also regional recipes. Grades 5–8.

The Sea Farmers, by John F. Waters, 1970. 120 p. $4.35. Hastings House, New York.

How millions are being fed through ocean farming of fish, lobsters, shrimp, oysters, mussels, clams and turtles, and the possibilities and experiments for future enlargement of such farming. Well researched with industries and government agencies. Glossary, bibliography and index. Grades 5–8.

Seeds of Plenty, Agriculture in the Scientific Age, by Lee Chadwick, 1968, 1969, 158 p. $3.86. Coward-McCann, New York.

Explores new methods of agriculture such as weather control experiments, transforming a desert into an oasis, filling the protein gap in underdeveloped nations. Population explosion and food production are also discussed. Grades 5–7.

The United States Department of Agriculture, a Story of Foods, Farms and Forests, by John Upton Terrell, 1966. 130 p. $3.50. Meredith, Des Moines, Iowa 50303.

The history, organization, laws, research and projects of this department. Useful information on pests, diseases, the surplus problems, 4-H Clubs, co-ops, careers and forestry. Others in the series deal with the U.S. Departments of State, Commerce, and Health, Education and Welfare. Grades 5–7.

What We Eat, the Origins and Travels of Foods Round the World, by Lois J. Johnson, 1969.

172. p. $4.95. Rand McNally, Chicago.

A history of foods and beverages throughout the world. Includes a brief section on the food of the astronauts and a projection into the food of the future. Grades 4–8.

Etiquette and Good Grooming

The Calling All Girls Party Book, by Rubie Saunders, 1966. 96 p. $2.95. Parents' Magazine Press, New York.

An attractive guide to giving parties by the editor of the children's magazine, *Calling All Girls.* Ideas are given for games, costumes, party food and inexpensive decorations. Grades 5 to 8.

The Leslie Uggams Beauty Book, by Leslie Uggams with Marie Fenton, 1966. 178 p. $4.95. Prentice Hall, Englewood Cliffs, N.J.

A glamorous approach to grooming by a popular black singer. Predates the Afro hairstyle. Grades 6 and up.

Let's Face It, the Guide to Good Grooming for Girls of Color, by Elsie Archer, 1959, '68. 208 p. $4.95. Lippincott, Philadelphia, Pa.

A revised edition of a unique guide written by a well-known counselor who is herself a black woman and whose experience has been largely working with young black pre-teens and teenagers. Also available in paper from the same publisher at $1.50. Grades 6 and up.

Manners Made Easy, by Mary Beery, 1966, 3rd Ed. 388 p. $5.95. McGraw-Hill, New York.

How good manners and good grooming can improve family, school and social relations for boys as well as girls. Includes information on styles of dress, modes of travel and how to evaluate services and prices. Grades 5 and up.

The New Seventeen Book of Etiquette and Young Living, by Enid A. Haupt, 1970. 325 p. $7.95. McKay, New York.

A guide to manners, dress, make up and general behavior at home, at school, at parties, and in all kinds of social occasions. Driving, traveling, eating in restaurants and how to find and keep a job are thoroughly discussed, as well as boy-girl relationships. Although addressed to young adults, older children find this book useful. Grades 6 and up.

CHILDREN AS MEMBERS OF SOCIETY

Business and Industry

Advertising, by Richard O. Pompian, 1970. 90 p. $2.75. Franklin Watts, New York.

A simple, entertaining coverage of all aspects of advertising and its effect on American society. Illustrated with photographs and reproductions of ads. "A First Book." Grades 5–8.

Electric Power in America, by Robert McCaig, 1970. 160 p. $3.94. Putnam's, New York.

Although primarily concerned with the history of electrical power in the United States, there is a chapter discussing the 1965 blackout and how the industry reacted and a chapter on projected plans for the future of electric power. Although largely from the standpoint of the industry, this is informative. Grades 5–8.

Helicopters and Other VTOL's, by Hall Hellman, 1970. 140 p. $3.95. Doubleday, New York.

A thorough historical and scientific account of VTOL's or Vertical Take Off and Landing Craft in rescue work, in peace and in war and as a safe and economical form of transportation for individuals. For older children. Glossary, bibliography and index. Grades 5 and up.

Man's Marvelous Computer, the Next Quarter Century, by Richard B. Rusch, 1970. 128 p. $4.75. Simon & Schuster, New York.

The situations the computer will create in the next twenty-five years—an exciting but alarming prospect. Some of the projections read like science—for instance grocery shopping by pushbutton. An interesting if rather complex book for older children and young adults. Grades 5 and up.

Men, Money and Automobiles, the Story of an Industry, by Leonard M. Fanning, 1969. 184 p. $4.50. World Publishing Co., Cleveland, Ohio.

A discussion of the growth of the automobile industry with attention to its effect on American economy, ecology, and safety. Grades 5–8.

Motorcycles, by Edward Radlauer, 1967. 32 p. $3.75. Bowmar, 622 Rodier Drive, Glendale, Calif. 91201.

Photographs in color and a line or two of text in large print tell about the popular sport of motorcycling. Other titles in a uniform series of non-condescending books for older boys with reading problems are *Slot Car Racing, Karting,* and *The Mighty Midgets.* Grades 3–8.

Motorcycles, Whirling Wire Wheels, by Edward Radlauer, 1969. 156 p. $4.50. Abelard-Schuman, New York.

An informal but detailed presentation of motorcycling when boys can enjoy even before they are old enough to have an operator's license. Grades 5 and up.

Motors and Engines and How They Work, by Harvey Weiss, 1969. 62 p. $4.50. T. Y. Crowell, New York.

Many instructive drawings clarify a brief text demonstrating the principles behind the operation of motors. For early elementary school children. Grades 3–5.

The New World of Paper, by Irmengarde Eberle, 1969. 79 p. $2.99. Dodd, Mead, New York.

A history of papermaking with an account of the industry today. Covers the modern conservation of forests and the uses of paper in such areas as fashion and building construction. Grades 5–7.

Weighing and Balancing, by Jane Jonas Srivastava, 1970. 32 p. $3.75. T. Y. Crowell, New York.

An introduction to the mathematics of measure and balance which includes simple experiments. A "Youth Math Book". Grades 3–5.

What Car Is That?, by Henry B. Lent, 1969. 127 p. $4.95. Dutton, New York.

Sixty cars with their distinguishing features are described for the reader to identify. Contemporary United States, foreign, sports and antique automobiles are included. An enjoyable book for older boys to test their knowledge of car models. Grades 5–8.

What Happens in a Car Factory, by Arthur Shay, 1969. np. $3.50. Reilly & Lee (Regnery), 114 West Illinois Street, Chicago, Ill. 60610.

Many photographs and a caption-like text give an overview of the assembly line process in an auto plant. Also considers the designing and testing of new models and the workers' problems involving "speed-up". Grades 3–5.

What Makes a Telephone Work?, by Len Darwin, 1970. 58 p. $2.95. Little, Brown, Boston.

A simple explanation of how sound travels, the telephone itself, and the equipment involved in transmitting calls. Includes a combined index and glossary. Grades 3–5.

Careers

Careers in Data Processing, by Stanley L. Englebardt, 1969. 127 p. $4.50. Lothrop, New York.

A discussion of all aspects of work in data processing—repair, programming, developing new uses in such fields as social science and law. Includes a short history of computers, a description of how some machines work and some career information. Grades 7 and up.

Careers in Music, by John Owen Ward, 1968. 127 p. $3.75. Walck, New York.

A practical and realistic approach, useful to students and their parents. Emphasis is on classical, operatic and solo careers but composition and publishing are touched on. Includes information on salaries, organizations and management. Grades 7 and up.

Towline, the Story of American Tugboats, by Robert Carse, 1969. 89 p. $3.95. W. W. Norton (Grosset), New York.

An experienced seaman describes tugboat operations and the skills required of the crew. Black and white photographs. Grades 5 and up.

What Does a Coast Guardsman Do? by Grant Compton, 1968. 64 p. $3.50. Dodd, Mead, New York.

This book describes the work of the United States Coast Guard, gives a history of the Service and tells how to qualify for a rating as a Coast Guardsman. Illustrated with many photographs. Grades 4–6.

You Can Work in the Transportation Industry, by Betty Warner Dietz, 1969. 95 p. $4.29. John Day, New York.

A textbook on all related job opportunities in the industry. Useful to vocational guidance teachers and 6th, 7th and 8th grade students. Illustrated with photographs. Also available in paperback from the same publisher at $2.45. Grades 6 and up.

Your Career in Film Making, by George N. Gordon and Irvin A. Falk, 1969. 224 p. $3.95. Messner (Simon & Schuster), New York.

Experts in the film industry from executive producers to union heads, discuss career possibilities and the means of achieving goals. Writing, acting, directing, editing and make-up are some of the areas explored in the making of commercial, educational and "underground" films. Grades 6 and up.

Law and Government

How a Law is Made, the Story of a Bill Against Air Pollution, by Leonard A. Stevens, 1970. 109 p. $3.95. T. Y. Crowell, New York.

A fictional account based on factual information which shows step by step how individuals or groups can alter the system by changing the law to improve the environment in which they live. Grades 5–8.

The Law and Economics, by Isodore Silver, 1970. 86 p. $3.95. Lerner Publications Co., 241 First Avenue N., Minneapolis, Minn. 55401.

A brief explanation of civil law embracing situations in which one person is harmed by another, e.g., injury due to negligence, the failure to fulfill contract responsibilities, or warranties on the quality of goods sold or produced. Grades 4–7.

On the Beat, Policemen at Work, by Barry Robinson and Martin Dain, 1968. np. $2.95 Harcourt, New York.

An easy-to-read text presents the daily duties of New York City policemen illustrated with black and white photographs which help younger children understand the role of policemen in any large city in the U.S.A. Grades 4–6.

Our Federal Government: How It Works, by Patricia C. Acheson, 1958, 1969. 210 p. $4.50. Dodd, Mead, New York.

The full text of the Constitution has been appended to a revised and expanded edition of this informative book which gives a clear explanation of the organization and functions of the major departments and agencies of the United States government. Grades 6–8.

The Policeman, by Walter Arm, 1969. 160 p. $4.95 Dutton, New York.

A readable and lucid account by a former Deputy Commissioner of the New York Police Department. Includes general organization of the force and special units and qualifications needed for the job. Grades 6 and up.

The Protectors, the Story of the Food and Drug Administration, by Harry Edward Neal, 1968. 190 p. $3.64. Messner, New York.

A detailed and informative account of the Food and Drug Administration's efforts to eliminate fraud, deception and the adulteration of food and medicine. Grades 5–8.

Silent Sentinels, by Robert Kraske, 1969. 127 p. $3.75. Doubleday, New York.

The development of locks, vaults, burglar alarms and other methods of protection against thieves. Includes accounts of some famous robberies and how such crimes can be prevented. Grades 5–8.

Under 21, a Young People's Guide to Legal Rights, by Michael Dorman, 1970. 210 p. $4.50. Delacorte, New York.

An informative book which encourages respect for individuals, the law and society while explaining the rights to which each child and young person is entitled. Agencies such as American Civil Liberties Union are discussed. Appended are tables of drivers' license age requirements by state, alcoholic beverage control laws concerning minimum age requirements, and marriage license requirements. Some chapters are headed: Student Rights, Censorship, Employment, Contracts, Crime and Justice, Drugs, Drinking, Marriage and Sex, Home and Parents, The Draft and Military Service. Indexed. Grades 7 and up.

Washington Alphabet, Seven Agencies That Regulate Business, by Mary Sagarin, 1968. 160 p. $3.95. Lothrop, New York.

Factual information on the seven independent commissions; Interstate Commerce, Federal Trade, Federal Power, Federal Communications, Security and Exchange, National Labor Relations, Civil Aeronautics, and how they function to protect the consumer. Grades 5–8.

CHILDREN'S SPECIAL INTERESTS

Art, Music, and Theatre

Behind the Scenes in Television, by David Coxe Cooke, 1967. 64 p. $2.99. Dodd, Mead, New York.

A brief picture of the preparation the work and the machinery that lie behind a TV show. An updated revision of an earlier edition of the title. Grades 3–6.

The Best in Magic, by Bruce Elliott, 1956. 246 p. $4.95. Harper, New York.

More than one hundred tricks clearly described and illustrated and requiring only a modest expenditure for equipment. Grades 5–8.

Guitar Years, Pop Music from Country and Western to Hard Rock, by Irwin Stambler, 1970. 137. p. $3.95. Doubleday, New York.

A lively history of the genre through personalities and styles as they have developed. While not including a formal discography, all important hits are identified throughout the text and fully indexed. The book thus takes on another dimension as a guide in setting up a basic record collection in the area of pop, country, western and hard rock music. Grades 5–8.

Horns, by Larry Kettelkamp, 1964. 48 p. $3.50. Morrow, New York.

Directions for making a horn at home from simple materials accompany a brief history and description of instruments in the horn family. *Drums, Rattles and Reels* and *Flutes, Whistles and Reeds* are attractive companion books in the same series. Grades 3–6.

How to Be a Puppeteer, by Eleanor Boylan, 1970. 132 p. $4.95. McCall Publishing, 230 Park Avenue, New York 10017.

This book gives brief advice on making puppets, stages and sets, and includes many short plays complete with stage directions plus suggestions for the adaptation of folk tales and a musical based on *Gulliver's Travels*, the score of which may be requested from the publisher for the use of non-profit groups. The information can be adapted to the use of elementary school teachers in consumer education courses. Grades 5 and up.

How to Have a Show, by Jeanne Bendick and Barbara Berk, 1957. 63 p. $3.75. Franklin Watts, New York.

Everything a child needs to know about amateur theatricals—from planning a show to getting the audience.

How to Make Music on the Harmonica, by P. V. Planta, revised edition, 1957. 124 p. $1.00, paper. Sentinel Books, 21 East 22nd Street, New York, New York, 10010.

A practical paperback which begins with a brief history of mouth organs, goes through all the stages of learning to play, lists abbreviations, words and phrases most often used in music, and concludes with several songs and directions for playing them. Grades 4–8.

Make Your Own Musical Instruments, by Muriel Mandell and Robert E. Wood, rev., 1959. 126 p. $2.95. Sterling, New York.

A practical little book which calls on the musical possibilities of everyday objects and odds and ends to make a variety of percussion, wind, and string instruments. There is a separate section on clay instruments and general suggestions for simple orchestrating and conducting. Grades 4–8.

Making Pictures Move, by Harry Helfman, 1969. 48 p. $3.50. Morrow, New York.

Several forms of animated art simply described and easy to master, including panorama, moving string, magic wheel, flip books, and comb animation. Good for school projects, for parties and for hobbies. Grades 4–8.

Marionettes, Easy to Make! Fun to Use! by Edith Flack Ackley, 1929, 1957. 115 p. $5.95. Lippincott, Philadelphia.

A handbook covering all aspects of marionette making and production. This gives detailed instructions on materials needed, how to make marionette animals and people, stages and stage settings, how to produce a play, and five plays for marionettes. Illustrated with diagrams and line drawings. Includes a pocket of paper patterns for the marionette bodies. Grades 5 and up.

Music and Instruments for Children to Make, by John Hawkinson and Martha Faulhaber, 1970. 47 p. $3.50. Albert Whitman, Chicago.

Small children are introduced to rhythm and song and the making of simple instruments. Grades K–4.

The Music of Africa, an Introduction, by Dr. Fred Warren and Lee Warren, 1970. 87 p. $4.25. Prentice-Hall, Englewood Cliffs, N.J. 07632.

"For the African, music is not a luxury but a part of the process of living itself". A unique book including many illustrations and a list of books and records. Grades 5 and up.

Musical Instruments of Africa, by Betty Warner Dietz and Michael Babatunde Olatunjii, 1965. 115 p. $5.95. John Day, New York.

How instruments of African countries south of the Sahara are made and used. A recording is included and a list of books and recordings. Illustrated with photographs. Grades 5 and up.

Paint, Brush and Palette, by Harvey Weiss, 1966. 64 p. $4.50. Young Scott.

An interesting and handsome book for the beginner which discusses color and various painting media. A companion book, *Pencil, Pen and Brush* shows children how to make pictures for pleasure, and *Paper, Ink and Roller* introduces the making of prints from press and wood blocks. Grades 3–6.

7 Plays and How to Produce Them, by Moyne Rice Smith, 1968. 148 p. $4.50. Walck, New York.

Plays for upper elementary children, many adapted from well known stories. Grades 5–8.

Sound All Around, by Ross Olney, 1967. $3.75. Prentice-Hall, Englewood Cliffs, N.J. 07632.

An introduction to high-fidelity and stereophonic sound systems, how they work and how to evaluate them. Grades 5–8.

Young Filmmakers, by Rodger Larson and Ellen Meade, 1969. 190 p. $5.95. Dutton, New York.

How to make 8 millimeter and 16 millimeter movies. A unique book which encourages creativity while giving practical advice on equipment and its use. Also available in paper at $3.95. Grades 5 and up.

Crafts

Bird Feeders and Shelters You Can Make, by Ted S. Pettit, 1970. 80 p. $3.95. Putnam's, New York.

Suggestions for the many ways of attracting birds are included in this Cub Scout Project Book which includes fully illustrated instructions for making feeders and shelters. Grades 2–5.

Creating With Wood, by James L. Seidelman and G. Mintonye, 1969. 56 p. $4.50. Crowell-Collier, New York.

A practical book with many illustrations and easy-to-follow directions for making a variety of useful articles. Tools and materials are easily obtainable. Grades 2–5.

Easy Does It, Things to Make and Do, by James Razzi, 1969. 61 p. $3.50. Parents' Magazine Press, New York.

Easy entertainments and simple crafts for young children including magic tricks as well as things to make. Materials needed are inexpensive. Grades K–3.

Fun With Leather, by Joseph Leeming, 1941. 88 p. $4.50. Lippincott, Philadelphia, Pa.

One of a series of craft books by the same author, this has step-by-step instructions and patterns for making such articles as belts, pocketbooks, notebooks, brief cases, book covers and picture frames. Beginning chapters describe the kinds of leather together with tools and methods for using them. Grades 4–7.

Holiday Cards for You to Make, by Susan Purdy, 1967. np. $4.95. Lippincott, Philadelphia.

Clear directions for making all kinds of greeting cards, place cards, and invitations with many illustrations and employing inexpensive materials. Grades 4–7.

The Joy of Woodworking, by Norman Pike, 1969. 170 p. $4.95. Pantheon, New York.

Information and facts about woods, woodworking and hand tools introduce instructions for making such articles as a letter opener, a tray, a stool, a jewel box, or a bench. Grades 5 and up.

Keeping the Plants You Pick, by Laura Louise Foster, 1970. 149 p. $4.95. T. Y. Crowell, New York.

How to preserve plants and their beauty. An attractive book of hobbies including mounting, pressing, things to make, and air drying. Grades 4–7.

Let's Make Presents, by Esther Hautzig, 1962. 191 p. $4.50. T. Y. Crowell, New York.

"One hundred gifts for less than one dollar." Clear diagrams and simple directions are given for easy-to-make gifts such as a family calendar, a belt with a change purse, sea-shell shadow box, cookies, etc. Grades 5–8.

Making Dolls, by H. Witzig and G. E. Kuhn, translated by Ingrid Froelich, 1969. 96 p. $3.95. Sterling Publishing Co., 419 Park Avenue, S., New York, 10116.

A practical book originally published in Switzerland under the title *Puppen*. It has very clear, step-by-step instructions and carefully designed illustrations. The various materials suggested for each project are easily and cheaply obtained. Grades 4–7.

Mascot Toys, by Brenda Morton, 1969. 79 p. $4.50. Taplinger Publishing Co. New York.

Concise instructions and clear diagrams show children how to make simple toys stuffed with sponges and plastic foam. Grades K–4.

Scrap Craft for Youth Groups, by Gerry Fleming, 1969. 216 p. $6.95. John Day, New York.

Materials for making these crafts seldom cost more than 10¢ and the directions are simple. An invaluable book for group leaders and teachers working with children. Grades 5 and up.

You Can Build Your Own Sailboat, by Donald and David Rouse, 1965. 87 p. $3.95. Harper, New York.

How to build a small "pram" type sailboat, perhaps the safest for children to handle, illustrated in the numerous photographs of the boy who built the boat taken by his father while the construction was going on. Drawings of parts of the boat with a list of materials accompanying the text. Grades 5 and up.

Models and Model Making

A Beginner's Guide to Building and Flying Model Airplanes, by Robert Lopshire, 1967. 128 p. $4.43. Harper, New York.

Instructions are simple and complete for making many types of models beginning with the easiest and going to the more complex. Illustrated with many clear diagrams and pictures of every tool one might use. Grades 4–8.

Bill Dean's Book of Balsa Models, by Bill Dean, 1970. 62 p. $5.00. Arco Publishing Co., 219 Park Avenue South, New York, 10003.

"Illustrated instructions for making 18 working models from balsa wood—planes, boats, cars and kites—each complete with full-scale plans . . ." Tools and materials are given for each model to be built. Grades 4–8.

How to Build Model Cars, by William Nordner, 1969. 60 p. $2.95. Meredith Press, Des Moines, Iowa.

Instructs children in building, operating, and racing all kinds of model cars. A section on the various tools and materials needed is included. Grades 4 and up.

How to Build Model Ships, by William Nordner, 1969. 60 p. $2.95. Meredith Press, Des Moines, Iowa.

How to build and operate models for many kinds of boats. Illustrations and diagrams demonstrate how to put pieces together, what tools to use and how to use them. Information on motors for power boats. For older children. Grades 4 and up.

How to Make and Fly Paper Airplanes, 1968. 70 p. $3.50. Four Winds Press, New York.

A craft book on the making of model airplanes is used to explain the basic principles of aerodynamics. Numerous diagrams illustrate the text. For boys and their fathers. Grades 4 and up.

Model Railroading, by Harry Zarchy, 1955. 172 p. $4.19. Knopf, New York.

Easy text and many diagrams show how to build model railroad tracks, accessories and scenery. The layout of the track, maintenance of equipment, painting and construction are covered. Grades 4 and up.

Model Railway Engines, by J. E. Minns, 1969. 120 p. $5.95. Putnam's, New York.

A history of model engines with specifications and comparisons between the models and their full-size prototypes. Grades 6 and up.

Models of America's Past and How to Make Them, by C. J. Maginley, 1969. 144 p. $3.75. Harcourt, Brace, New York.

Furniture, bridges and vehicles from our colonial and pioneer past described for experienced young carpenters or for fathers working with their children. Grades 5 and up.

Pets

Catnip, Selecting and Training Your Cat, by Kurt Unkelbach, 1970. 103 p. $3.95. Prentice-Hall, Englewood Cliffs, N.J. 07632.

Up-to-date information on the selection, training and care of cats as pets. It is not as complete as *Doris Bryant's New Cat Book* which addresses all ages but it is a very good handbook for children. Grades 3–7.

Dogs, Best Breeds for Young People, by Wilfred S. Bronson, 1969. 96 p. $3.95. (Harcourt), New York.

How to select and train a satisfactory pet is related in an informative book copiously and amusingly illustrated by the author. Includes a list of books and pamphlets on pet dogs. Grades 3–7.

Doris Bryant's New Cat Book, by Doris Bryant, 1969. 181 p. $4.50. Ives Washburn (McKay), New York.

This handbook for cat owners updates earlier manuals by the author who is a recognized authority on the many facets of the care of pet cats. It is a serious book reflecting recent progress in nutrition, equipment, veterinary science and feline psychology. For cat lovers of all ages—children, young adult and adult. Grades 7 and up.

Gerbils, by Arnold Dobrin, 1970. 63 p. $3.75. Lothrop, New York.

A clearly written and illustrated guide to the purchase, care and breeding of the gerbil, a desert rodent that makes an engaging and satisfactory pet. Grades 2–4.

How to Raise a Dog in the City and in the Suburbs, by James R. Kinney and Ann Honeycutt, 1969. 187 p. 3d ed. $5.95. Simon & Schuster, New York.

Amusing but informative book by a confirmed dog-lover for anyone who has or is going to get a dog. Older children and adults. Illustrated with James Thurber drawings. Grades 6 and up.

Sewing

Costumes to Make, by Peggy Parish, 1970. 111 p. $3.95. Macmillan, New York.

Simple and inexpensive costumes for plays and parties using basic dress and pajama patterns. Grades 5–7.

McCall's Needlework Treasury, compiled by McCall's Needlework and Crafts Magazine, editors, 1964. 390 p. $7.95. Random House, New York.

This practical and attractive book is the most useful and up-to-date handbook of knitting, crocheting, weaving and other needlecraft skills that can be found. For all ages. Grades 4 and up.

Of Course You Can Sew, by Barbara Corcoran, 1971. 127 p. $4.95. Doubleday, New York.

Advice on purchasing needed equipment and materials is included in this useful, readable and attractive guide to the basics of sewing for the young beginner. Clear directions are accompanied by many drawings and diagrams. Author is a professional dressmaker as well as an author and illustrator of children's books. Grades 4–7.

Redecorating Your Room for Practically Nothing, by Esther Hautzig, 1967. 203 p. $4.50 T. Y. Crowell, New York.

An entertaining and practical book of useful and original projects for girls. Grades 5 and up.

Singer Sewing Book, by Gladys Cunningham, 1969. 420 p. $7.95. Singer Co. New York.

A comprehensive guide for would-be sewers of all ages. New techniques to fit new fabrics and sewing machines with colorful and instructive illustrations and diagrams. Grades 6 and up.

The Stitchery Book, Embroidery for Beginners, by Irene Preston Miller and Winifred Lubell, 1965. 96 p. $4.95. Doubleday, New York.

A fascinating and easy to understand book of interest to all ages. Grades 5 and up.

Sports and Hobbies

Anyone Can Camp in Comfort, by James Ralph Johnson, 1964. 154 p. $3.75. McKay, New York.

A veteran camper's practical guide. Emphasis is on economy and comfort. One chapter is devoted to finding the best buy for the best need. Grades 5 and up.

Baseball for Young Champions, by Robert J. Antonacci and Jene Barr, 1956. 156 p. $3.95. McGraw-Hill, New York.

Simple explanations, well-organized chapters and a good index make this a useful introduction to playing and understanding the game. Grades 3–7.

Basketball for Young Champions, by Robert J. Antonacci and Jene Barr, 1960. 160 p. $3.95. McGraw-Hill, New York.

A book on how to play basketball and how to understand it as a spectator. It is a companion book to *Baseball for Young Champions* and *Football for Young Champions.* Grades 3–7.

Better Fishing for Boys, by James P. Kenealy, 1968. 64 p. $2.95. Dodd, Mead, New York.

A well-known fisherman gives detailed advice on how to select equipment and fishing accessories, how to care for and maintain it and the best ways to be a successful fisherman.

Better Football for Boys, by David D. Cooke, 1958. 64 p. $3.25. Dodd, Mead, New York.

Many photographs and diagrams illustrate a guide to tackling, blocking and playing every position on the team. One of a good series of sports books for boys. Grades 5 and up.

Bike-Ways, 101 Things to Do With a Bike, by Lillian and Godfrey Frankel, 1968. 128 p. $2.95. Sterling Publishing Co., 419 Park Ave., S., New York, N.Y. 10016.

Clear and concise information on selection, care and repair of bicycles, what to wear, games and races, camping and other practical information. Illustrated with many photographs and diagrams. This new edition of an older title includes new features such as hand brakes, multiple gears and generator type lights. Grades 3–8.

Coins You Can Collect, by Burton Hobson, 1970. 128 p. $4.95. Hawthorn Books, New York.

A new and revised edition of a beginner's guide to collecting coins from many countries of the world with photographic illustrations. Grades 5 and up.

The Complete Book of Bicycling, by Eugene A. Sloane, 1970. 342 p. $9.95. Trident Press (division of Simon & Schuster), New York.

This definitive guide is of interest to all cyclists, children, young adults and adults. The chapters on safety should be must reading for those who buy bicycles for children as well as all who ride them. Includes history, touring, and camping information, material on repairs and advice on purchasing the right bicycle for the individual person. Grades 6 and up.

Flower Gardening, by Elizabeth Abell, 1969. 84 p. $2.95. Franklin Watts, New York.

A first book for the amateur gardener. Grades 3–7.

Fun with Stamp Collecting, by Fred Reinfeld, 1957. 88 p. $4.50. Doubleday, New York.

Concise and easily understood information on all phases of stamp collecting presented in a large flat book with many illustrations. Grades 4 to 7.

Getting Started in Coin Collecting, by Burton Hobson, revised edition, 1967. 124 p. $2.95. Sterling Publishing Co., New York.

A concise book for the beginner with photographs and descriptions of the coinage of many countries in North and South America, Europe, Africa and Asia. Index and glossary. Grades 6 and up.

A Guide to Fresh and Salt-Water Fishing, by George S. Fichter and Phil Francis, 1965. 160 p. $1.25, paper. Golden Press-Western Pub., New York.

A practical pocket handbook with more than 650 illustrations in full color. A bibliography is appended. Grades 5 and up.

Junior Skipper, by Pearsall, 1965. 99 p. $3.95. Norton, New York.

This manual of seamanship has the backing of The New York State Young Boatman's Safety Course for which a certificate is given. Illustrations clearly depict the information carried in the text. Water skiing, skindiving and sailboating are also discussed. Grades 4 and up.

Kites, by Marion Downer, 1959. 64 p. $3.50. Lothrop.

A practical book on making and flying kites and how to choose the necessary materials. Information on kite-flying contests is included and proper safety rules. Grades 3–8.

Riding Step by Step, by Margaret Cabell Self, 1965. 169 p. $4.95. A. S. Barnes, Forsgate Drive, Cranbury, N.J., 08512.

A handbook addressed to young but experienced riders. Illustrated with many drawings and photographs of children riding and grooming horses and caring for tack. Grades 3–7.

Spinning Tops, by Larry Kettelkamp, 1966. 63 p. $3.50. Morrow, New York.

A simple explanation of the use of children's tops throughout history and in different parts of the world with instructions for making many of them and for playing fourteen top games and stunts. Lively and informative illustrations. Grades 3–7.

The Young Sportsman's Guide to Water Safety, by Pat Wilson, 1966. 96 p. $2.75. Nelson, Copewood and Davis Station, Camden, N.J. 08103.

Covers safety rules for boating, water-skiing, skin-diving, swimming, and diving with brief comments on surfing and a chapter on life saving. A complete guide. Grades 7 and up.

SUBJECT INDEX

Books and articles have been indexed by their major topics only. No attempt has been made to index all subjects covered by books of broad scope. The reader may therefore find it helpful to consult general works as well as those indexed under a specific topic.

Numbers after a decimal point indicate the position of an entry on the page. Thus 32.6 indicates the sixth entry on page 32, counting entries from top to bottom beginning with the left column.

☆ U. S. GOVERNMENT PRINTING OFFICE: 1971 O—421-220